SECRET MISSIONS 5

VEILED DESTINIES

Crossroads At The Axis of Circumstance

WALTER BOSLEY

Corvos Books
USA

Secret Missions 5: Veiled Destinies

Inquiries should be addressed to:
LCL Publishing Co.
7231 Boulder Ave #292
Highland CA 92346

FIRST PRINTING JULY 2021

Published in the United States of America

9 781312 814424

DEDICATIONS

DR. ZIAD KHAN
DR. MATTHEW WHEALON
DR. EMAN AHMAD
LILIANA BOUTTAVONG
MARY & ERVIN CAVER
MALEINA KEYES
KEN KHASTEDAI
NURSING STAFF, ONCOLOGY CLINIC,
OF ARROWHEAD REGIONAL MEDICAL CENTER
and
LIVE CHAT MEMBERS OF
THE WALTER BOSLEY CHANNEL

Prologue

The actual prologue to this book is the material in the books which precede it.

I should have known this book would happen, for as the *Empire of the Wheel* mystery unfolded before my eyes, the data that would result in *Secret Missions: The Hidden Legacy of Old California* was already presenting itself. It had also become apparent rather quickly that aspects of the *Latitude 33: Key to the Kingdom* research which led directly to the EOTW research would reveal yet more data which all three lines of research shared in common. This would continue for an additional eleven years and shows no sign of abatement. A few volumes back, I decided that I would need to present more context for the series volumes to date at some point and, with the publication of *Secret Missions 4: The Esoteric Napoleon Volume 1*, I decided this was the right time.

If you haven't read any of my previous nonfiction works, it would be best if you did. However, a good partial set would suffice in *Latitude 33*, *EOTW1*, *Secret Missions 1*, and *Shimmering Light*. Be advised, though, that the devil is in the details so you may not completely appreciate references here to any unread volumes in my catalogue. Of course, there is the option that this book may be an interesting starting point before reading any of my other books so, by all means, read on.

Two particular threads running through my nonfiction works are what inspired this idea to consider why my path keeps going in this direction. One thread is the somewhat mysterious goddess Hekate, the other being the equally mysterious beings known as the Tuatha de Danann. That these entities repeatedly show up in my research, whether it be about Disneyland or mysterious 1915 deaths or explorers from the Age of Discovery, is a curious thing to me. That they show up also in my investigations of breakaway organizations, ufology, the airship mystery, and Napoleon Bonaparte is likewise very curious. A close third is the thread of telluric current/gravity anomalies, specifically the popular notion of the World Grid, and should not be disregarded in deference to the other two. On the contrary, this network of energy coursing through the planet has its links to both of the main threads, the shadowy goddess and the elusive race of otherworldly beings.

This book is an attempt to fill in some blanks left in the previous material and answer remaining questions, to some extent. As always, I have tried to support any supposition or hypotheses with as much evidence as possible and to provide references to my sources. The impact of this research on my personal perspective makes speculative possibilities inevitable, but at least the reader will come away with a better appreciation of this series in seeing how they fit within the proper order of historical events and figures.

Though the initial objective of my nonfiction research has always been to present and determine what may actually have happened within the context of my hypotheses, there remains a necessary and valuable consideration of metaphysical possibilities and even the paranormal, where it appears to have manifested. In this book more than the others, that may be necessary as the very nature of the identified threads demands such consideration. The answer to the question of why these threads are present, and why they connect to seemingly unrelated topics, appears to be related to our very existence and also to our individual identities and expression of human will. Strict materialists are not going to find much here to rejoice over, but I've never actually written for them anyway so this should come as no surprise.

Venturing into any significant details will result in new material, thus details of the past material can be referenced in the previous volumes. The benefit here is that this book is not simply a rehash of books you have already read. I am attempting a fresh analysis here, and further extrapolation upon previous opinions and hypotheses. Ultimately, I had to to do what I don't really like to do and discuss my personal experience with those two common threads through all my work, but that's because it's how it all came to me in the first place.

So let's get on with this...

Chapter One

Joan & Juan

I came to the *Secret Missions* series from a desire to write about something other than the *Empire of the Wheel*. Not because I was bored with those books, but because I had to get away from that milieu for a while. I had written three of those books in a four and a half year period which had followed two and a half years of investigation fraught with ceaseless revelation of and through synchronicity and, at times, startling paranormal manifestation. There were also the facts of the cases: three murdered children, four likely murdered adults, evidence of a motive torn right out of a pulp era horror novel. Ironically, it wasn't the negative or clandestine attention my investigation indeed earned, I simply desired a break from it all.

There was also the presence of Juan Cabrillo who had popped up on my research radar, almost at the same time as did Saint Catherine of Alexandria aka Hekate. Her Cabrillo thread, of course, was her association with Catalina Island. Pulling it led to Joan of Arc. The rest is, admittedly, hypothesis and speculation with a fair amount of history, and it all resonates.

For those who have not read the book, *Secret Missions: The Hidden Legacy of Old California* presents my idea that Juan Cabrillo was *hidalgo de sangre*, blood descendant of a Templar knight, specifically the son of Pedro Cabral, the explorer credited with claiming Brazil for Portugal. I also propose therein that Cabrillo took on a new identity following a ritualistic faking of his death through which he became a full-fledged Templar. Why? It is my proposal that Cabrillo took possession of the legendary - and missing - sword of Joan of Arc, serving as its custodian possibly for the remainder of his days.

I also propose, with analyses of pertinent history and the physical description of the sword, including that proposed by sword maker Lance Bernard, that the historical weapon may have been the legendary Excalibur of Arthurian lore, be it literally so or perhaps a copy by technical design and properties. This, in my opinion, makes Hekate the Lady of the Lake.

Joan of Arc claimed to have had direct contact with three supernatural entities known to her as Saint Michael, Saint Margaret, and Saint Catherine of Alexandria, the last one known to my readers as St Catherine of the Wheel aka Hekate. It was specifically St Catherine among these three who took the lead in communication with young Joan, ultimately directing her to a church in Fierbois where waited the special sword behind the altar, right where Charles Martel had left it seven hundred years prior. Joan went on to victory after victory with the sword in her possession, finally being captured during a battle in which she did not have the sword. She had handed it over to her brothers and it quickly disappeared.

Interestingly, the trial through which Joan was condemned reflected the court's obsession with the sword in question. A read of the transcript reveals the inquisitors' keen interest in what had happened to the weapon, documenting their repeated demands as to its location. That the English were behind the trial is rather suggestive: Believing that it may have been the very sword of King Arthur, someone in England sought the power it would put into their hands, either literally or figuratively. But Joan claimed ignorance of the sword's disposition and was sent to burn at the stake on 30 May 1431 AD, made a grim example of what happens when one dares not cooperate with aristocratic determination.

Joan's fate is not uncommon among those who encounter supernatural beings. It seems Joan's reward for following the guidance of the saints was martyrdom, but what if it had been her fate to be killed in battle or executed anyway? Could it be that St Catherine/Hekate intervened in Joan's life to alter the girl's path in a manner suitable to the cause?

It's worthy to consider that an entity such as St Catherine/Hekate can see a little farther down the line of someone's life than can said person and that Hekate/Catherine simply manipulated the fated circumstances. Hekate wanted France to have Joan and she knew that Joan would need help: an 'Excalibur' sword.

Possessed of knowledge of the heroine's sad fate, Hekate could have seen to it that the sword was not in Joan's possession at the time of her capture. It would appear that Hekate did not want England to wield Excalibur ever again, at least not the Germanic usurpers of the England after Arthur's day. I propose in the book that the sword was secreted away by Templars to their secret vault in 'undiscovered' America.

The scenario: A Templar secret, the sword is moved across the northern continent after the New World is revealed and the colonists multiply, until put into the care of Juan Cabrillo almost exactly one hundred and twelve years after Joan's execution. What has become of the sword remains a mystery to this day. This is my proposal.

Regarding the sword's present location, I think I may have a decent proposition on where it was taken after California. If one accepts my hypothesis that a Templar guardian, in this case Juan Cabrillo with a new identity, carried it as far away from California as his own path could take it, we may be able to identify some interesting circumstances and evidence worthy of consideration.

The circumstances of Juan Cabrillo's reported death are that he was wounded either in the shoulder or on the leg, take your pick. He was buried somewhere on or near what we know as Catalina Island (historically associated with St Catherine of Alexandria aka Hekate) yet his remains have never been found. Members of the expedition told differing versions of their leader's death. Curiously, immediately upon return to their port in what is today Mexico, many of these crewmen were sent to Peru and never heard from again. As mysterious as was his birth, Juan Cabrillo's exit from history was just as perplexing. In *Secret Missions Vol 1*, I propose that Cabrillo did not die on the expedition.

So if Cabrillo did not die, and if he was the Templar custodian of the Excalibur sword of Joan of Arc, what happened to him and where did he take the sword?

Since I proposed that the Templars brought the sword to the Americas and moved it across the northern continent as more and more colonial immigrants arrived, I suggest further that the objective was to keep moving the relic westward. Therefore, I suggest that Cabrillo, under whatever identity he assumed, took the sword across the Pacific. I have considered the possibilities and suggest the following locations for Cabrillo's tenure as custodian of the Templar vault: Midway Islands, Nan Madol, or Pitcairn Island.

Additionally, I think I know the ultimate resting place of Juan Cabrillo, though it is not among the proposed vault sites. First, where might the sword have been taken after California?

Midway Islands

The actual location of the proposed Templar vault site could be anywhere in the greater area spanned by the archipelago of Pacific US Minor Outlying Islands and the Hawaiian Islands, and I do have a specific candidate that is not the Midway Atoll itself.

Midway is a roughly two and a half square mile atoll called so for being essentially halfway between the continental United States and the eastern shores of Asia. Sighted in 1859 by Captain Middlebrooks of the *Gambia*, possession of the atoll was not taken by the United States until the summer of 1867 by Captain William Reynolds of the USS *Lackawanna*. Will Reynolds served for some years with the U.S. Exploring Expedition and before that had journeyed to Brazil, Africa, and

Malaysia. Reynolds was also among the American crews that first sighted Antarctica.[1] Midway would also become the center of a major WW2 victory for the US Navy in June of 1942.

But I don't think my proposed Templar vault would have been on the Midway Atoll. Of this particular group of islands, the best candidate, in my analysis, is Palmyra Island.

Essentially a reef, some multiple islets and two shallow lagoons, Palmyra itself is technically also an atoll but it differs from Midway and the others in its group in that it has more vegetation.[2] History tells us that the first known sighting of it was by the American vessel *Betsy* in 1798.[3] A subsequent report claimed in 1802 that no sign of prior habitation nor fresh water was found by the crew of the USS *Palmyra* shipwrecked on the reef, subsequently lending its name to the place.[4] The report is limited in the extent to which the crew explored the location thus leaving open the possibility that finding neither habitation nor fresh water doesn't guarantee their absence.

It so happens that an interesting story of lost Inca treasure is linked to Palmyra Island. In 1816, the story goes, a hoard of gold, silver and gemstones was loaded aboard the *Esperanza* which sailed from Callao on the first day of January but was caught in a storm and subsequently raided by pirates who stole

---

[1] *The Private Journal of William Reynolds: United States Exploring Expedition, 1838-1842*; Penguin 2004; Stanton, William R, *The Great United States Exploring Expedition*, Berkeley 1975; Reynolds will come up again in this volume.

[2] Wikipedia

[3] Capt Edmund Fanning, *Voyages and Discoveries in the South Seas 1792-1832*, Marine Research Society 1924.

[4] Captain Cornelius Sowle, *The Naval Chronicle*, Volume XII Pgs 464-465, July-Dec 1805, Royal Navy

the treasure and headed west toward Macao. Weeks later, however, they too met a storm and were driven onto the reef at Palmyra. The crewmen buried some of the treasure then repaired their vessel and departed, leaving ten men behind. The departing crew was never heard from again, though a year later six of those ten men left behind managed to escape the island in a boat of their own construction. Ultimately they all died for the effort.[5]

Allegedly, the *Esperanza* itself was the venture of merchant seamen and Peruvian natives looting ancient temples, according to an article published in the Honolulu Star-Bulletin in 1923. Also according to the report, there was an abundance of fish and fruit on the islands. The stranded crew never had to touch the food stores from their salvaged shipwreck. The ten who were left behind obviously had plenty to eat and somehow had to have found fresh water despite the earlier report. Of the four men who stayed behind on Palmyra when the second group fled, nothing is known.[6]

Henry Cooper, Minister of Public Affairs for the Republic of Hawaii and a well known figure in the history of US involvement with the territory, purchased the Palmyra Atoll in 1911, though the land court kept him from buying up all the islets.[7] Cooper went hunting for the lost Inca treasure but whether he found any of it is unknown.[8] In 1913, he took

---

[5] Martin Connor, *Priceless Treasures of the Incas May Be Buried on Island in Palmyras*, Honolulu Star-Bulletin Pg 1, 14 April 1923.

[6] Ibid

[7] *Contest Cooper's Claim to Palmyra*, Hawaiian Gazette 1912

[8] *Judge Cooper Off for Pirates' Treasure Isle of Palmyra*, Honolulu Star-Advertiser 29 July 1911.

Austrian born scientist-explorer Joseph Rock to explore Palmyra. Rock would later explore Tibet and investigate its mysteries. With such interests, who knows what all Rock and Cooper could have been looking for on the islands.[9] What might these two men have known about Palmyra that they weren't saying?

Henry Cooper was a Freemason, member of Hawaiian Lodge #21 to which King Kamehamea V had also belonged, as well as Prince William Pitt Leleiohoku, brother of the Hawaiian monarch David Kalakaua. When Prince William died, his sister Lydia Lili'oukalani became monarch and she was deposed by none other than Henry Cooper himself.[10] No stranger to controversy as a public servant, Cooper certainly fit the bill of a guy looking for an advantage. Was treasure-hunting an objective all along?

In his reminiscence of exploring his Palmyra isles with Rock, Cooper remains rather vague about what they were doing, commenting mostly on the sights and making camp and dealing with sand crabs. He tells of finding relics of previous Japanese inhabitants of the islands and admits to his inability to determine exactly what they were doing there. Cooper also refers to the first mention of the Palmyra islets in an 1851 book dedicated to Sir Edward Bulwer-Lytton, a book whose author remained anonymous.[11] Lytton, of course, was the author of a

---

[9] Joseph F. Rock, *Palmyra Island With A Description of Its Flora*, College of Hawaii Bulletin No.4, April 1916; Wikipedia.

[10] Hawaiian Lodge 21 historical record; Hawaii state archives; Wikipedia bio.

[11] Henry E. Cooper, *My Palmyra*, Mid-Pacific Magazine November 1915. Note the date: This issue was released the month Cora Stanton and the two Estep children met their doom. Also, I have an ancestor named Henry Cooper. Synchronicity alert.

classic hidden race novel that takes place inside the subterranean world of the hollow Earth.

What clues do we have in Henry Cooper's associations and interests to suggest that he may have been on a quest for a hidden Templar vault? Having been a Freemason is suggestive. Referencing a book dedicated by an unknown author to a well known dabbler in the occult, who was also a lost civilization enthusiast, could be a clue. Exploring the islands with a scientist who himself was keen on mysterious civilizations is yet another. What Cooper's limited biography neglects to address is very likely the answer to the question, He may indeed have become aware of even a mere rumor of a treasure vault, whether he was aware of any Templar association or not. The man's interests and associations certainly suggest it.

Might Joseph Rock have been his source of the knowledge? Rock explored much the same territory as did Nicholas Roerich and Henning Haslund. His knowledge of mountain ranges in China was so extensive that American pilots enlisted his aid during WW2. But the first clue that Joseph Rock could have been interested in lost relics and arcane mysteries is his family home. His first years were spent living on the Count Potocki estate, for whom Rock's father was major domo.[12]

Yes, *that* Potocki family. Count Alfred Jozef Potocki was the grandson of the author of *The Manuscript Found in Saragossa*, Jan Potocki. A book which is discussed in my analyses of both Richard Burton and Napoleon Bonaparte. I agree with Jeffrey

[12] Gwen Bell, *The Story of Joseph Rock*, Journal of the American Rhododendron Society, Virginia Tech Univ Library; Jeffrey Hays, *Joseph Rock and the Naxis*, factsanddetails.com 2008.

Hays when he surmises that young Joseph Rock likely enjoyed exposure to the Potocki family library which was certain to include arcane volumes once studied by the mysterious Jan himself, whom some scholars link to Cagliostro's Egyptian Rite Lodge of Freemasonry.[13] It can be reasonably suggested that young Rock's wanderlust and curiosity about the far and mystical corners of the world may very well have been directly inspired by the influence of the adventuring ancestor of his father's employer.

If that was indeed the case, Joseph Rock is likely the best candidate as a personal source for Henry Cooper of any rumors of treasure vaults linked to Palmyra. But we don't know for certain, as is typical with these things. However, there remains the curious Japanese presence which may reveal more than it seems. Recall that Cooper and Rock found relics of Japanese habitation on the islets. How far back did this go?

I suspect Japanese sailors and adventurers heard the same rumors of a treasure vault somewhere among the Palmyra islets. How could that have happened? Pirates certainly could have spread the rumor, of course, but might there have been a more direct source?

This brings us back to Juan Cabrillo.

As readers of my first *Secret Missions* book know, Juan Cabrillo's origin and especially his death are cloaked in mystery. Readers will also know why I am convinced that he was definitely Portuguese, through his father and perhaps his

[13] Gary Lachman, *The Mystical Count*, Fortean Times Nov 2000; Wikipedia bio of Potocki family.

mother also. It is what happened after Cabrillo's reported death which factors here. I have previously proposed that he assumed a new identity and spent a portion of the remainder of his life as custodian of the special sword, and that's where I left it until now.

Subsequent research and analysis which I have conducted proved invaluable to a hunch I developed a couple of years ago. I was still curious about where Cabrillo truly ended up and my suspicion about where he took the sword led me further west into the Pacific. Until my recent hunch, I didn't venture a guess as to upon which island I suspected the sword to be hidden away. So I decided to step back and look at the bigger picture yet again, reconsidering a greater span of history of the region in question. This led me to look at Japan for reasons I will state soon enough. For now, follow me.

I had to get Cabrillo to the islands after the proposed hoax of his death. Assuming he was operating alone, I overlooked a clue that didn't mean anything until doing research for this chapter: the disappearance of his crew shortly after their return to New Spain (Mexico). As discussed in the first volume, they were immediately refitted, supplied and then deployed to Peru, where it is said they disappeared. Instead of merely slipping away into the freedom of obscurity on a vast wild continent, might they actually have been in an arrangement with Cabrillo?

I suggest that enough of Cabrillo's men loyal enough to participate in the faking of his death. Instead of disappearing into the vast territories of South America they could instead have met up with their captain at Lima or some other harbor and then sailed west to the Pacific islands.

It was the story of the *Esperanza* that made me wonder if this was possible. Since men of Cabrillo's expedition had reportedly disappeared, it is as good a possibility as any. Though I can't propose that the Templar Cabrillo would expose his custodial vault mission to a crew of men who were not likely members of the order, the arrangement could certainly have been to take Cabrillo to a specified location and then part ways. Particularly if they were compensated enough to start a new and better life elsewhere. He could then proceed alone to a prescribed site of a vault yet to be constructed. However, it may be that Cabrillo's first Templar mission was merely to take custody of the sword in California and transport it to other knights already in place in a prepared location.

Cabrillo could merely have been delivering the sword to its actual custodians who would remain on whatever island the vault had been located. Cabrillo could have continued on from there and there is a possibility that he may indeed have, though it is indeed speculative. Moving on may have been his plan all along. But to where?

Portuguese mariners and explorers are at the heart of the hidden cartographic tradition involving lost portolan maps likely obtained via the Fourth Crusade at Constantinople. The Templars weren't supposed to be directly involved, but they provided logistics. Sixty-nine years later, Marco Polo departed from the Templar city of Acre on his famous voyage to Asia. Joseph Farrell suspects that Polo, himself possibly a Templar, was testing the knowledge of secret maps he possessed. Farrell cites two clues: that Polo gave the first copy of his travels to the Templar Grand Master Thibault de Cepoy and because a Templar envoy was sent to Polo while he was a war captive.[14] Polo is known to have visited Japan on his legendary journey east, but what has been assumed to refer to Japan in his account may actually been a camouflaged journey to the Americas.

The details of Polo's journey to 'Cipangu' are actually a better fit for North America than for Japan. Farrell cites the described distances between China and Cipangu, as well as certain traditions for which Native Americans are known, including placing pearls in the mouth of the dead and the eating of human flesh, the latter once very popular with the people of the Iroquois nation.[15] This suggests, by virtue of suspected Templar Polo gifting his book to a Templar Grand Master, that the Templars gained knowledge of the Americas and certainly the actual Japan.

What's the Portuguese connection?

Merely a dozen years after Marco Polo's return to Italy, the Templar order is toppled by their persecution, sending most of the knights and their retinue fleeing to Scotland or joining their brothers in Portugal, where King Denis refused to arrest any Templars. Instead, he founded the Order of Christ which simply absorbed the existing Templars. These knights in Portugal, as I have discussed in previous volumes, carried on the traditions of the Templars, especially that of exploration. Thus did these

[14] Joseph P Farrell, *Thrice Great Hermetica and the Janus Age*, (AUP 2014) Pgs 143-146; Wikipedia

[15] Ibid, Pgs 144-145; Bosley, *EOTW3: The Nameless Ones*, Pgs 87-91.

Portuguese explorers likely gain the knowledge and documents of the hidden cartographic tradition, as well as access to Polo's information including knowledge of Japan and America.

Is it any surprise that Christopher Columbus is suspected of being a Templar and already knew what he would find prior to his famous voyage of 1492? Joseph Farrell writes of this: "*Because according to the Celestine monk Marco Beneventano, Columbus 'discovered those lands in the company of the Portuguese and not the Spaniards' thus indicating some unknown prior voyage of Columbus to the New World before that undertaken for the Spanish monarchs Ferdinand and Isabella in 1492.*"[16]

This suggests that Portuguese mariners would likely have been aware of Japan almost sixty years before Cabrillo's disappearance. Does this, in turn, suggest that Portuguese *hidalgo* Cabrillo also knew of Japan?

It so happens that in the same year that Cabrillo allegedly died, 1543AD, the first Portuguese mariners arrived in Japan, landing at Tanegashima. Juan Cabrillo could have delivered the sword to its Pacific island destination and then continued on with his loyal crew, reaching Japan. Might Cabrillo have brokered Portuguese merchant trade with Japan? It certainly provides a line of evidence to consider. If it is indeed so, then we have something upon which to hang the proposal.

I do suspect this is the case. I also propose that Japan is where Cabrillo spent the remainder of his days. It comes from an unexpected yet logical circumstance: Juan Cabrillo may have become an honorary samurai.

---

[16] Farrell, *Thrice Great Hermetica*, Pg 143.

Already a soldier, likely *hidalgo de sangre* and presumably a secretly knighted Templar, Cabrillo would have fit in with the military culture of Japan. It so happens that certain Shinto temples there honor the remains of and are dedicated to foreign warriors, a sort of tomb of unknown soldiers.[17] Presently I am pursuing further data on this speculation as I have reason to suspect that Juan Cabrillo may have been associated with a particular Japanese clan.[18]

With a Japanese connection proposed, what might they have learned from Cabrillo about a powerful Templar treasure somewhere in the Pacific? Considering the alliance with Nazi Germany during WW2, might Japan's aggressive campaign of conquest have had a little to do with a desire to seize a powerful item of lost ancient technology?

Was Japan after the sword of Joan of Arc?

The Battle of Midway was a major American victory. Though it indeed took place only months after Pearl Harbor, and the United States needed to make a point, was there an even deeper impetus to the tenacious fighting? Was there a classified factor of which only a few at the top were aware?

Consider how obsessed with relics certain Nazis were. Did they convince the Japanese that the Templars had secreted a

---

[17] Unfortunately I'm unable to find my source for this but I found an email to Lyn Buchanan dated 21 March 2018 in which I share this apparent fact.

[18] I was reluctant to include this suggestion of a clan because of how I came to it: remote viewing. In the session, a specific color and scent dominated the data. That color and scent I subsequently found to be associated with said particular clan. This data led to the information regarding the Shinto temple honoring foreign born warriors, which I now unfortunately cannot find. When I can back up these specific suspicions with a source, I will include them in a main body of work. For now all this must remain a footnote.

powerful ancient weapon somewhere in the Pacific? Might the Nazis suspect there was something powerful hidden in the Midway Islands?

The only Pacific engagements by Nazi Germany in WWII that we know of involve the island of Nauru, first between the 6th and 8th of December 1940 and on the 27th that same month.[19] The attacks were intended to interfere with important Allied phosphate shipments bound for Australia. Interestingly, one of the German ships involved, *Orion*, operated as a mine-layer outfitted with a Japanese float plane. She attacked an Allied freighter in the South Atlantic and continued around Cape Horn for operations in the South Pacific. *Orion* also spent six months of 1941 in the Indian Ocean during which time we are told nothing happened and the ship encountered no engagements. But why would the Kriegsmarine have let a valuable asset do nothing for so long?

Perhaps when you consider that German colonial ambitions were aimed at Pacific islands, it becomes more interesting to wonder what the Orion may actually have actually been doing all those months. The anthropologist Felix von Luschan had established a department devoted to Oceania. By his death in 1924, German scientists had been enthusiastically crawling all over these islands, primarily in pursuit of eugenic measurement of skulls and other such tomfoolery inspired by the hackneyed

---

[19]Military History Now, "The Battle of Nauru – Nazi Germany's Forgotten Foray into the Pacific" 24 Jan 2014; "Nauru Island Heavily Shelled" The Mercury, 28 Dec 1940; "Raider Used Japanese Flag" The Canberra Times 31 Dec 1940; German Attacks On Nauru, Wikipedia.

perspectives of Helena Blavatsky.[20] But that's simply what we know they were doing in the Pacific, it shouldn't be a stretch to suspect they were looking for other things. Also quite active in India, what might the Germans have had *Orion* doing all those months without engagement?

It could have been anything. *Orion* could have been a clandestine escort protecting a scientific vessel engaged in exploration or perhaps transporting German scientists to and from Indian ports from either East Africa or Malaysia and anywhere in between, such as Thailand or Burma to the north or even Antarctica to the south, itself an obviously enticing possibility. The Germans had first gone there in 1872 with the Eduard Dallman whaling expeditions. Pertinent to the *Orion*'s allegedly uneventful six-month cruise of the Indian Ocean are the Kerguelen Islands where during the First German Antarctic Expedition, 1901-1903, the *Gauss* dropped off personnel who established a German station and the ship continued on to explore an 'unknown area' between the islands and the mysterious South Polar continent. The Kerguelen Islands are in a convenient spot of the south Indian Ocean. The Second German Antarctic Expedition followed a decade later and the third, the German Antarctic Expedition of 1938-1939, had Nazi Germany 'looking for whaling stations'. By the time the *Orion* was cruising the Indian Ocean for six months unencumbered, German scientists had been onto Antarctica for almost seventy years.

---

[20]Christopher Hale, *Himmler's Crusade:The Nazi Expedition To Find The Origins of the Aryan Race* (Castle Books 2003) Pgs 91-92.

The *Orion* wasn't alone in the attacks on Nauru Island in 1940. The *Komet,* a 'commerce raider disguised sometimes as a Japanese freighter, participated in the attacks and also subsequently sailed into the Indian Ocean as did *Orion.* In February of 1941, *Komet* made shore on Antarctica and also at the Kerguelen Islands. During the summer of 1941, the German raider operated again in the pacific, as far north as the Galapagos Islands, putting her within range of various locations of interest to the thesis of this chapter. Again, like with the *Orion*, what else might this vessel have been doing in support of a search for suspected ancient relics on Pacific Islands?

The well known activities of *Orion* and *Komet* positively place Nazi German assets in the Pacific during the time in question. The activities of German scientific 'colonists' establishes German anthropologists establishes a definitive presence of such interests across the Pacific for almost seventy years by the time of WWII. This provides a reasonable foundation for the hypothetical suggestion that the Nazis may have suspected something of historical arcane value somewhere among the Midway Islands, as well as the other possible sites I shall further propose. *Orion* and *Komet* were certainly not the only Kriegsmarine vessels operating in the Pacific so any of these ships, especially 'civilian' commerce raiders, could have supported the search for such relics, specifically the sword of Joan of Arc, of course.

If the Japanese were armed with intelligence from German anthropologists and historians who had uncovered such information, might not Allied scholars have also? President

Roosevelt had, after all, been involved with the Oak Island mystery which is associated with the Templars. Was there more at stake than control of the Pacific and did the United States Navy have no choice but victory at Midway in an effort to protect a secret at Palmyra?

With Cooper and Rock at Palmyra before that, and signs that Japanese sailors had been there doing some unidentified business, I propose that the conflict at Midway may have had at stake the capture of the mysterious and powerful sword. The existing problem with this Midway/Palmyra scenario is that my available telluric world grid mapping does not cover these particular islands, though a major world grid line does appear to flow right through the nearby Hawaiian Islands. Still, there are many years between the disappearance of Juan Cabrillo and the Battle of Midway and perhaps the sword came there after a stop elsewhere.

Nan Madol

I propose this mysterious city at Pohnpei in Micronesia because its very existence remains unanswered by conventional archaeology. Its construction is linked to legends of floating stones and forgotten civilizations[21] and that suggests to me the sort of thing that fuels the pursuit of the lost and forgotten world at the center of my *Secret Missions* investigations. There is also an interesting creepy story about Victor Berg, the

---

[21] David H. Childress, *The Lost World of Cham* (AUP 2017), Chapter 6; *Ancient Micronesia & The Lost City of Nan Madol* (AUP 1998).

German governor who in 1907 stayed overnight in the ancient ruin, opened a tomb, and was found dead the following morning.[22] There is also a tradition with the locals that if they tell what they know, they will also die.[23]

One story that may have a threadbare connection to the hypothesis of this chapter is about the Japanese control of the site starting in 1911 and their pearl divers in the early decades of 20th Century. The story goes that these divers claimed to find a "House of the Dead" in an underwater chamber in Nan Madol. In this chamber were supposedly watertight sarcophagi made of platinum.[24] They also claimed to have found other precious metals, bars of silver, and pearls, of course. Further operations by more Japanese divers actually did bring up platinum for years, until two of them did not return to the surface. The beginning of WWII happened shortly after that and the Japanese pulled out of Nan Madol. Unfortunately for these tales, Jason Colavito was unable to find any documented evidence of platinum extraction associated with Nan Madol.[25]

Fortunately for me, I'm not trying to prove those claims, I am merely pointing out the Japanese control over Nan Madol in the decades leading up to WWII, providing them an opportunity to have been looking for relics. They did receive the site from German landlords, which is notable within our context here. The Japanese maintained a presence on adjacent Pohnpei for

---

[22]Peter O'Loughlin, "Mystery Surrounds Nan Mahdol, Pacific's Great Ruined City" (AP News 24 Aug 89); William Gleeson, *Before the Delusion: Secret Vatican Files of the Pyramids and Stonehenge* (SCB 2012) Chap 47.Postscript.

[23]Childress *Nan Madol* Pg 19; Von Daniken, *Gold of the Gods* (Putnam 1973)

[24]Herbert Rittlinger, *The Measureless Ocean* (Germany 1939).

[25]Jason Colavito, "Are There Ancient Platinum Coffins off Nan Madol?" (12 Nov 12)

several years, including a garrison during the Second World War years.[26] Thus do we have the Axis powers controlling this unique site of Nan Madol for several decades. Whether they got platinum out of any mysterious 'house of the dead' or not, what might they have looked for there? What might have they hoped to find? What clues might they have actually found of any possible Templar presence?

With canal-like waterways running between towering structures, long tunnels cut through coral, and tales of spectres haunting the place after dark to scare away the curious[27], Nan Madol impresses me as a site possibly known to and used by our hypothetical Templar vault-keepers. With the first European discovery of the site not being recognized until the early 19th Century, it would have been the perfect hiding spot in the 16th Century, far away from civilization and somewhat imposing.

Nan Madol provides a maze of difficulties for would-be treasure hunters seeking to capture a powerful relic. It also provides a defensible position for protectors. Raiders would be at the disadvantage and likely be vanquished before ever coming close to the vault. Probably most important, within the context of the Templar vaults as I propose them, their function being linked to the world grid, my available telluric world grid mapping shows a major line flowing right through the area.

But an imposing structure is also a noticeable one and that can be a problem if you're trying to hide something. The better site

---

[26]Japan took control of Pohnpei from Germany per the Treaty of Versailles 1919.
[27] Childress, *Cham* and *Nan Madol.*

would be even farther away from civilization and a little more subtle, preferably negligible.

The next candidate offers this advantage.

Pitcairn's Island

Actually a group of four islands, Pitcairn forms the least populated nation in the world. East of French Polynesia and west of Easter Island, the namesake island of Pitcairn has a five hundred year history of Polynesian habitation. The British sighted it in 1767 and named it after the teenage lad who called it out. However, before the infamous arrival of the mutineers of the HMS *Bounty* twenty-three years later, it so happens that a Portuguese explorer, Pedro Fernandes de Queiros found the Pitcairns one hundred and sixty-one years prior.[28]

Queiros was born forty years after Cabrillo disappeared, but might he have known the Pitcairn isles were there? He was on the Neira expedition exploring the Pacific when he took command after Neira died and then set his sights on locating the ancient legendary Terra Australis[29] which raises the question of whether Queiros may have been armed with secret cartographic knowledge. He was the navigator, after all, and he did go in search of an ancient land suggestive of territories on the legendary Piri Reis map. Was Queiros part of a brotherhood, dare I say *hidalgo de sangre*, and privy to where a Templar vault was located?

[28] Wikipedia
[29] Wikipedia

Queiros was seventeen years old when the swashbuckling Luiz Vaz de Camoes died in 1580AD, leaving behind his masterpiece *Os Lusiados*, the epic tale of exploration and discovery[30] which so fascinated Richard Burton and influenced Jan Potocki before him. Queiros began his own adventure by entering the Spanish navy that very year. During the next fifteen years, as he developed himself into a seaman and navigator, might Queiros have become privy to the secret cartographic tradition as Columbus is also suspected?

Because of the Portuguese connection and the associated milieu I've explored in my books about Cabrillo and Burton, I have to wonder if Queiros might have indeed known that Pitcairn was there before 'finding' it. If that's possible, then we must consider the possibility that the same source of his secret cartographic knowledge provided him knowledge of a Templar vault on the island. Additionally, might the subsequent British sighting have been an indication that the Crown (and its resident oligarchy) were still searching for their lost Excalibur?

I have to wonder if there is some yet to be deciphered secret regarding the *Bounty* mutiny. Was Fletcher Christian an intelligence agent, a status unknown to Bligh? Christian did come from a family of Deemsters on the Isle of Man, judges and legal officials through multiple generations of his family. Had the admiralty recruited him for a special assignment aboard the *Bounty*?

---

[30] Wil & Ariel Durant, *The Age of Reason Begins* (Simon & Schuster 1961), Pgs 290-293.

Captain Cook had been given sealed orders not to be opened until he departed Bora Bora. The classified instructions ordered Cook to search for the aforementioned Terra Australis at the bottom of the world. We are told he didn't find it and that Antarctica was not sighted until 1820, so might this have been the objective of a secret mission linked to the *Bounty* or Fletcher Christian?

Or could there have been another objective embedded within the search for the elusive land to the south?

Perhaps the infamous mutineer was not so much lazing around in Tahiti as he was looking for something, some object hidden there by another agent and waiting for his retrieval. Could some unexpected turns outside Christian's classified mission have driven him to steal the ship in order to follow a lead to Pitcairn, suspecting that a Templar vault was there? There are conflicting stories regarding the mutineer's death and no burial site. It is believed by some that Fletcher Christian faked his demise. Remember that Christian's family came from the Isle of Man, linked to Scotland during the time of the Templar persecution when knights of the order fled there.[31]

Might Fletcher Christian have actually been working on behalf of the Templars? Had they placed him in the Royal Navy as a double agent? It could even be that his secret mission was to transport the sword from Tahiti to Pitcairn Island. It's worth consideration.

And what about Pitcairn during WWII?

---

[31] Wikipedia bio

It was certainly within reach of the German merchant raiders, *Orion*, *Komet* and *Atlantis*.[32] Japan also was occupying many of the Pacific islands. The Pitcairn islands were pretty much in the Axis playground so any relic hunting expedition supported by the much and varied disguised merchant raiders of the Kriegsmarine could have easily carried out a search for the sword there. The problem is that there is more than one island and the relic could be on any of them and the residents have been completely unaware, thus no help even on the chance they would have been willing to help the enemy.

If any Templar relic, including the sword of Joan of Arc, was on any of these islands in the middle of nowhere, it doesn't seem to have been found. But we may never know and that is the case for Nan Madol and the Midway islands as potential Templar hidden vaults. The Battle for Midway had starkly obvious strategic value and need not have had anything to do with any archaeological mysteries, yet the possibility remains intriguing that Joan's special sword could be anywhere on this planet and most certainly is somewhere.

Whatever the case may be in all of this, I am confident that Juan Cabrillo did not die in 1543 as history tells us. I stand by my proposal that he assumed a new identity and entered service to a clandestine purpose which involves Hekate and a hidden culture. Will we ever know for sure what Juan Cabrillo was looking for in the Bay Area? I think that question could be answered by examination of whatever Spanish explorers knew

[32]"A Distant Tempest – How Nazi Merchant Raiders Carried the War to the South Pacific" (Military History Now 28 Nov 16)

of California before arriving in California and that we shall explore in a subsequent chapter.

We’re just getting started...

Chapter Two

Not To Be Overlooked

Returning to the historical period between the Cabrillo saga and my examination of Napoleon Bonaparte is something I have not yet covered to any substantial depth, and my continued research on the French emperor is covered in a second volume on his role in this series. But let us take a look at some other things that might have bearing on what is of interest here.

Following the period discussed in the previous chapter, specifically looking forward from the late 16th Century, the expansion of human knowledge in geography of our world continued significantly with Spanish and Portuguese exploration of the Pacific. The Solomon Islands, Australia, New Zealand, Siam, Burma and Indochina were all added to the maps of the known world. Much of the knowledge of the Orient was filtered through the Jesuits (a problem I address in a later chapter). French explorers added Nova Scotia, the St Lawrence River and Quebec to the roster, which leads to an interesting mystery we will discuss soon enough. Mercator's projection maps emerged at this time, as did his great atlas. Longitude and latitude were expressed in a manner reflecting an improved scientific grasp on the nature of our world.[33] Galileo,

[33] Wil and Ariel Durant, *The Age of Reason Begins* (Simon & Schuster 1961), Pgs. 589-590

Copernicus, Tycho Brahe and Kepler were the driving forces behind the foundation of modern astronomy[34], the first science to truly foreshadow our own space age.

It was also the era of Giordano Bruno and scholars believe that the Illuminati was born of Bruno's philosophy. His hermetic view of Christ and frank expressions on religion ultimately led to his arrest by the Inquisition which subsequently burned Bruno at the stake, another fine example set by the sadists of the Roman church. Joseph Farrell writes: "*...It remains true that Bruno's hermeticism was the repudiation of all religions...Bruno, like many Hermeticists of the High Renaissance, viewed the origin of all positive or revealed religion as being from Egypt.*"[35]

Farrell explains how Bruno saw the Hebrew mythologies as having been drawn from Egypt, the same for mythologies of all the Mediterranean cultures. Bruno saw no need for revelation nor the authority which its systems projected. Hermetic cosmological doctrine needed neither Catholicism nor Protestant Christianity, from his perspective.[36] This was dangerous stuff, to suggest the Church was superfluous, back then. It was the sort of thinking that led to the Enlightenment. As Joseph Farrell says: "*Bruno, in other words, is advocating the very revolutionary principle of the sovereignty of the individual person.*" [37]

---

[34] Ibid, Pgs.594-612

[35] Farrell, *Financial Vipers of Venice* (Feral House 2010) Pgs. 15-16

[36] Farrell, *Financial Vipers*, Pg.16

[37] Ibid, Pg.17

In these times lived William Shakespeare and the 7th Earl of Oxford (whom I agree wrote the plays) along with Christopher Marlowe, secret agent. Elizabeth and Mary, Queen of Scots, came and went with all that came with them. Sir Francis Bacon, too. And yet, for all its high thought and scientific advancement, it was a time of superstition run rampant.

The Durants write: "*Nearly all these occultisms flourished among the Britons under Elizabeth and the early Stuarts. In 1597, King James VI published an authoritative Demonologie, which is one of the horrors of literature. He ascribed to witches the power to haunt houses, to make men and women love or hate, to transfer disease from one person to another, to kill by roasting a wax effigy, and to raise devastating storms...*"[38]

James advocated that witches and magicians, and those who patronized them, should receive the death penalty. In the span of forty years in Scotland alone, eight thousand women accused of witchcraft were burned at the stake. Interestingly, when he transferred from Scotland to the English throne, James became somewhat of an advocate of the accused, exposing false confessions, insisting on fair trials, and even overturning certain doom for a group of women accused by a petulant child.[39]

This era of superstition was an atmosphere from which emerged the Puritans. Democratic theocracy was their political ideal. They disdained the idle nobility while defending the wealthy. Puritans were excessive in their morality yet some consider this just what 'loose' England needed at the time.

---

[38] Durant, *The Age of Reason Begins,* Pg.162.

[39] Ibid, Pg.163.

Parliamentary government and trial by jury were hallmarks of the Puritan legacy and from their ranks came men and women who engaged in the settling of America. British character and society are credited to them.[40]

Of course, with the Puritans also came the shutdown of theaters. Suffering a severe lack of humor, they declared most music and all dancing to be devilish, every pace 'a step to hell'. William Prynne, a particularly tight rectum of a man, determined that theater was invented by Satan. It was all devil worship.[41] Unfortunately, among those stalwart bastions of proper society who went to settle America were the fanatics who carried on the mad tradition of executing women accused of witchcraft, allegations based solely upon insidiously dubious testimony[42]. The Puritans basically made a nuisance of themselves and even their champion Oliver Cromwell, a 'self styled Puritan Moses', came to be so despised that after he died his remains were dug up so that he could be executed![43]

Fortunately for the western world, there were places other than England of that time. In France, Poussin would paint the now legendary 'Shepherds of Arcadia' contributing later to the Rennes le Chateau mystery and suggesting a personal knowledge of a secret and special source of gold[44]. In Spain, Cervantes would write *Don Quixote*. Portuguese adventurer Camoes' *Lusiadas* would suggest what I suspect today -- that

---

[40] Ibid, Pg.192.
[41] Durant, *The Age of Reason Begins*, Pgs.192-193.
[42] Kind of like US Congressmen with the impeachment of a recent president.
[43] Wikipedia.
[44] Farrell, *Thrice Great Hermetica*, Pgs. 131-134.

Vasco da Gama, his maternal ancestor, actually had gone to Brazil and was shown the city of Manuscript 512 before Cabral claimed the territory, long before the *bandereista* patrol went there and filed their report, which Richard Burton and his wife subsequently translated in a later century. England would have its hat in the secret missions ring with Drake's exploration of the Pacific coast of North America. It was a great age for its resonance in our times.

Though it may seem to the reader unfamiliar with my works as if I am stringing together a hodgepodge, the fact is that I have just pointed out some threads running through all my previous works: Bruno's reference to Egypt as the source of mythologies naturally must include Hekate. His advocacy of individual freedom was the objective of the Enlightenment which led to the revolutions in America and France, and these events led to Napoleon Bonaparte, though not exclusively. The Hermetic influence on science, literature and the arts, such as Poussin's work, also served to make Napoleon who he was. Napoleon would go to Egypt, after all, and emerge enlightened.

As suggested by his intellectual passions and my speculative analysis, even Camoes' epic and Manuscript 512 would touch Napoleon's life, his father's ancestor likely having been an associate of Columbus via the banking family into which said ancestral Buonaparte married. In 1532, Pizarro would journey into the Peru of the Inca who misidentified the Spanish explorers with a mysterious ancient race of men who came from the sky and built the amazing megalithic structures, possibly among these the enigmatic ruins at Lake Titicaca in Tiwanaku and Puma Punku. In the second volume of my examination of Napoleon, I provide a closer look at the undercover exile's possible forays into South America.

But there remain many years yet between the curious fate of Juan Cabrillo and the birth of Napoleon. For one thing, there was Drake's exploration of the California coast thirty some years after Cabrillo, during which Drake most likely did explore the same extent of the bay at San Francisco as did his Portuguese rival and in an equally secret mission. I am personally convinced that Drake would have been looking for and indeed observed the same remnants or landmarks of the forgotten civilization as did Cabrillo. In my opinion, what we're talking about here is among the reasons Napoleon would express an interest in California when considering the prospects of his impending exile. The curious facts surrounding Drake's true foray to California, and into the mouth of the Arctic, have been published.[45]

Forty some years after Drake, the Rosicrucians reportedly announced themselves in Paris via posted announcements plastered all over the city.[46] Thus do we come to what the life of Napoleon Bonaparte suggests to me: A secret society of some as yet unidentified composition was behind his development, sponsorship, and rise to power. In my opinion, this places Napoleon among the secret missions milieu with Cabrillo, Drake, Burton and others.

---

[45] Samuel Bawlf, *The Secret Voyage of Sir Francis Drake*, Penguin 2003.
[46] Pauwels & Bergier, *The Morning of the Magicians*, Destiny 1960, Pgs 25-26.

Louis Pauwels and Jacques Bergier put it well: "*The notion of a secret international society composed of men of the highest intelligence, desirous of protecting their scientific discoveries against officialdom and the curiosity and greed of other men, and reserving for themselves the right to use their discoveries at the right moment, or else to conceal them for a number of years to allow only an insignificant fraction of them to be published -- such a notion is both ancient and an ultramodern one.*"[47]

The authors go on to quote historian Serge Hutin, in reference to the Rosicrucians yet applicable to any such secret (or breakaway?) society: "*They then represented a group of human beings who had reached a higher state than the mass of humanity, and thus possessed similar internal characteristics which enabled them to recognize one another at all times.*"[48]

I suspect, and therefore propose as suggested in *The Esoteric Napoleon,* that such a group planned, selected, developed, and assisted Napoleon Bonaparte in order to place in Europe a driving force that would change the sociopolitical structure of that continent, and the UK, irrevocably. Despite the pernicious propaganda, the misnamed wars[49], and the ultimate defeat of Napoleon at Waterloo, the oligarchy so desperate to destroy this movement ultimately failed to stop it. As an expression of the forces driving the Ages of Reason and of Enlightenment, Napoleon was a success.

---

[47] Ibid, Pgs 26-27.

[48] Ibid, Pg.27

[49] Eight of the nine so called 'Napoleonic' wars were initiated by England either directly or via their European/Prussian allies and thus should be referred to as 'The Wars of English and Prussian Aggression'. WBB

From my perspective, the oligarchy and its puppet nations understood this success and this is why the lies and negative spin about Napoleon continued for almost two hundred years. They had to stop their own bleeding, so to speak. I think Marxism in addition to the power of central banking, itself magnified through purposeful elimination of a gold standard, were direct tactics used like a tourniquet, you might say, with the escalation of war exponentially expanding the establishment of military-industrial complexes in the 20th Century added for good measure. Marxism provided a threat to non-Marxist nations, financial manipulations caused depressions from which war most quickly lifted those nations, and the (and all) Cold War perpetuated the circular strategy.

Has it worked? Increasingly, the common masses have moved away from the enlightened elegance of intellectual liberty and artistic expression and are willingly handing over their hard won freedom to a deep security state monster, with its odd companion leftist social terror, created by the very oligarchs whom Napoleon threatened in the first place. Just look at American popular culture in our times and you might never guess that the Enlightenment had ever happened, and we're not the only nation which has been dumbed down.

Where is the secret group today? Though faced with candidates of diminished character to work with, in our times, I suspect they are at work in a similar fashion as they were in those late years of the 18th Century. Though arguably not as brilliant as Napoleon Bonaparte (and who is, these days?), there was recently a national leader who invokes the same contrast of adulation and hatred as did Napoleon in his times. This individual was the target of the same type of insidious character assassination as was Napoleon and from much the same culture: the puppets of the Oligarchy behind the oligarchy.

It is my suspicion that a private group was behind this individual's political upset over the presumed candidate whom he defeated. I see the hand of a secretive organization[50], itself as powerful as the elite inner Oligarchy, which I suspect made its presence known to the insiders during that election and continues to exert influence and maneuvers against the will of the frantic collectivists whose plan had been upset and have since swindled their way back into power.

We cannot underestimate the important role of France's direct influence upon the development of the New World. The beginning of open resistance to the oligarchy of Europe was the very establishment of the Knights Templar for their existence and particular rise to power gave them an independence that became dangerous to the rule of dynasties and the Church. Out of that applied independence, and especially from its subsequent persecution, sprung ideals which would deeply irk the ruling class and change the world greatly in the interests of the masses. No, not a perfect world, but definitely a better one. We owe much to that group of French knights who were, in my opinion, behind the opening of the New World to the oppressed of Europe and England.

---

[50] I am not referring to any idiotic bullshit fantasy 'alliance' which the likes of New Age cult gurus and their dubious associates have peddled for a number of years, nor do I refer to the Q Anon gamester nonsense. I think the organization I describe has its roots in centuries past. WB

It would be a long fight that not even the American revolution would completely win and ultimately demanded the appearance of Napoleon who, like it or not, left an indelible impression upon the continent that defines modern western municipalities to this day. In his own lifetime, even after his defeat at Waterloo, Napoleon may have continued to impact the western world through clandestine influence made possible by a clever ruse.

But that is to be examined in further detail in *The Esoteric Napoleon Volume 2.* Before we can look more closely at Napoleon Bonaparte, we must examine the aforementioned thread revealed by the French exploration of Canadian territory, specifically a particularly curious culture associated with it and, further, the mystery shrouding that culture as suggested in the works of two artists, one a painter of enigmas, the other a poet.

Where we're going next might explain Napoleon's interest in America.

Chapter Three

Et In Arcadia Ego

This chapter is a necessity and I warn the reader to not expect a neatly tied up package. This is a thread which must be pulled further than this book can take it so I present the following as merely my introduction of this material to the *Secret Missions* field of play. I am speaking of the mystery of the Acadians of North America.

There is no mystery to the known events involving this particular French Canadian sub-culture and its expulsion by the British from the territory in which they had settled. The diaspora of these people called Acadians is well known. The mystery, from my perspective, relates to the period before that, the murky past of pre-Columbian America. I suspect therein lies a more accurate motive for pushing the Acadians out than we are usually offered. Why do I think that?

My suspicions about the Louisiana Territory involve the mysterious and ancient Mound Culture, the legend of Prince Madoc, and a Merovingian thread via the curious tale of Father Berenger Sauniere and Rennes-le-Chateau. Through all of this runs an obvious French thread and a less obvious Napoleonic one. With LaSalle being the first to explore the Mississippi River from Illinois to the Gulf of Mexico, and the subsequent Bonapartist refugee demi-soldes establishing a colony, for a time, in the Alabama landscape linked to the Prince Madoc legend, my suspicion that Sauniere discovered a secret possibly less to do with Christ than it did with a Vatican role in the suppression of a French royal bloodline suggests to me that the Acadians may factor more significantly in the mysterious history of the Americas.

Giovanni da Verrazzano, the Italian explorer in the service of French King Francis I, was the first to use the spelling 'Arcadia' on a North American map, which included territory as far south as the entire Atlantic coast north of Virginia.[51] Suggesting candidacy for a *Secret Missions* book himself, the Florentine born Verrazzano's life is greatly a mystery, including his alleged death after reportedly rowing away from his ship anchored somewhere off a Caribbean island where, as one story claims, he was eaten by cannibals[52] thus was there found no body. Some believed he re-emerged as a pirate. Curiously, in the following century, Samuel de Champlain chose to remove the 'r' from the spelling of Arcadia, changing the area to 'Acadia'. Despite some resistance to Acadia having any link to the legendary Arcadia, the fact remains that it was indeed first called the latter, more traditional, name. Is there any significance to this?

I think so. Mythologically, Arcadia is the pastoral paradise home of the god Pan. Arcadia was also an actual place in Greece which, following the fall of the Romans, became an idyllic territory of the Byzantine Empire. Therein have we a

---

[51] Verrazzano bio, Wikipedia; Various

[52] Ibid

resonant association to matters discussed in *Esoteric Napoleon* for in the story of the lost Merovingian princess Albsuinda have I proposed a possible bloodline connection between Napoleon's mother and the Merovingian dynasty. As discussed in that book, Albsuinda was taken to Constantinople never to be heard from again. Might she have lived the rest of her days in the Grecian Arcadia? Might the trail of Napoleon's maternal bloodline have found its way to Italy through Greece? What would this have to do with an American Arcadia?

The answer to that might be that infamous Fourth Crusade. I have discussed this enough in previous volumes that the reader should be familiar with the notion of Templar knights and other such knightly orders getting their hands on valuable secret documents, specifically portolans and charts depicting previously unknown journeys to and exploitation of the New World prior to Columbus. I suggested that among possible secret documents obtained by the Templars, as a result of the sacking of the Byzantine capitol, may have been the record of Merovingian ancestry including the true fate of Albsuinda and her descendants to that time.[53] I further suggested these documents and maps played a role in the alleged explorations to the Americas by Templars in the nearly two centuries preceding Columbus. All this may lead us to Prince Madoc.

Believed by some to have journeyed to the Americas in the late 12th Century, Madoc is traditionally a Welsh nobleman who crossed the Atlantic and landed somewhere in the American southeast, specifically today's Mobile or somewhere

[53] *Esoteric Napoleon* Vol 1

in the Mississippi Delta, by way of the Caribbean and Florida, of course. But Madoc was also purported to have landed on Newfoundland, or Nova Scotia, possibly Newport in Rhode Island and even Virginia, all places subsequently identified with the Canadian Arcadia/Acadia mapped by Verrazzano four centuries later. With the Fourth Crusade happening just over thirty years after Madoc's alleged disappearance in America, Verrazzano could have been armed with knowledge previously seized by the Templar agent forces sacking Constantinople. Verrazzano had previously lived in Egypt and when he pitched his idea for an expedition to the New World, he made his argument with a poem by Jacopo Sannazaro, a Neapolitan born scholar who fought in the War of Ferrara with condottieri Alfonso of Calabria against the forces of Pope Sixtus IV.[54] That poem was *Arcadia.*

What was special about Sannazaro's poem that an explorer would use it to find a particular territory in the New World? I couldn't tell you because there exists a single English translation and even used copies go for around $125. The only English bit I've read is a portion of the legendary final chapter which, according to scholars[55], transforms Sannazaro's entire work. It is this final chapter of *Arcadia* which is represented in Poussin's painting of the three shepherds, famously known as 'Et In Arcadia Ego'. As near as I can tell, it is about the death of the narrator and his return to paradise, realizing that he had been given a glimpse of it earlier in life but had walked away.

[54]Readers of *The Esoteric Napoleon* will be interested to know that Ercole of the House of Este led this particular war against the papal forces.
[55]Anthony Madrid, "Et In Arcadia Ego" (The Paris Review 15 May 2019)

Point being that Arcadia is a paradise – more specifically, a hidden paradise which one must be carefully guided to reach. Sounds like an allegory for a secret land which one must have special directions to reach, which in turn sounds like what many suspect the Americas were before Columbus' revelation.

But there had to have been something more specific in *Arcadia* to make it valuable to Verrazzano in his pitch for sponsorship, right? There likely is and it's probably in a description of a landscape or a route taken by the protagonist narrator. I would guess that it's not going to be obvious even now but it would have been something that an esoteric scholar like Verrazzano would have been able to decipher. My best initial suspicion is that it all ties in with the theme of the dead or dying and 'sailing away to the Land of the West', a popular afterlife theme in Western European literature for centuries, from Arthurian legend to Tolkien. Where do people go, ideally, when they die? To Paradise. Why would the West be associated with a paradise? Possibly because explorers who had come to the 'unknown' Americas were enchanted with its abundance and exotic secrets. Perhaps even because ancient travelers who ventured from the known world beyond the ocean's horizon and never returned were believed to have found a better place. Whatever the reason, the mysterious West became associated with paradise, with Arcadia.

Did Verrazzano put the truth to the western Arcadia myth? Did he find evidence of Prince Madoc or Viking settlers in North America? Might Verrazzano's 16th Century discovery be the reason for the thematic link between Sannazaro's poem and

Poussin's painting? 17th Century Poussin could have gained access to details of a particular territory in the Americas, thanks to both Sannazaro and Verrazzano carefully revealing a landscape which the artist may have in turn revealed through his art, specifically those paintings dealing with the Three Shepherds aka 'Et In Arcadia Ego'. This brings us to how all this finds its way into the Rennes le Chateau intrigue three centuries after Poussin.

It's simple, really. The implication is that Albsuinda is somehow linked to the Americas, specifically 'Arcadia', and it may be through Prince Madoc's legendary venture west. The New World was colonized by Europeans under the ways and rules of their world in the 15th Century. Who gets somewhere first claims it and owns it. Imagine the problem for the crowned heads of Spain, England, and France, if in any way Prince Madoc had ventured to the Americas and set up there, thus establishing a claim in the eyes of European law three centuries before Columbus. Now add to that a direct-line descendant of Albsuinda being a part of that colony, that claim to the Americas. It would, according to their own rules, negate any claim by the known European and British colonizers of that specific territory of North America, perhaps all the known territory of that continent at that time.

Now consider my argument for Albsuinda being the secret bloodline ingredient making Napoleon Bonaparte a true Merovingian heir to the throne of France[56], a claim predating all other dynasties in Europe, and throw in an additional claim via

---

[56] Volume 4 of this series, *The Esoteric Napoleon*

Madoc's exploration, giving Napoleon much of North America. (And that's not even yet considering the speculative possibility that there's a drop of Mary Magdalene's blood in the mix but let's throw that suspicion in for good measure). What you have is a potential conspiracy between the Vatican and the French Crown to suppress that information in order to protect oligarchic control of Europe, with a good shot at explaining how Berenger Sauniere used what he found at Rennes le Chateau to leverage power and wealth in Paris: the evidence that Napoleon Bonaparte was not only the true heir to the lands he claimed for France but to a big chunk of North America as well. Napoleon may have had a legal claim to the North American Arcadia, possibly in the most expansive sense – and all within the rules of the game in those times. It gives new meaning to what secrets were to be found in the Louisiana Territory.

Is it then any real surprise that the North American Arcadia/Acadia was subsequently populated by French colonists? The Knights Templar were a French established order. Verrazzano was working for France. Poussin was French. All are implicated in the secret cartographic tradition, ie knowledge of lost ancient awareness of the Americas from documents captured at Constantinople. The players on this team would have been no real friend to the European or British oligarchy.

It would require a major effort of investigation and analysis to identify the landscapes of the Poussin paintings in North America, if my suspicion is correct, but I argue that it should be considered. Since exploration and colonization was well established by the time he was painting, we must ponder what else might Poussin's purpose have been beyond mere depiction of a landscape. Was he trying to map a veil hiding something specific within the terrain? Or *about* the terrain? Might Nicolas Poussin have known something about the geomorphology of the American 'Arcadia'?

Speculating for a moment that Poussin's landscapes in the pertinent works are in North America, landscapes which by the 17th Century were generally known, we must further suspect that there was something encoded deeper within the images. The Sesh Heri telluric current/gravity anomaly map I have owned for over a decade shows a good amount of telluric/gravity lines flowing through Verrazzano's Arcadia, thus would I start my search for Poussin's landscapes in accordance with this data. Poussin may have been identifying nodal points of gravity wells since associated with particular landmarks.

It should be noted that the North American Arcadian Expulsion, forced by those unsurprisingly duplicitous British, saw most of its French residents make their way to Louisiana, many settling around New Orleans. By this time they had been called 'Acadians', of course, ancestors of today's 'Cajuns. Following Napoleon's defeat at Waterloo in 1815, many Bonapartist refugees settled in the new Acadian Louisiana drawn by the comfort of a familiar culture. Three decades later, Henry Wadsworth Longfellow would write his epic poem about Acadia and it would echo Sannazaro. for *Evangeline* is about wandering from a homeland paradise and lost love found again, much like *Arcadia* except that poem's protagonist realizes his love is the homeland paradise itself. One may be able to confirm that Sannazaro's protagonist indeed dies at the end for the similar *Evangeline* sees the titular character die before her true love can find her. Evangeline has crossed the river of death as does the narrator of *Arcadia*. In this there may be a clue as to what happens in the afterlife.

Longfellow got the idea for *Evangeline* from Nathaniel Hawthorne but clearly drew inspiration and some plot structure from Sannazaro. But might Longfellow have known something about what Nicolas Poussin knew? Longfellow was the first American to translate Dante's classic trilogy about what happens to a soul after death. Did he understand the Three Shepherds painting aka 'Et In Arcadia Ego' by the inscription on the tomb depicted in the work?[57] Scholar Andrew Gough demonstrates in his analysis that the 'three shepherds' are likely the same man at different stages of life and the tomb is his own. Who, then, is the woman in the painting?

I say the female figure is Hekate and she is there to greet and then usher the dead man to the afterlife. Poussin understood Sannazaro's ending and this painting is proof. But that is the superficial analysis. We are still left with Poussin's role in the Rennes le Chateau mystery, as these paintings are specifically involved. And there is the question of the landscapes: where are they and what will be found there? Is there a connection

---

[57]Todd Wood & Walter Bosley, *The Mystery of Ingersoll Lockwood* (Corvos 2020) Chapter 5.

between telluric-gravitic nodal points and the journey into the afterlife – more specifically the Underworld?

What Sannazaro's *Arcadia* offers upon closer inspection is a journey his narrator protagonist takes to the hollow earth.[58] A literal Underworld – the very domain of Hekate. As Poussin's painting is thematically associated with Sannazaro's poem, and the shepherds are indeed contemplating death, the female figure has to be Hekate, the goddess of the Underworld who specifically controls the triple intersection at the gate beyond death. I conclude that the woman in the painting is indeed her and that the man is depicted in triplicate makes it even more obvious.

What did Longfellow know of Poussin's secret? The poet clearly was aware of Sannazaro's *Arcadia* as his own *Evangeline* reflects. The only clue we have as to a Poussin influence on Longfellow is that the poet's own tomb somewhat resembles the sarcophagus tomb in the Poussin paintings--except Longfellow's is 'horned' on the corners. This feature can be found on ancient altars as well and represents immortality.[59] There is an eerie chapter in the Longfellow story involving the family tomb where it was discovered six family members were discovered to be -- and to this day remain – missing from their graves. Would Henry Longfellow's grave be empty if opened today?

In my *Empire of the Wheel* books, an argument is made for an association between Hekate and the telluric current/gravity

---

[58]Anthony Madrid

[59]Wood & Bosley

anomaly energy lines of the earth. With nodal point energy increased at intersections, along with gravity wells which can theoretically affect time and space, might one encounter portals to some 'paradise' after death, some liminal doorway to an Arcadia in another dimension? Did Sannazaro, Poussin and Longfellow believe such an idea? Did Verrazzano find such doorways? Is such knowledge to be found among the ancient secrets of the treasures of the Fourth Crusade?

Just as with Juan Cabrillo, no one really knows exactly what happened to Giovanni de Verrazzano. And according to Sesh Heri's map, a telluric/gravity line runs right through the Mt Auburn Cemetery where that horned sarcophagus tells us Henry Wadsworth Longfellow is interred. No one seems to want to open it to be certain, even after six of his family members disappeared from theirs. One has to wonder what Lovecraft might have known about that mysterious 'Arcadia' for his poem of the same name is among his surprisingly bright works.

Then again, Arcadia may wait beyond the gates of death so it should be no surprise that he would find it promising. The more important point of all this, I think, is that it may indeed be a clue that someone in Europe knew specifics about the Americas before 1492. This talk of a place beyond death linked to the New World shouldn't be new to readers of this series for in the first volume we learn of the *humqaq* of the Chumash of California, located specifically at Point Conception.[60] Talk about Lovecraftian. The *humqaq* is reportedly an interdimensional gateway between the land of the living and the

[60]SM1 Chapter 14

land of the dead. The Zodiac Killer's first known victims were murdered at Gaviota Beach just south from the point from where souls begin their journey to the afterlife. Perhaps to some Arcadia of the Pacific?

A more pertinent question is whether there is an east coast Acadian equivalent of the *humqaq*? It is called the 'Western Gate' by the Chumash, after all. Does that in itself indicate the same tradition as among Europeans and Celts, that the land of the dead is in 'the west'? Or could it suggest that the Chumash believed there was also an 'eastern gate'? Indeed they did and it's at Montauk Point, Long Island, according to a Chumash elder of the Owl clan who has even visited the Eastern Gate as a guest of a counterpart Shinnecock elder.[61]

As if Montauk Point doesn't have enough going on with its reputation, might this Shinnecock and Algonquin 'Eastern Gate' be the source of all the weird tales associated with the place? Long Island is certainly well within Verrazzano's original boundaries of his North American Arcadia. Whether you choose to believe in the mystical claims about said 'Eastern Gate', the sources associate it to the Chumash *humqaq*, the western gate that is supposed to be a portal to the afterlife. This alone brings us back to our questions regarding what Longfellow and Poussin knew about Arcadia and death. These gates don't have to actually be portals, it's the suggestion that Verrazzano and select others could have known about it, specifically that they could have been aware of a native belief

[61]Theo Radic, "The Chumash As The Keepers Of The Western Gate" (Acta Americana Vol 8 No 1, 2000, Uppsala University)

or custom in a part of the world they weren't supposed to know anything about until they went there. We might also ask what the subsequent French Arcadians learned about the 'Eastern Gate' at Montauk for an interesting cultural coincidence emerges when we look to where the ousted 'Acadians': New Orleans

The voodoo traditions of New Orleans include the concept of seven gates to the Underworld right there in the city. Known as the Gates of Guinee, they are located in specific spots of the French Quarter.[62] Acadian refugees arrived at Louisiana in 1765 and many settled in New Orleans. Voodoo wouldn't have been so foreign to some Acadians as they were known to practice a European witchcraft blended with Mi'kmaw sorcery learned in the northeast before the British forced them to leave Canadian Acadia(Arcadia).[63] Certainly the concept of a gate to the land of the dead at Montauk wouldn't have taken them by surprise and neither would the voodoo Gates of Guinee. My point is that the concept of such things had been in North America since before Columbus, with the Shinnecock of Montauk and the Chumash of California. So how would Verrazzano and others before him have possibly known about these traditions before Columbus' sponsors opened it all up?

Templar explorers. The 'French knights', by that time an organization whose members spanned European cultures and embraced their need to operate 'in the dark'. Perhaps something

---

[62]Atlas Obscura.

[63]Susan Janet Harmon, "Mi'kmaw Shamans and Acadian Sorcerers: A Study in Cultural Transmissions, Transferences and Transformations" (University of Maine, Dissertation, PhD awarded 2014)

made believers out of those clandestine explorers and they shared knowledge of the evidence only among a select specially initiated inner circle. This might be how whatever prompted Poussin to produce his art encoded where it possibly pertained to North American Arcadia got started. It didn't even need to actually be a belief in gates to the underworld in Poussin's case, it could actually have been that such lore was used as a veil for hidden Templar vaults. Locations of such vaults could be what Poussin depicted in particular paintings. The references to Hekate and the triplicate man and the tomb with the skull could simply be clues to a treasure hidden at or near places the local natives believed to be gates to the afterlife and the allusions merely another way of saying 'Look in the graveyard' or 'Look where the natives say dead people embark to the afterlife'.

Neither Poussin nor Sannazaro nor even Verrazzano need have believed in a literal gate to another dimension to suggest that North American Arcadia was scouted for subsequent settlement by pre-Columbian European explorers. Templar vaults linked to the secrets these men were involved with would be enough. But did Henry Wadsworth Longfellow take the dimensional gate concept seriously?

Did the Templars? Did subsequent French sorcerers learn something of an otherworldly nature from their time in the New World Arcadia before fleeing south to Louisiana and other places, including Argentina? Might what they have learned have anything to do with the sort of thing Sesh Heri identifies on maps via his study of geomorphology and topography?

Just as the Chumash *humqaq* at Point Conception in California has the telluric/gravity anomaly energy running right through it, the map shows the natural phenomena running right through Montauk, Long Island. You don't even have to read the various works of Peter Moon to entertain the possibility that something very strange may indeed be going there.[64] And I do think something extraordinary may be going in both these places. I am convinced that Cabrillo and Verrazzano knew more than they ever let on. Whatever Cabrillo learned in California, and whatever Verrazzano learned in American Arcadia, it was extraordinary enough for both men to walk away from their already extraordinary lives. They might as well have passed through gates to another dimension.

Now let's move on to an interesting figure who knew secrets and believed peculiar things.

[64]I can't vouch for Moon, but his Montauk books offer a fun ride through a trippy perspective on all manner of high strangeness popularly associated with Montauk, and a whole lot more. I recommend a 'nuggets of truth' approach to his material because even a broken clock is right two times a day.

Chapter Four

Unsung Mystery

In previous volumes of this series, I have discussed the Polish adventurer, soldier, author Jan Potocki. Though deserving of his own book, I could not yet again discuss the influence of this fascinating yet relatively obscure figure without telling more about the man himself.

Born in the spring of 1761, Jan Potocki was a contemporary of Napoleon Bonaparte, and you could say he was very much a man of those times. Born of a noble lineage, Potocki was a Captain of Engineers in the Polish army. He also became a linguist, ethnologist and an Egyptologist. Educated in Switzerland, at Geneva and Lausanne, Potocki's life of travels took him through Europe, Africa, and Asia. He would be the first of his countrymen to fly in a hot air balloon. Intrigued with secret societies, Potocki would experience service at sea as a novice for the Knights of Malta fighting Berber pirates. Having spent time in France, he was fluent in French and wrote in the language. Potocki would start his own publishing firm and was one of the original travel writers, his wealth taking him across the Mediterranean, through the Balkans and into Russia,

Turkey, Egypt, Morocco, and even Mongolia, among several corners of the world.[65]

Potocki's single lasting contribution to history, so far, has been a work of esoteric fiction that has fascinated scholars and esoteric literature enthusiasts for over two hundred years, titled *The Manuscript Found In Saragossa*. Commenced in the late 18th Century, the novel was completed in the early 19th Century. It was written in French and told through a structure of stories within a story, similar to *The Arabian Nights*. The tale begins during the so-called Napoleonic wars[66] but covers events which take place in prior decades. The main plot concerns a Walloon officer making his way through Spain when he encounters assorted characters who put him through a mystical ordeal nestled between narrative episodes of a gypsy king, ultimately leading to a revelation about his personal destiny. Gothic themes, cabalistic intrigues, secret society shenanigans, and supernatural Orientalism make for a fascinating journey for the reader, if you can keep track of all the intertwined threads. First published in 1805, a complete text was not available until 1989 and the English translation wasn't properly accomplished until the 1990s.[67]

It is not my intention to provide an in depth analysis of the structure of Potocki's *Manuscript*, for it is the themes and allusions which are most pertinent to the focus of this book.

---

[65] Janusz R. Kowalczyk, 'Jan Potocki', Culture.PL, 2013; Fortean Times, *The Mystical Count Potocki*, Aug 2002; Ian Maclean, Introduction to *The Manuscript Found in Saragossa,* 1992; Wikipedia.

[66] Only one of those wars was started by Napoleon.

[67] Maclean; 'Jan Potocki' entry at sf-encyclopedia.com; Wikipedia

That the protagonist, Alphonse the Walloon[68], is being put through an initiation before his true family history and subsequent destiny will be revealed to him is the main point of the story. To what extent this plot reveals anything about the personal life of author Potocki is naturally of interest but the more I learned about him the more I began to wonder about whom else he might have been speaking. Does the story reveal anything about Napoleon Bonaparte?

This is not an unreasonable question for, in *The Esoteric Napoleon*, I explore clues and put forth the hypothesis that Napoleon's ancestry holds ancient secrets and the man's obvious curiosity for the unknown and the arcane also resonate quite well with the hermetical aspects of Potocki's novel. Might Potocki have used Napoleon as the model for Alphonse? This question itself begs the question whether Potocki might have been personally acquainted on some level with Bonaparte. There is record of a Count Potocki having visited Napoleon sometime between 1801-1815,[69] and Napoleon's affair with Marie Walewska was commenced via a ball hosted by Count Stanislaw Potocki, a relative of the author. This was likely the Count Potocki identified but, even so, with Jan Potocki's interests and pursuits, Napoleon had to have been some influence on his life.

Jan Potocki was born into a powerful family, the first documented member dating to the early mid 12th Century, though they were not officially recognized until the 15th

[68] A French-speaking ethnic group of southern Belgium.

[69]John Goldworth Alger, *Napoleon's British Visitors and Captives 1801-1815* (Archibald Constable 1904) Pg.156.

Century. They exist today as one of the wealthiest families in Polish aristocracy. Among the titles applied to members of this family is *hetman*, which is assigned to military commanders. Until 1776, Polish hetmen enjoyed autonomy from the crown. The title was still used when referring to a commander or leader. One of the well known Polish aristocrats to be titled hetman was Janusz Radziwill, ancestor of a mid 20th Century Prince 'Stash' who married a daughter descended from a Bonapartist family named Bouvier.[70] Was *hetman* commiserate with *hidalgo de sangre*?

Potocki was awarded by the Order of the White Eagle, the Order of St. Vladimir, and the Order of Saint Stanislaus which was a recognized order of knighthood until 1831. Interestingly, the Order of St. Vladimir bestowed hereditary rights of nobility until well after Potocki's death. He was awarded first class status in both the Stanislaus and St. Vladimir orders which, along with hereditary nobility rights, may suggest *hidalgo de sangre* status of the Polish stripe. In our times, Grand Duchess Maria Vladimirovna bestows knighthood to recipients of the Order of St. Vladimir, though this (and she) are contested.[71] But the question remains: does this suggest the *hidalgo de sangre* status for Jan Potocki?

Ironically, it might not need to, for Potocki was identified as a novice with the Knights of Malta, specifically affiliated with their naval operations against the Berber pirates in the Mediterranean. Did he secure knighthood from the order? The

[70] Yes, THAT Bouvier family. Encyclopedia Britannica, 1911 Edition; 'Stash married Lee, Jackie Kennedy's sister; Wikipedia

[71] Burke's Peerage; Wikipedia

record does not reflect it but remember that, following the persecution of their order, several Knights Templar were absorbed into the Maltese order.[72] And with the Templar order officially disbanded and outlawed, they are believed to have gone underground, which suggests that Potocki could have been recruited into their ranks secretly or even under a cover identity. Having already demonstrated a knightly status via his family's *hetman* history and his own awards from three Polish orders, we can legitimately suggest that Potocki could very well indeed have been a Templar and therefore *hidalgo de sangre* in its original and truest sense. And there indeed was a Templar presence in Poland.

In the late 12th Century, Duke Henryk of Sandiomerz invited a contingent of Knights Templar to Poland to defend Polish nobility against the Turks.[73] There were also Templars in parts of western Poland, Templar control of the town of Sulecin, and Templars established the chapel at Chwarszczany. But it is with Duke Henryk where we may find our connection between the Templar order and the Potockis, for the son of that first documented member of the family was Aleksander Potocki, the governor of Sandomierz.[74] That puts Templars and Potocki *hetmen* in the same place at the same time, and with Jan's later association with the Knights of Malta, an inheritor of some Templar knights and assets, it is quite reasonable to suspect *hidalgo de sangre* status for the author. Any one of his

[72] Bosley, *SM4:The Esoteric Napoleon* V1, Pgs 59-61; Various.

[73] 'The Knights Templar and the Secret of Infinitives', polishtutor.org, Feb 2017.

[74] Potocki family bio, Wikipedia

ancestors could have become a member of the Templari before he had the opportunity via his Malta adventure.

Having demonstrated that Potocki could reasonably have been an undercover Templar knight, it makes his travels and exploits all the more interesting. Can we determine whether Potocki was on a private quest, seeking evidence of the forgotten civilization, and does his literary masterpiece reflect this?

The easiest place to start is the last part of the question. Potocki sets up the main narrative in Spain, from which all the subplots project. From the work of E. M. Whishaw, *Atlantis In Spain* (1928), we have reason to consider Spain to be where surviving colonists from Atlantis (whatever it was) ended up after the alleged cataclysm destroyed their mainland. The controversial Lady of Elche has been proposed by Whishaw as evidence. More specifically, Potocki features the Sierra Morena mountain range, which has a history as the chosen hermitage of Juan Severino, a Lithuanian healer of sorts who lived there while in possession of a skull to which the Inquisition took offense.[75] This mountain range is also associated with a legend of a giant snake, which could suggest late survival of prehistoric species, but it's the mining history of the Sierra Morena which most suggests the presence of the forgotten civilization. In the time of the Punic Wars, the range was known by the invading Carthaginians for its gold and silver mines.[76] Potocki may very

[75] Henry Lea Charles, *A History of the Inquisition of Spain*, Vol 4, Macmillan 1922, Pg.200.

[76] Robert L. O'Connell, *The Ghosts of Cannae: Hannibal and the Darkest Hour of the Roman Republic*, Random House 2011, Pg.81.

well have suspected the same as Whishaw and selected Spain as a setting for this reason.

From the outset, we have this story set in various locations of Andalusia. I bring to the reader's attention that the original title of Whishaw's *Atlantis In Spain* was *Atlantis In Andalucia*[77] so already we have the hint of lost civilization presence in the background of Potocki's saga. Very old gold mines are also an important part of the story which further reflects the forgotten civilization idea. Potocki's novel features a Baetican gold mine and this dates back to the pre-Roman days. Whishaw's examination of proposed Atlantean colonies in Iberian Spain focuses on ancient mining in Niebla and the Rio Tinto. The Sierra Morena Mountains stretch through the heart of both Whishaw's proposed Atlantean mining colony and is, as already discussed, the mountain range featured in Potocki's novel. Certainly Potocki knew something of this Atlantean tradition in the region of which Whishaw writes for she specifically discusses the tradition of Atlantis in folk memory of the region dating back to the time of Columbus and he used this folk memory in his appeal to recruit sailors from the region.[78] There is also Potocki's service against Berber pirates as one potential source of his knowledge of ancient times.

Whishaw devotes a fair portion of her hypothesis to the role of Berbers in the interaction with her proposed Atlantean colony in Iberian Spain. As a soldier of the Knights of Malta, is it unreasonable to suggest that Potocki, a student of history,

---

[77]1928

[78]Whishaw, Chapter 6.

might have learned something more of this Atlantean colony of Iberia from this order of knights? Surely their scholars would have a grasp on any Atlantis-Berber association, especially after the Fourth Crusade. I say that any knowledge of Atlantean presence in Spain on Potocki's part is implied through the setting of the saga and in the ancient family mining element of his work. And this Iberian Atlantis colony is not where Potocki's interest in the forgotten civilization ends.

Recall Richard Francis Burton's mysterious missing months in South American jungles, in particular the curious similarity between key portions of Camoens' *Os Lusiadas* and Manuscript 512, that most interesting document of 1753 which purports to relate the actual discovery of a lost city abandoned by a forgotten civilization.[79] In the poet Camoens' epic verse is featured the Portuguese national hero Pacheco who also appears in Potocki's *Manuscript Found In Saragossa*. It makes no sense for Potocki to not have been familiar with *Os Lusiadas* and therefore also the details of the portion pertaining to what Vasco de Gama is shown of the lost city so resonant with that in Manuscript 512. Yes, Pacheco was an historic figure in Portugal and one didn't need to have read Camoens to be aware of him, but Potocki was a man who shared interests with Burton, if not an era, and they were both students of Kabbalist Abraham Abulafia. This is reflected in the character of Pedro de Uzeda, the Cabbalist in Potocki's work.

There is another curious possibility in Potocki's novel of a link to either Napoleon or Arcadia (or even both) in the

---

[79]Bosley, *SM2: Burton*, Pgs 106-110

character of one of the Moro Brothers, he who reveals the protagonist's inherited wealth to him in the end. Called 'Moro', this character reveals more 'secrets of the caves' owned by the family and also tells Alphonse of an 'uncle in the Indies', meaning either India or East Asia, who died and left him nothing. It could have nothing to do with Bonaparte. But at the same time Moro tells Alphonse this information, he also reveals that Alphonse has inherited a treasure of wealth and advises him to spread investments between Belgium, Spain and America. With the subject of secret caves and wealth and America discussed in the same scene, might we be looking at a clue about a hidden treasure in the New World? Might Potocki's use of 'Indies' have been a clever ruse actually meaning the *West* Indies?

There's also the naming of the character 'Moro'. In *The Esoteric Napoleon* we learn that one of Charles Bonaparte's ancestors was Francesco Buonaparte of the late 15th and early 16th Centuries. This Francesco was *condotierre*, a mounted soldier or mercenary knight. He was married into the Casa de San Giorgio family who owned the bank which financed Christopher Columbus. I suggested in the Napoleon volume that Francesco could even have sailed with Columbus on the alleged secret 1485 voyage to the New World. It so happens that his nickname was Il Mauro.[80]

In the Napoleon volume, I also propose that Francesco, Il Mauro, or 'the dark one', may have earned his moniker from being a Moor or even an Iberian, by blood. This requires us to

[80]Bosley, *The Esoteric Napoleon*, Pgs.136-142

consider that Il Mauro could just as easily come from 'Il Maure', suggesting an ancestry from Mauretania, source of many ancient immigrants from North Africa into Iberian Spain. If this is the case, then Francesco may have been an heir to a family treasure in Spain dating back to ancient times or even gold mines. 'Moro' of Potocki's novel could be a somewhat veiled 'Il Mauro', thus connecting the Bonapartes to a hidden treasure. And if the Bonapartes were connected to a hidden treasure then we must consider what Napoleon's access or rights to that treasure might have been. Add Moro's instruction for Alphonse to put the money in three places, one being America. This could be a veiled reference to some Bonaparte family treasure having been 'invested' in America when Francesco aka 'Il Mauro' traveled there with Columbus in 1485, if that voyage indeed happened.

Was the secret 1802 expedition to the Louisiana Territory which Napoleon ordered[81] actually an attempt to locate something hidden – or found – in America by Francesco Buonaparte in 1485?

There is the serious possibility discussed in T*he Esoteric Napoleon* that Letizia Ramolino's dowry could easily have included ancient documents complementing charts and maps which Charles Bonaparte inherited from his family.[82] Napoleon's keen fascination with America could have been supported by such maps and documents if they were to alleged to have led one to ancestral treasure or gold mines there. Since

[81]More on this later.

[82]*Esoteric Napoleon*, Pgs 182-184.

Napoleon turned around the next year and practically gave the Louisiana Territory to the United States for an unexpectedly low sum, are we to wonder if Napoleon's secret expedition of 1802 found the hidden inheritance?

Moro instructing Alphonse to place the money in America isn't the only clue we have, for the suggestions of Brabant and Spain are equally loaded. Spain is easy as *The Manuscript Found in Saragossa* is set in Spain and we get plenty of allusions as to why. Now add the possibility that Charles Bonaparte's ancestor Francesco aka 'Il Mauro' may have had Iberian blood. And don't forget about Joseph Bonaparte being made the King of Spain by his brother. Who knows what of Francesco's family secrets Joseph may have learned while on that throne.

It is in Moro's instruction for Alphonse to place some of his inheritance in the Brabant province of Belgium where we find a very intriguing implication. Brabant, specifically the town of Genappe, ends up being Napoleon's headquarters during Waterloo. Of course, Potocki could not have known that when he wrote his novel because *Manuscript* was finished in 1814, the year before the fateful battle. Is there anything else about this particular spot in Brabant indicating any other contextual interest here?

There certainly is: Genappe is the birthplace of Godfrey de Bouillon, a founding member of the Knights Templar.[83] The Napoleonic implications of this choice by the emperor general

[83]L. Bréhier, "Godfrey of Bouillon" in The Catholic Encyclopedia (1909), citing Haigneré, Mémoires lus à la Sorbonne, Paris, 1868, 213

are to be discussed in the second volume of *Esoteric Napoleon*. For purposes here, we have a clear reference to the Knights Templar by Moro to Alphonse in Potocki's novel. When you put them together, what might we get? Brabant (Genappe) plus Spain plus America might very well be saying Knights Templar plus Spain plus America and that suggests the secret of Christopher Columbus having been a Templar, as now suspected. I think this suspected status had everything to do with Columbus' role in revealing the New World of America – and is a veiled revelation made by Jan Potocki in 1814, almost two hundred years before it has become popular to suspect Columbus of being a member of the then outlawed Templar order.

We could stop right here, as far as Potocki is concerned. However, there is so much more about the man and his amazing novel that I will continue my pursuit to learn as much as I can about Potocki and his secrets. Since I think it would be best served with a dedicated volume, I will save it for that.

But we will leave you with something to whet your appetite: Jan Potocki committed suicide at the age of 54, in December of 1815. He shot himself with a homemade silver bullet.

He believed that he was becoming a werewolf.

Chapter Five

Unspoken Archeaology, Gold, & Murder?

It's difficult to entirely avoid Napoleon, by this point. However, that material is better served in two dedicated volumes in this series. Therefore we will go around Napoleon by way of Lewis and Clark, for I cannot shake the nagging suspicion that there remains a big secret to their expedition which, if I'm right, is astonishingly still classified over two centuries following their exploits and Lewis' suspicious death.

My suspicions about the Louisiana Purchase arise for multiple reasons, one of them being President Thomas Jefferson using executive power to more than double the size of the United States. The Louisiana Territory, a vast landscape north of the 33rd latitude[84], and with famously unspecified boundaries to the north and west, was sold to the United States for a bargain basement price by our friend Napoleon Bonaparte for multiple reasons, not the least of which was to strengthen the young nation and flip the proverbial (and well deserved) offending finger to the British. What makes the whole episode interesting to my mind is a sense that we don't know the whole story, either of the place or the deal to obtain it.

Thomas Jefferson envisioned the expedition before commissioning the two explorers and his scientific interests

---

[84] Oh my. THAT latitude...

were as keenly aroused, as were his savvy political wits regarding the clear boon this would be to the still fledgling country. I strongly suspect that Jefferson had Lewis and Clark looking for more than flora, fauna, and diplomatic terms with the natives. So what might they have been looking for that remains unspoken of today?

Let's engage in some further speculation.

As discussed in *The Esoteric Napoleon Volume 1*[85], the skulduggery of Nicholas Biddle and the controversial death of Meriwether Lewis gives one pause to wonder what was or possibly remains in the vast former territory.

We know that Thomas Jefferson was very much engaged in scientific and historical knowledge, possessing the largest personal library in the US at the time. Jefferson would send Meriwether Lewis and William Clark to explore the newly acquired territory. Lewis would end up dead, some say leaving an early example of 'suiciding' in America, just a few years after returning from that expedition. Biddle's involvement in both the financial and archaeological details of the expedition would appear even more suspicious with his subsequent actions regarding central banking. It appears that Biddle could have enriched himself through knowledge of some as yet unidentified thing or information discovered on the expedition, quite possibly impressive sources of gold.[86] But before that legendary expedition, there is the much lesser known secret

---

[85] *Secret Missions 4* by Walter Bosley, Chapter 12.

[86] Ibid

French expedition just a year prior to Napoleon's sale of the real estate.

As stated in the previous chapter, and in *Esoteric Napoleon*, on page 291: In 1802 Napoleon instructed his naval minister, Denis Decres, to prepare assets for the exploration of the Louisiana Territory, thus an expeditionary military unit was formed, with maps of the Louisiana coastline known to have been commissioned though by no means should it be assumed these were the only ones. Napoleon's specific words on this: "*My intention is that we take possession in the shortest time possible...**and that the expedition be made in deepest secrecy**.*"[87]

It is known that France taking back control of Louisiana from Spain was kept quiet for a while, thus Napoleon's instruction that the French expedition be done in secrecy makes historical sense. However, might there have been a deeper reason for this secret expedition? If Napoleon turned around the following year and practically gave it all to the United States, why would he have bothered with the expedition? I suspect that he was looking for something in particular and I wonder if it was found. Because of the uprising in Saint-Domingue, and Napoleon's clear mishandling of it (his regret is well documented), most anglophilic historians make no mention of this expedition, so we have no material evidence that it ever happened. In the volume on Napoleon I suggest that this expedition indeed happened.

What were they looking for?

---

[87] Ines Murat, *Napoleon and the American Dream*, Pg.11

There are a few possibilities. First there is the personal family treasure mentioned in the previous chapter. That could include looking for any evidence of Prince Madoc's colony, first in the environs of Mobile, Alabama, then in the greater New Orleans area (specifically that which would later become the state territory), and any additional places known to be linked to the Acadian diaspora, as far as New England and Canada. However, these places were somewhat populated and that doesn't serve the 'deepest secrecy' which Napoleon instructed. The family treasure could also have been hidden anywhere in the vast Louisiana Territory, which would take the secret expedition up the Mississippi River, then across the plains and up into Canadian territory. Such an expedition might have still been in the field by the time of the Lewis and Clark operation, but it would have had almost a two year head start, though the territory was owned by the US as of 30 April 1803, suggesting anything found would legally belong to the United States. There was time for whatever they were looking for to be found before this happened or the United States government found out about any discoveries on their newly acquired property.

Though something of a personal stake for Napoleon is my first choice, the covert French expedition could have been looking for evidence of the forgotten civilization. Just north of the boundary of the northern part of the Louisiana Territory is Cahokia, the curious mound culture site where many argue can be observed one of the world's largest pyramid bases. Whatever archaeological treasures might have been found there would certainly have interested Napoleon. One could argue for this with any potential ancient site marking the presence of a lost or forgotten civilization. There is just one problem with the idea of a secret French expedition finding such relics and this problem precludes the idea that anything of archaeological value would have been taken back to France in secret.

Napoleon seized numerous works of art and relics over the years with the purpose of displaying them in museums, particularly in The Louvre. It was not in his character, one could argue, for him to have sent an expedition to find lost relics and not say a word about any such discovery. Two instances come to mind, which I present in *The Esoteric Napoleon*, and admittedly they are rather speculative: the unidentified painting Napoleon seized from the Duke of Modena which, so far, only Walter Scott mentions; and the Rosetta Stone, which I propose was actually translated earlier than history tells us. If I prove correct, there still can only be one explanation for why Napoleon would not want to bask in the triumph of such a decoding of the ancient Egyptian language and that would be if some personal stake in it were involved, aka something very special to Napoleon himself.

What could have been so special? The first thing which comes to mind is if Napoleon believed in some personal bloodline connection to ancient Egypt. Any advantage over other scholars of Egypt in his day would serve his purpose in any such claim. Remember, we're talking about dynastic politics wherein much wealth and power are at stake. Apply this to the secret 1802 expedition to investigate the Louisiana Territory. What personal stake might Napoleon have had there? Again, I presently can only offer that it would have been something Napoleon may have believed was linked to his family, which I can only guess he would have learned through information Charles Bonaparte left behind or that his mother's family revealed to him. The other bloodline possibility is that the Prince Madoc story is basically true and, as discussed previously in this volume, Napoleon might have believed he had a claim to the New World based in dynastic authority.

But there is yet one more possibility I can think of as it plays a prominent role in the westward expansion of the United States, and is discussed in more depth later in this volume: Gold.

Napoleon's savant advisors may have convinced him that sources of gold could be found by reading the terrain. If anyone with Napoleon's ear understood geomorphology, it would have been those scientists and scholars of the arcane whom he so valued. The search for gold could explain the secret expedition of 1802. France was at war and needed money and resources. Napoleon could have used the gold, or any other such valuable mineral that might be found. That alone, relatively mundane in comparison to thrilling possibilities of ancient relics and forgotten civilizations though it may be, is a very practical consideration here. And the reasons to keep it secret are obvious: Napoleon wouldn't want any rivals or enemies to know where he was getting it, of course. Mystery solved?

Before you let disappointment set in, keep in mind that I still suggest that Napoleon's secret explorers were looking for *legendary* sources of gold, as in Phoenicians and Ophir and

King Solomon's mines. I'm also suggesting that Napoleon's scientists would have required the expedition to look for signs in the soil and features in the topography that would reveal the likely presence of gold. Did they find it?

Who knows? Napoleon certainly sold the territory to the United States fairly early the following year. Would he have done that if the expedition found a gold mine or mines or especially a hidden mother lode? That doesn't make sense. It's more likely that whatever they were doing, nothing of the sort was found. It would only make sense if something of great personal value to Napoleon was found and then we're back to the issue of why was it not made public, if so. Think about it. If something was found to prove Napoleon's Merovingian claim on much of Europe and a fairly significant portion of North America, the man would have let that be known in order to rebut the conflict surrounding him. He would have announced it to the world.[88] Since nothing like that happened, I must return to the most logical possibility, until other information is revealed: It was the gold.

Why am I confident in this assertion? Because of subsequent events surrounding the California Gold Rush which will be discussed shortly, in this book. While I also imply that Napoleon's time in the Americas after 1815 would have

[88]It must also be considered that whatever Napoleon was looking for was outside the Louisiana Territory, either in the Spanish southwest territories of Arizona and New Mexico or in North American Arcadia/Acadia which would place it in US or Canadian territory. I doubt Napoleon would provoke a conflict over it, if that was the case. Either of these possible locations outside the Louisiana Territory could, however, explain any interest Napoleon would have in them while living in the US as 'Joseph'.

involved secret explorations, there is a very practical reason for that. In 1802, he had a very public need to not be so secretive about what might have been found. Napoleon's life was very different after 1815, in my opinion.[89]

We may never know what any such secret French expedition found in 1802, but I have to wonder if it had anything to do with the likely murder of Meriwether Lewis. A possibility that I will throw out there involves my suspicions about Nicholas Biddle, as discussed in *The Esoteric Napoleon*. Biddle had been assigned the task of converting the journals of the Lewis and Clark Expedition Expedition into books. I basically describe a scenario in which Biddle was serving the globalist banking oligarchy, as he was a big wheel in central banking in the young United States. He had also conducted the financial accounting analysis of the expedition. Between adapting the journals to books and gaining an intimate knowledge of what was found on the expedition, Biddle would have known if Lewis and Clark had found any signs of gold deposits. There may have been some unethical act on the part of the banker and Lewis discovered it.

If Lewis was going to expose Biddle's duplicity in service of the world bankers, Biddle's associates might have had him killed. If Lewis was going to expose whatever Biddle personally gained with his intimate knowledge of the expedition, Biddle may have had him killed. Other options might have had nothing directly to do with Nicholas Biddle's actions but might have involved Lewis threatening to expose a

---

[89]Refer to *SM4: The Esoteric Napoleon, Volume 1.*

well kept secret knowledge of said gold deposits and some other group did not want that to happen. This takes us farther out on the limb of speculation as it implies some underground group with a possible stake in the young United States being the beneficiary of said suspected gold deposits.

Sesh Heri lays out the role he thinks gold played in the westward expansion of the United States, specifically the acquisition of California, in his book *The Handprint of Atlas*.[90] In his lengthy hypothesis, Heri identifies Fort Knox as being located right on a major gravity anomaly world grid telluric energy line. He asks the question if alchemically produced gold is actually stored there, a most intriguing question.[91] Within our context here, I must add the question: Did sensitive knowledge of where the earth manufactures gold and how to locate it lead the United States to somehow influence the natural process or take advantage of it in a manner to expedite it? Could such knowledge of making gold be a deeply classified secret explaining mysteries surrounding our gold supply as examined by Joseph Farrell in *Babylon's Banksters*?[92]

In his book, Farrell lays out the ancient association between the banking oligarchs and religious temples for their value in arcane knowledge and its application to the esoteric arts and science of money as well as its value in manipulation of the masses. Farrell goes further to suggest that such an association involved a well guarded knowledge of a lost science of a

[90]Corvos Books, 2010. Out of circulation.

[91]Heri, *Handprint of Atlas*, Pg 83.

[92]Farrell, *Babylon's Banksters: The Alchemy of Deep Physics, High Finance and Ancient Religion* (Feral House 2010).

forgotten civilization and this explains a European dynastic fascination with alchemy and the transmutation of base metals into gold.[93] As Farrell plainly states: *"...they are indeed trying to reconstruct a lost mythical past: a global 'golden age' with a supremely sophisticated science with which they can dominate and subjugate the earth. But to reconstruct it, on the scale required and implied by their enterprise itself, will require that virtually the entire planet and its resources must be at their disposal.*"[94]

Farrell is describing the objectives of the global banking oligarchy and in so doing has provided a motive, bringing us back to the mysterious death, more likely murder, of Meriwether Lewis and the question of Nicholas Biddle's loyalties, for the above describes central bankers for whom Biddle was an advocate and enthusiastic ally. Farrell's analysis also provides an unexpected yet possible classified objective of the Lewis and Clark Expedition, that being a revelation as to the nature of what I suspect Biddle may have done with his intimate knowledge of the expedition journals, and possibly even an explanation for the War of 1812.

Thomas Jefferson was a man deeply interested in science and its relative subjects thus the earth's process of producing gold and also subjects such as alchemy would have intrigued him. Such information relative to the Louisiana Territory could have been conveyed to Jefferson by Napoleon after his secret expeditionary team reported what they found. This could explain Jefferson's bold use of executive order in making the purchase on his own judgment.

[93]Ibid, Farrell summarizes these points on Pgs 294-295.

[94]Ibid Pg 296

As auditor and then literary adapter of the journals of the Lewis and Clark Expedition, Nicholas Biddle, loyal to his central banking friends and masters, was in the position to communicate to the oligarchs of the City of London any data relative to whatever Lewis and Clark discovered of gold deposits in the territory. Meriwether Lewis could have discovered this duplicity and threatened to expose Biddle, but was murdered before he could spill the beans.

England attempting to overthrow the United States in the War of 1812 could actually have been all about gaining control of the gold deposits of the Louisiana Territory, as directed by the banking oligarchy representatives in their London headquarters. England had been dealing with North American native tribes in an effort to block westward expansion of the United States, the Louisiana Purchase becoming a major wrench in that plan. While the American forces were indeed trying to gain Canadian territory in the northeast, England's focus on the frontier to the west is telling. The attempt to take New Orleans late in the conflict might have been England making its play to capture the mouth of the Mississippi and control the waterway thus also gain the freedom to search for the suspected gold deposit sites as reported by Biddle.

As you can see, the central bankster oligarchy of Joseph Farrell's grand scenario offers an eerily resonant explanation for the mystery surrounding the Louisiana Territory. Whatever Napoleon's secret expedition may have found, it appears to me that perhaps it didn't go far enough west, for the reader will soon learn that the suspected, possibly expected, mother lode was waiting in California.

But that doesn't mean California had all the gold. The mother lode of the west might just be part of a much larger vein. Consider Fort Knox again, situated on a world grid line. The gold vault of the United States is merely fifty miles west of a place called Muldraugh Hill which was the site of old Fort Duffield, at the confluence of the Salt and Ohio rivers. Sesh Heri writes that the confluence of rivers can be a signpost for gold deposits for complex geomorphological reasons, not simply sediment deposits. The fortifications for Fort Knox were built the same year Fort Duffield was constructed, in 1861. Might gold deposits have been discovered at Muldraugh Hill during that construction? We are told that Kentucky does not possess the conditions for gold but if you didn't want anyone to know about your natural gold deposits, wouldn't you say that? You might especially put that word out if you wanted to discourage any poking around in the ground anywhere near Fort Knox.

What if the US could withdraw the gold from a Muldraugh Hill area deposit without anyone knowing about it?

Consider that Mammoth Caves are only fifty miles south of Fort Knox. These caves are identified as the longest cave system in the world. Over 400 miles of passageway has been reported. How much passageway might exist underground between Muldraugh Hill and Fort Knox? Are we to believe that the US Army has not taken advantage of this?

Now consider the possibility that underground passages linking Mammoth Caves and Fort Knox might also extend west, much farther west to other cave systems deep into the old Louisiana Territory. Could this have been the big secret of the Lewis and Clark Expedition? Might they have seen massive gold veins under the ground? What else might Lewis and Clark have found in such a cavern system if they indeed found such a thing?

Who knows?

Let this question lead us to the next chapter...

Chapter Six

From Poe to the Pole, By Way of NYMZANIA

By the time which I propose that Napoleon Bonaparte actually died in 1844, the Royal Society had been taken over by the materialist bean-counting science technicians fourteen years prior and Sir Richard Francis Burton was a twenty-three year old commissioned officer in the East India Company. The Prussians had been relieved of their concerns over the Enlightenment upstart emperor for almost three decades and were well on their way toward unification of Germany. Ambrose Bierce was two years old.

As I proposed in *Origin: The Nineteenth Century Emergence of the 20th Century Breakaway Civilizations*, the shadowy organization NJMZa, an acronym which I extrapolated from NYMZA[95], was likely already founded and on its way to sponsorship of the Sonora Aero Club and others like it, according to Charles Dellschau. Prussia was working hard on its vision of a Reich that might make possible the expansion of its duplicitous method of invasion via alliance and betrayal.

[95] I offered a possible translation of Dellschau's acronym back in 2013 and again in 2015, for good measure. The only people who tend to have a problem with it also just happen to disagree with my hypotheses in general. A convenience not lost on me. WB

Where exactly might NYMZA/NJMZa have been by the 1840s? Certainly setting itself up as a corporate organization that would take it beyond a mere society of like-minded philosopher-scientist industrialists, as proposed in *Origin*. As of this writing, I have no further details to present on the pre-Dellschau NYMZA. However, I have elsewhere presented my opinion of the Prussian invasion strategy mentioned above, and offered in stark resonance with known history, by author Paul Winkler in his 1937 book *The Thousand Year Conspiracy*.

Written before WW2 and published during the hostilities, Winkler's book is troublesome. While it does not offer footnoted sources, the book indeed makes perfect historical sense and disturbingly foretells a post WW2 perspective on America. I was never more convinced of a Nazi influence on the military-industrial complex of the United States, imported per the Prussian method, than after reading Winkler's book. And, by the way, Paul Winkler was greatly responsible for bringing Mickey Mouse to Europe as he personally negotiated a merchandise rights deal with Walt Disney in 1930.[96] How's that for synchronicity with my book *Latitude 33: Key to the Kingdom*?

I sadly suspect the fascist grip on our political culture was particularly strong between WW2 and 2001. Read Winkler's book for yourself before it disappears. Much of it concerns the medieval history of the faux 'Prussian' Junkers and how they used and then betrayed the Teutonic Knights. The book might

---

[96]Disney Dream Makers History

additionally provide an interesting perspective on the early 19th Century NYMZA/NJMZa question.

Among the topics of interest to various parties discussed here were lost civilizations and the extraordinary proposition that our world is hollow. This is worthy of consideration because some traditions around the world tell of the literal emergence and disappearance of entire populations. Might a hollow Earth have provided them refuge? A new world separate from the surface people?

Edgar Allan Poe was certainly intrigued by the idea. He was famously an admirer of one J. N. Reynolds, himself an associate and promoter of 'hollow Earth' advocate John Cleves Symmes. Poe publicly lauded the ideas of these men and even based some of his fiction on their beliefs. His only published novel, *The Narrative of Arthur Gordon Pym*, is the product of the influence of Symmes' hypothesis and Reynolds' 1827 work, *Remarks On A Review of Symmes' Theory*.[97]

Though Reynolds would pull away from Symmes' idea that a hole at the North Pole leads to the inner Earth territory, he would remain a strong advocate for American polar exploration. Interestingly, in 1828 Reynolds would convince the US Congress to back a Pacific Ocean expedition but once Andrew Jackson got into office in 1829, it was canceled. However, that same year, Reynolds convinced private investors to back an expedition and he got to go along. Unfortunately, there was

---

[97] David Standish, *Hollow Earth: The Long and Curious History of Imagining Strange Lands, Fantastical Creatures, Advanced Civilizations and Marvelous Machines Below the Earth's Surface*, DeCapo Press 2006, Pg.87 (How long does the subtitle need to be??); Poe, from *The Complete Tales and Poems*, July 1838, Pg.723

some trouble after arriving at Tierra del Fuego. The expedition reached the icy edge of the southern continent but the crew mutinied. Reynolds and a doctor named Watson were put in a boat to make it back to the South American mainland on their own and the mutineers stole the ship to embark on a new career in piracy.[98] Did they take their lead from the Bounty mutineers?

It is my opinion that Poe and J. N. Reynolds had met and were personally acquainted for a while. Poe's public commentary and his mysterious muttering of the name 'Reynolds' on the day he died, disheveled and semi-coherent in Baltimore, are convincing.[99] One wonders what exactly happened to Poe in those missing days, every bit as mysterious as Burton's missing months in South America twenty years later. Perhaps the author intended to embark on an adventure of his own and was waylaid?

There is an interesting side note here. There was a US Navy officer named William Reynolds who served with the United States Exploring Expedition of 1838-1842. This Reynolds also saw Antarctica. The pertinent issue here is that this very expedition, known informally as the 'Wilkes Expedition', was the result of J. N. Reynolds' persistent lobbying to the US Congress, himself unable to secure passage for this expedition because he had pissed off so many people in his efforts. Was William Reynolds related to J. N. Reynolds? Might Poe have also known William? Could William have been the Reynolds whom Poe referred to in his dying days? Both J. N. Reynolds

[98] Standish, Pgs.88, 91-93.

[99] Ibid, Chapter Three; Kenneth Silverman, *Edgar A. Poe: Mournful and Never-ending Rememberance*, Harper 1991, Pgs.432-436

and William Reynolds were born in Pennsylvania, though sixteen years apart, William being the younger of the two. There is the chance these men were indeed related, perhaps cousins. Since the younger Reynolds also saw Antarctica, we must wonder what Poe could have learned from him, if they ever met.

The hidden civilization theme runs thick through the tale of *Arthur Gordon Pym*, which ends with the sudden appearance of a giant pale and shrouded figure emerging from the chasm of a whirlpool.100 Could this have been a projection of a vanguard of the Tuatha de Danann

But of course, that is fiction. Right? We are looking at historical curiosities and particular threads that connect some of these together. In order to further grasp the meaning of any suggested secret mission of Richard Francis Burton, we have considered how that thread runs from the 15th Century to the Napoleonic Era and on to Burton's adventures, a thread spanning more than three hundred years and involving the enigmatic Jan Potocki, as examined in a previous chapter, and also discussed in *Secret Missions 2: The Lost Expedition of Sir Richard Francis Burton,* a mission which involved those pesky Prussians.

The Prussian thread, specifically NYMZA/NJMZa, runs prominently through our narrative from this point forward. For the time being there is enough to look at here, where Burton and Bierce are concerned so, since it is taking me another volume to properly cover Napoleon Bonaparte, we shall stick with these two. The mysterious Prussians were treated mostly on the periphery in my books on Bierce and Burton, but they had to have been present when these two men lived and chased their exploits, both known and suggested.

Neither Burton nor England were operating in India in a vacuum. Prussians had been there for two centuries by the time Burton arrived. Mostly missionaries, the Prussians were sponsored by organizations such as the Francke Foundation, itself backed up by the King of Prussia and the Electorate of Brandenburg, two possible sources of Nymzania if any there ever were.

The kingdom was the product of the House of Hohenzollern and the Duchy of Prussia which itself had sprung forth from the Teutonic Knights. With such lineage and sponsorship, it's no surprise that August Hermann Francke, namesake of the foundation, was a teacher of natural sciences, a category into which things like alchemy and other Hermetical pursuits were placed in those days. It is from these pursuits we can draw the source of whatever NYMZA may have been, if it existed.

I have identified possible participants and fields of expertise of NYMZA in my book *Origin*, so here I will proceed to what such an organization might have found worthy to pursue in South America. Gold is always the first obvious objective and likely prevailed over all. This would have logically led to an investigation of mining opportunities and certainly an interest in what the Inca and other cultures on the southern continent knew about ancient sources of precious minerals. That might lead to whatever the native cultures would have been willing to share about the legendary tunnels, I think, and here is where things could get really interesting. It just may be that the 20th Century Nazi Ahnenerbe interest in Tibetan tales of underground tunnels and Shamballah had a precedent in what Prussian explorers of NYMZA learned about the South American underworld of ancient tunnels and secret vaults. Even if NYMZA didn't exist, the various German explorers of 19th Century South America would have collected the same information for future reference.

But at present I think NYMZA existed so we will go with it for it could hypothetically lead to what or who might actually be down there, which brings us back to Poe and Reynolds. What had they learned about that mysterious land to the south? Is it merely coincidence that Burton's missing period was down there and that Bierce disappeared into Mexico, making it clear that he intended to head further south into the same continent? We could guess that Burton would have been intrigued by the works of Poe and equally Poe's sources of inspiration, but Bierce was actually friends with a known acquaintance of Poe: Mayne Reid, a former drinking buddy of the legendary gothicist, and himself a popular author.

Ireland-born Reid's adventuring ways were admired by Poe. In 1846, Mayne Reid had moved to Rhode Island, the heart of Lovecraft country (before Lovecraft) and subsequently went off to Mexico when war broke out, where he fought at the Battle of Chapultepec, once the site of an Aztec fortification. Among Bierce's regular circle of friends while in England, Reid was in the position to convey all manner of whatever he might have learned about ancient Mexico while there during the war. Reid became a very popular adventure writer and his last published work is about Tierra del Fuego, the tip of South America across from Antarctica, where Poe's associate Reynolds had been abandoned by mutineers long before.[100] Reid's friendship with Bierce would be one of several through which the American might have learned something of that continent with which he would be so fascinated. Between the possibilities offered by Reid's knowledge and the known activities of German scientific explorers, Bierce's keen interest in South America would only have been more stoked by the possibility of NYMZA activity to the extent his link to the airship mystery afforded, if true.

But it appears we may never know what role any of this played in Bierce's decision to disappear into Mexico, though I do my best with the information at hand in the third volume of this series. Questions posed in that book are only speculatively answered. We do know that during Bierce's life we can lay the timeline of the purported NYMZA and it appears a crucial period in the lore of this organization spans the years during which Bierce's life grew more curious, leading up to his disappearance. Between Bierce's arrival in England in 1872 and his disappearance in 1913, Germany experienced a blossoming of occult culture and industrial growth. Herein we find the thread of Theosophy, woven however precariously, via German occult players, and hypothetically NYMZA, to Bierce via the airship mystery and John W Keely. Theosophy would lead German occultists to various fraternal magick orders, their trail led by the likes of Rudolf Steiner, Guido von List, the OTO,

---

[100]I have seen one source that has proliferated the mutiny as having happened at Valparaiso, Chile.

associations with Annie Besant and *episcopi vagante* Charles Leadbeater. Among the Theosophists in America was Clara Bloomfield-Moore who championed Keely and his inventions, and linked to the Keely saga is NYMZA. Is there any clue to Bierce's fate in this?

There may be, for in 1912, the year before Ambrose Bierce disappeared, Dellschau stopped referencing NYMZA in his drawings. Later that same year, unknown airships would begin to appear over much of England but over France and Holland as well, into early 1913. With WWI then merely a year away, most scholars write off the airship scare as German zeppelins testing England and France's defenses.[101] Did this event mark the beginning of NYMZA's absorption into the growing German war machine? Might certain in-the-know players in the United States have been concerned about where NYMZA disappeared to, suspecting that the mystery organization was indeed gearing up Germany for war? Was Bierce indeed sent on an intelligence collection mission into Latin America to find any valuable data on German spies and secret societies, or NYMZA, in South America?

In my book *Origin*, I have presented my hypothesis on the connection between NYMZA and the rise of Nazi Germany, and additionally the organization's possible participation in the hypothetical Nazi International of Joseph Farrell. Where the original and only documented source of NYMZA is concerned,

---

[101]Theo Paijmans, *Free Energy Pioneer: John Worrell Keely* (AUP 2004) Pgs.393-396; Brett Holman, 'The Phantom Airship Panic of 1913: Imagining Aerial Warfare in Britain before the Great War' (Cambridge Univ Press Jan 2016); Holman, 'Mapping the 1913 Phantom Airship Scare' (Airminded, 2013).

there is no allusion to it in Dellschau's remaining works by 1912. Only through its association with exotic technology per the Sonora Aero Club story can we guess at the organization's involvement in the pursuit of such things by the time of 20th Century Germany, especially in the Nazi era. As even my willingness to climb out onto the edge of speculation knows its limit, we will leave NYMZA right there for the moment and will instead end this chapter with an interesting anecdote.

The following is from the New York Times, 9 Oct 88:

Body of Adm. Byrd's Son, 68, Found in Empty Warehouse

By Peter Kerr

Richard E. Byrd Jr., ...son of the admiral and Arctic explorer, was found dead last week in the darkness of an abandoned warehouse in Baltimore, his emaciated body clad in dirt-blackened clothes and one scuffed shoe, the police there said yesterday.

The 68-year-old Mr. Byrd, a graduate of Harvard University who as a young naval officer escorted his father on a journey to Antarctica in 1947, apparently died of malnutrition and dehydration, the police said.

The body was discovered Monday by a custodian who said he had chased Mr. Byrd and another man from the area on Sept. 28, according to Detective Charles Gilbert of the Baltimore police homicide squad. It was unclear, the police said, how the elderly member of a prominent Massachusetts family had come to wander and sleep in an area of warehouses and factories in the city's Hampden section.

"He was just wearing a shirt and pants and one shoe, and they all looked dirty," Detective Gilbert said, adding that the custodian who had chased Mr. Byrd and the other man recalled that "they had booze with them in a paper bag at the time."

Resident of Beacon Hill

Mr. Byrd's family described him as a resident of the affluent Beacon Hill section of Boston.

His son, Leverett Byrd of Needham, Mass., was quoted in The Baltimore Sun yesterday as saying that Mr. Byrd left Boston on Sept. 13 to attend a ceremony at the Washington headquarters of the National Geographic Society. The ceremony honored his father, Adm. Richard E. Byrd, the pioneer aviator and polar explorer, who achieved fame with his long-distance flights over the Arctic and expeditions in Antarctica from 1924 to 1956.

"I put him on a train, and my wife was supposed to meet him," Leverett Byrd said. "What happened in between, I don't know. It's very strange, this whole thing. We're trying to come to grips with it."[102]

Byrd was unkempt, wearing dirty clothes that were apparently not what he was wearing when he left home, and he was allegedly seen with booze in a brown paper sack, hobo style. He did not seem to be his usual self. There is a story there. It could possibly be explained by the terrible affliction of Alzheimer's Disease. But it surprised his family. It would have to have been a sudden and complete amnesia of sorts for a somewhat affluent man on a train bound for a ceremony in Washington DC to end up like a bum in an abandoned Baltimore warehouse. Though that could indeed have been the sad case, there remains reason

[102]AP News 10 October 88; Peter Kerr NYT, 9 Oct 88; Various.

to wonder about a couple of things. First, what did Richard Byrd Jr know about the secrets of Antarctica and could that have had anything to do with how his life ended? Could someone have thought he was going to start talking? If so, why not just kill him quickly? He was 68, it would have been easy to cause an accident. Instead, the man is missing for three weeks.

Where was he exactly? Might he have really been in Baltimore all that time? Or could he have been somewhere else and dumped off in Baltimore in a destructive mental state? It's all very questionable but could possibly have a more mundane explanation. In fact, the usually labeled 'mystery' turns out to not be so much of a mystery. One source reveals that Byrd Jr had been rather eccentric for many years. Sleeping in warehouses seems to have been something he had done on occasion, or sometimes in railroad cars. Byrd Jr was also known to not spend his wealth on himself, often dressed well below what was expected for a man of his station. Even more telling was the distinct downturn of his personality in the years after he accompanied his father on Operation Highjump, and especially by the time his admiral father died in 1957. Byrd Jr's eccentricity settled in deeper following his divorce in 1960. By 1988, years of increasingly offbeat behavior – except for a focused and determined desire to preserve his father's legacy – meant that Byrd Jr's ultimate fate was not entirely a surprise.[103]

So why do I suggest that something more interesting may be at play here?

Because of Edgar Allan Poe.

In 1849, on the 3rd of October, after having departed his home in Richmond on 27 September, Poe was found in a confused state, laid out on a street gutter in Baltimore. The

[103]J Garland Pollard, "The Strange Death of Commander Byrd" (Style Weekly, 13 Dec 88)

clothes he was wearing were not his own. He was indeed known to be a drinker but this is not necessarily thought to be the cause of his condition. Poe was mostly incoherent yet he kept muttering the name 'Reynolds' and eventually died on the 7th of October.

The common details between Poe's and Byrd's deaths are obvious: Both died in Baltimore, both were found in indigent circumstances, one in an old warehouse, the other in a street gutter. Both were found in dirty raggedy clothes not their own. Both men had departed their homes on a September day, en route to important business in two cities which are somewhat close together. Both men were linked to alcohol use in relation to their unexpected conditions. It is also interesting that both men had been missing for days before dying in the early days of October, 139 years apart. Both men had been born in Boston, 111 years apart, a number to which some would attribute a mystical meaning. It is also interesting that Byrd Jr was 68, the same age at which his famous father died. Yet there is even more that I find curious about this.

Edgar Allan Poe was fascinated with polar exploration. His only novel is about a ship entering the hollow Earth at the South Pole. Scholars say that Poe drew inspiration from a hollow Earth advocate of the day named J. N. Reynolds, the name Poe muttered shortly before he died. Why is it that a man whose tragic end is so much like the tragic end of Richard Byrd Jr is obsessed with Antarctica and hollow Earth theory, two subjects at the center of Byrd's father's life both through actual endeavor and the lore that has sprouted from it after he died?

Admiral Byrd is alleged by many to have seen a North Polar entrance into our allegedly hollow planet. And with Operation Highjump, he is also believed by many to have encountered some dark secret in Antarctica, perhaps as doom-laden and mysterious as the ending of Poe's novel. Is the resonance between Poe and Richard Byrd Jr some manifestation of a karmic frequency existing between these two men? If so, was Admiral Byrd filling the karmic role of Reynolds, himself a member of an Antarctic expedition that is said to have inspired Poe? Was Byrd Sr a karmic recurrence of William Reynolds of an Antarctic expedition and who would himself achieve the rank of admiral?

Does the same drama play out from century to century, merely with other actors in the various fate-determined roles, only the cosmetic differences between events engineered to discourage most people from noticing? With these two men, we enter the high strange territory of Hekate herself, for she stands at the crossroads of the secret of individual human destiny. Though we may not be able to sufficiently explain the curious phenomena that links Poe and Byrd Jr much like Abraham Lincoln and JFK are linked through significant details in their lives, we cannot ignore it. Do events and circumstances appear predetermined because they are actually cogs in a machinery of a self-winding timepiece which governs our plane of reality?

Are such curious and strange similarities encoded in the details of connected lives pointing the way to hidden truths we are expected to unveil in some process of enlightenment about some forgotten ancestral past?

Is whatever might be going on in Antarctica the reason why Richard Byrd Jr ended up the way he did? Was he, as many suspect with Poe, victimized by unseen players and purposely left in a condition that would lead to his death? Did any of this have anything to do with Antarctica and what may be down there? And what of NYMZA in all this?

The one piece missing from Poe's part of this mystery is Germans. Part of the popular lore built up around Admiral Byrd was that he allegedly encountered postwar Nazis with astounding technology in Antarctica during Operation Highjump. His son was there with him and would also have seen these legendary super-aircraft along with everyone else, all 4,700 of them, we must assume. The popular telling of this story always centers on what the admiral saw, without any comment about the other personnel who would have had to encounter the alleged Nazi mystery craft. There is sufficient reason to doubt the popular version of the story, but there is a nugget of truth to German presence in Antarctica because history shows that Germany indeed conducted explorations there. It's not practical that Nazi supercraft emerged to chase off the US Navy, but if something like that did happen, might it have been someone else?

Might it have been another group of Germans who had been operating in South America for a century by the time Nazi Germany fell? Could Poe's fascination with the South Pole and Reynolds' research have exposed them to NYMZA? That would fill in the one major blank in Poe's similarity to the fate of Byrd Jr. Though stories of Nazi super saucers taking on the US Navy in 1947 isn't likely, there have been curious visitations to Antarctica in recent decades. Apollo astronaut Buzz Aldrin blurted out after his eventful visit that something of great 'evil' waits at the South Pole. What is it? Might Poe's novel actually offer a clue? Could the secret of Antarctica have been one of the major gifts bestowed upon Nazi Germany by NYMZA?

I will leave the reader with one last tidbit in this hall of mirrored questions on Antarctica and those players on our stage. This concerns a naval vessel which may weave yet another thread of mystery into this curious fabric. I am speaking of the USS *E.A.Poe*, once simply called the *Edgar Allan Poe.*

Officially categorized as an 'unclassified miscellaneous vessel' registered under the number IX-103, the ship was originally chartered from Weyerhaeuser by the US Navy, built in Oregon in 1942, but was damaged by a torpedo that same year and not brought back into active military service until February 1945, or so we are told.[104] The *Poe* served in the South Pacific islands, specifically southeast of Australia, and not far from Antarctica, until March of 1946 when the ship was taken out of service at Subic Bay, PI, and stricken from the US Naval register two weeks later. The record states that the Poe was released to the new owner, identified as Asia Development Corporation.

But that sale didn't occur until two years later, in March 1948. Where was the *Poe* all that time? Was the ship really just floating there in Subic Bay for two years? It's interesting to think about the possibilities of a ship officially decommissioned by the US Navy and stricken from the register. Imagine the potential uses the US government might have for an unregistered ship it still owned in the first few years of the Cold War. And who and what exactly was the Asia Development Corporation? I could not find this company by name for 1946, rather I found the same name for a company incorporated in 2005 again for another company of the same name incorporated in 2018. There is the Asia Development Bank founded 'in the early 1960s' and is notably headquartered in Manila, just 166km from Subic Bay where the *Poe* was decommissioned and unregistered in 1946. Where did Asia Development Corporation go after buying the *Poe*?

The record states that the former USS *E.A.Poe* was wrecked in 1949 and then scrapped, thus ceasing to exist apparently along with its owner. Was Asia Development Corporation involved with the US intelligence community which had been

[104]NavSource Online; Dictionary of American Naval Fighting Ships.

developing ventures under the guise business diplomacy, a brainchild of Nelson Rockefeller and the OSS?[105]

Weyerhaeuser had been actively involved in providing lumber products and shipping troops and supplies to the US military starting in WWI and continued these activities during WWII, nearly sixty of their vessels sunk in conflict.[106] Was it really the company that ordered the construction of the *Edgar Allan Poe* in 1942, or was Weyerhaeuser merely the front through which possibly the Office of Naval Intelligence was commissioning the ship? And why the name *Edgar Allan Poe* for a ship that spent all of its service in the very south of the South Pacific, not far from the shores of Antarctica?

Was the USS *E.A.Poe* named such because of Poe's literary fascination with – or what he learned about – Antarctica? Is there anything suspicious in the vessel being decommissioned, and then unregistered with no activity listed conveniently during the period of Operation Highjump?

The mystery of the last days of Edgar Allan Poe is directly connected to the mystery of Antarctica and the idea that a lost civilization looms in the forgotten past of this world. The years between Napoleon Bonaparte's reign and the US Civil War was an era in which the mystery of the ancient past faced off with mysteries yet to come. It was also the era in which a particularly abundant territory long believed to represent a forgotten world was finally claimed by the gold seekers who had been following a secret trail since the day Thomas Jefferson made the deal of the century.

All along, that trail may have been leading to California...

---

[105]USAID, Wikipedia; Institute of Inter-American Affairs, Us National Archives; The Office of Strategic Services:America's First Intelligence Agency, CIA Public Affairs, May 2000; various.

[106]Weyerhaeuser Company History (fundinguniverse.com); Company history (Weyerhaeuser.com); Weyerhaeuser (HistoryLink.org).

Chapter Seven

Manifest Ambition

The Golden State is the geography of much of my nonfiction work so far and not merely a simple point on the *Secret Missions* map. There is just something about the place. There seems to have always been something about the place, well before it was explored by Juan Cabrillo in the mid 16th Century.

Believed to have emerged far back in the mists of time, the history of California begins with a fabled island realm. Superficially, the island of the Amazons would appear to be just that, a fantasy legend. However, there are intriguing clues which might suggest otherwise. It may be that California was indeed part of a now lost civilization, as has long been considered before I got in on the act. We shall be considering the legendary aspects of California and see how it is reflected in the historical and geographical Golden State, for I propose that the tales and beliefs about the California of a long lost past may have some basis in fact: That California was an island, that this island territory was part of an ancient realm of 'Amazons', and that the Amazonian gold legend associated with California played an important role in its eventual statehood.

But through all of this lore and history, there has existed a centuries long struggle to dominate California and the secret war continues today. At the heart of why so many have coveted possession of California lies its geomorphology. The clues to this covert campaign date back to the role Spain played in the New World. I will illustrate here the rivalry between two forces of conquest and a bit of their conflict over the territorial republic that would become America's 31st state. Behind all of it may lie the presence of a mysterious culture and a lost empire.

The Source

Our starting point is that fulcrum between the historical and the mythical, the early 16th Century romance adventure by Garci Rodriguez de Montalvo, *Las Sergas de Esplandian*, his second sequential contribution to the 14th Century Chivalric literary classic, *Amadis of Gaul*. Montalvo was among the political class of his day, at one time serving as the alderman of Medina del Campo from where, in 1482, he was sent with a military force to maintain possession of a city in Granada, the southern province in Spain which had been previously occupied by the Moors. Montalvo had three sons. His grandson Garcia de Montalvo was a soldier in the conquest of Peru and Venezuela around the time that Juan Cabrillo was preparing for his historical voyage of exploration of the coastline north from the Baja peninsula. Garcia became a source for Fernandez de Oviedo who authored the first European literary work produced in the Americas, a romance adventure about a knight. Oviedo claimed he conceived and wrote the work while serving in Santo Domingo as supervisor of a gold smelting operation. It so happens that Oviedo dedicated his novel to Ferdinand the Duke of Calabria. As heir to the Kingdom of Naples, Ferdinand, we are told, was 'influential'. Testament to that may be the vague history available where he is concerned.[107]

Fernandez de Oviedo himself is how Europeans first learned of tobacco, hammocks and pineapples. You might say the seed of popular tiki culture was planted with him, as he was the first European to reach the West Indies islands in 1492, after Christopher Columbus, and wrote *Natural y General Hystoria de las Indias* which was widely read in 16th Century Europe. The book, and Oviedo himself, was despised and his work described as lies by Dominican Bishop Bartolome de las Casas who labeled Oviedo a tyrant.[108] Whatever he was in the New World, Oviedo had been educated at the court of Ferdinand and Isabella and was obviously politically connected in some practical manner as he dedicated his book to the aforementioned Duke of Calabria and had previously served as personal page to Prince John of Asturias, son of Ferdinand and Isabella.[109] Becoming a supervisory level bureaucrat directly involved with the acquisition and processing of gold suggests that someone at court had expended influence on Oviedo's behalf and herein lies his pertinence to California's allure for the Europeans, in particular for Spain.

---

[107]Garci Rodriguez de Montalvo, Fernandez de Oviedo, Duke of Calabria, *Amadis de Gaula, Las Sergas de Esplandian* (Encyclopedia Britannica; Wikipedia)

[108] Las Casas was the author of *A Short Account of the Destruction of the Indies* (1542). Historical revisionist Howard Zinn cites Las Casas in his socialist-leaning work.

[109]Kirstin Downey, *Isabella The Warrior Queen* (Anchor 2014) Pg. 253; Wikipedia biography.

Gold is at the heart of all things California and one journeys through adventure, fantasy and hazy mythology to get to it. Oviedo's book was quite popular through the 16th Century but disappeared from the presses of Spain for a century and a half. When it did emerge again, some of the manuscript was missing. According to the Huntington Library in California, the reasons for this are not known.[110] What were these missing parts? Professor Daymond Turner cites eighteen segments missing from the second volume and suggests that Oviedo's death in 1557 is the reason.[111] But could there have been another reason?

What did these missing eighteen segments have in them? Turner cited that parts 8-28, making up the second volume of Oviedo's work, were missing entirely and the third volume was missing the initial portion of Part 29 and all of 32.[112] We are told that the Volume 2 material was returned by the 1852 edition but where had it been and why? Was there something in the text that someone didn't want out there for three hundred years? The contents of Volume 1, Chapter 8 involve an accounting "Of some peculiarities of these people of the giants" as well as of birds and fish and news of an armada. Most scholars classify giants and the like as mythology, of course.

---

[110] Carrillo, Jesús (2002). *"The 'Historia General y Natural de las Indias' by Gonzalo Fernández de Oviedo"*. Huntington Library Quarterly. 65 (3/4): 321–344.

[111]Daymond Turner *The Aborted First Printing of the Second Part of Oviedo's "General and Natural History of the Indies"* Huntington Library Quarterly Vol. 46, No. 2 (Spring, 1983), pp. 105-125.

[112]Daymond Turner, *Forgotten Treasure from the Indies: The Illustrations and Drawings of Fernández de Oviedo*, Huntington Library Quarterly, Vol 48, No. 1, American Issue (Winter 1985), Pgs.1-46.

With such material in the first volume, what had been missing from the second volume of Oviedo's book for three centuries?

Finding these supposedly restored segments was not easy. I did manage to find and translate Book 29 of the second part of Volume 2, which was not missing, but is mostly an account of Vasco Nunez de Balboa who was searching for gold when he became the first European to see the Pacific Ocean. Oviedo also writes of Balboa at Darien, a place which subsequently plays a role in the Napoleonic link to South America three centuries later.[113] Balboa was betrayed and murdered by his friend, and soon-to-be father-in-law, Pedrarias Davila who beguiled Francisco Pizarro into believing that Balboa was usurping his authority. Consequently, Pizarro had Balboa and four of his friends beheaded. It took the executioner three blows to sever the explorer's head while his lying betrayer, the jealous and duplicitous Pedrarias, watched quietly from behind safe cover.[114] One cannot help but wonder what Balboa may have taken to his grave regarding the search for gold and its trail to the Pacific, leading Spain ever closer to California. Ultimately, I was able to find the part of the book containing the once missing segments and it proves quite interesting.

Mostly chronicling activities and events in the Philippines, the first segments are about Ferdinand Magellan in Patagonia. What we know of the popular account of giants in Patagonia comes

---

[113]The rumored clandestine military expedition into South America by refugee Bonapartist soldiers as briefly discussed in *SM4: The Esoteric Napoleon Vol 1*. This will be explored further in the second volume of that subject.

[114]William H. Prescott, *History of the Conquest of Peru* (1847, Modern Library Edition 1998) Pg 146; Octavio Mendez Pereira, 'Muerte de Balboa'; Wikipedia biography.

from the scholar who was along for the ride, Antonio Pigafetta, who wrote *Magellan's Voyage: A Narrative Account of the First Circumnavigation.* This is where we get the story of the ten foot tall giants whom the Spaniards were not fortunate enough to bring back with them as proof. Matt Simon of *Wired* points out that the Tehuelche people of what Magellan called Patagonia were in fact of larger stature than average. Simon cites that Magellan even got the name Patagonia from a popular novel titled *Primaleon* which depicts a wild tribe referred to as 'Patagonians'.[115] Once again, like with *Esplandian*, we have stories of the New World being influenced by popular fiction of the day, this one by Francisco Vasquez, dating to the early 16th Century. The *Primaleon* is a follow up to a previous work Vasquez penned in the genre of chivalric adventure romance and was published a decade prior to Magellan's voyage.

Although the case for exaggeration has been made strongly by authors from Sir Francis Drake to present day scholars galore, might there have been something embedded in Magellan's account, and others like it, which would have been classified as legitimate information the Spanish didn't want everyone knowing about?

It's interesting that the *Primaleon* describes its contents with the following bit: *"The famous and renovvned historie of Primaleon of Greece, sonne to the great and mighty Prince Palmerin d'Oliua, Emperour of Constantinople...".* This is where these legends of the New World which cast Spanish

[115]Matt Simon, "Fantastically Wrong: Magellan's Strange Encounter With the 10-Foot Giants of Patagonia" (Wired.com, 17 Sep 2014)

explorers off on their visions of discovery and conquest become something other than mere fantasy driven opportunism, for reference to Constantinople suggests something potentially very real behind all this. The previously mentioned *Amadis of Gaul* was a similar and very popular chivalric romance adventure of the time but with an origin that remains unclear, predating the *Primaleon*. In this earlier saga, the title character journeys to Constantinople and there finds the princess who will be married to our aforementioned Esplandian, he whose story will involve the 'giant' Amazon queen Califia and a siege of the 'Rome' of the eastern empire, which throws into the mix the question of what certain Europeans knew about the New World before Columbus' 1492 voyage.

The Infamous Sacking of the Imperial Archive

To quickly summarize, in 1198AD Pope Innocent III instigated yet another crusade, as if the first three were not enough. Crusades require logistics and supply. This is how war profiteers make their fortunes, by the way. However, two major supply centers of the day, Genoa and Pisa, were at war with each other, much to the delight of the Venetian shipping and trade magnates who sent six French knights – usually code for Knights Templar – to negotiate terms between suppliers and their bellicose client. The agreement ultimately included the critical phrase "to serve God and Christendom, wherever that may take us", which would come in handy when, following the duplicitous negotiations between Venice and the Viceroy of

Egypt, those in command of the transport vessels took their sweet time in kicking off said crusade. The agreement with the client in Rome allowed a year for preparation and departure, after all. Those crafty Venetians waited until winter, when it was too late to proceed to Acre and the resultant frustration on the part of the military and diplomatic parties led to a calculated change in plan: the Crusaders would target Constantinople itself. In the end, the Byzantine capitol was usurped by Venetian puppets of the Latin hierarchy, giving Venice control over trade between east and west, thereby pushing aside bickering rivals Genoa and Pisa.[116] A brilliant series of maneuvers by Venice, indeed.

But that wasn't all there was to it. Some scholars see an ulterior motive on the part of the 'French knights' involved in negotiating for the Venetians. That motive was suspected to be a treasure trove of knowledge, specifically a practical intelligence about the known and 'unknown' geography of the world as well as relics and artifacts some considered mere legend or myth. This might suggest a motive for the double-crossing secrecy behind the agreement on Venetian behalf negotiated between the 'French knights' and the Viceroy of Egypt, for the Byzantine Empire had enjoyed access to the material knowledge of Egypt including the legendary spoils of the ancient Library of Alexandria. Constantinople had its Imperial Archive which many described as housing some of the very scrolls and relics of that ill fated Egyptian institution, thus

[116]Encyclopedia Britannica; New World Encyclopedia; Joseph Farrell, *Financial Vipers of Venice: Alchemical Money, Magical Physics, and Banking in the Middle Ages and Renaissance* (Feral House 2010) Pgs. 75-80

the keen interest of Fourth Crusade participants to get their hands on it.[117]

What was so valuable to the 'French knights' and their associates? Joseph Farrell debates whether the Knights Templar were or were not aware of Venice's secret intention of sacking Constantinople, through their trickery with Egypt and false designs on the Middle Eastern targets, as the Templars allegedly believed.[118] But more pertinent to our examination here is what the Knights Templar and their European associate orders hoped to get their hands upon. The answer may lie in the hypothesis that human civilization has been highly advanced in the remote past, essentially suggesting that high civilization comes and goes with human foibles and natural disasters. Professor Charles Hapgood was a proponent of this hypothesis and has been labeled a 'pseudo scientist' ever since. Here's what he said about the idea in 1966:

"*In one field, ancient sea charts, it appears that accurate information has been passed down from people to people. It appears that the charts must have originated with a people unknown; that they were passed on perhaps by the Minoans and the Phoenicians, who were for a thousand years and more the greatest sailors of the ancient world. Wee have evidence that they were collected and studied in the great library of Alexandria and that compilations of them were made by the cartographers who worked there.*"[119]

---

[117]Farrell, *Financial Vipers*, Pg. 80

[118]Farrell, *Thrice Great Hermetica And The Janus Age: Hermetic Cosmology, Finance, Politics and Culture In the Middle Ages Through The Late Renaissance* (AUP 2014) Pgs.60-66

[119]Charles H. Hapgood, Preface to *Maps of the Ancient Sea Kings* (AUP 1996 Edition) Published 1966.

Hapgood points out further that, although most of the maps of these ancient times charted the Mediterranean and the Black Sea, there were others depicting the allegedly then unknown Americas, and specifically Arctic and Antarctic terrains also officially argued to have been unknown to Europeans at the time. Hapgood concluded from these charts that ancient mapmakers had journeyed from pole to pole. The accuracy of the Antarctic coastline of the old maps when displayed alongside modern charts of the same terrain – land presently having been covered by ice for centuries – convinced Hapgood that these lost cartographers possessed an instrument for reading longitude long before our known civilization even thought of doing so, and that it was superior to anything our civilization developed until our modern times. One need only refer to the controversial Piri Re'is Map of 1513AD to understand why Hapgood considered these ancient maps to be evidence of a lost advanced civilization in the distant past.[120]

Though the Piri Re'is Map was discovered in 1929, Professor Hapgood pointed out that the ancient maps in question "have all been known for a long time". He was convinced that mainstream science cannot dismiss them, for they are evidence of the lost advanced civilization. But what exactly did Hapgood mean that the maps have been known for a long time?

In his book, Hapgood cites Oronteus Finaeus who drew maps in the early 16th Century --- the same period of Spanish exploration and conquest of the Americas. Finaeus' World Map of 1532AD includes a prominent display of the Antarctic

---

[120]Ibid.

continent which we are taught was not discovered until the early 19th Century. The general accuracy is rather surprising, considering we allegedly didn't know it was there in the 16th Century.[121] Hapgood also presents the Hadji Ahmed map of 1559AD as an astonishing example of knowledge of lands supposedly not yet discovered at the time he drew it. Likewise with Gerhard Kremer, aka Mercator, upon whose shoulders modern cartography was founded. He, too, produced a 16th Century map of South America and an Antarctic land mass with limited yet surprising accuracy. And yet, none of these were as accurate as the map which preceded them all, the Piri Re'is Map of 1513, which suggests indeed that older maps were out there and they were far more accurate than what was being produced in known history.[122]

There is also the letter from USAF Captain Lorenzo Burroughs, Chief of the Cartographic Section of the 8th Reconnaissance Technical Squadron (Strategic Air Command), who on 14 August 1961 stated officially that the Air Force considers Hapgood's theories valid, following an extensive study of the Piri Re'is Map of 1513AD, using all cartographic technology available to their unit.[123] Speaking as a veteran of the USAF, I find the Burroughs letter quite an intriguing opinion for a USAF officer representing a technical unit to commit to letterhead.

But remember, mainstream scientists and historians will tell you that Hapgood was a pseudo scientist to be dismissed,

[121]Ibid, Pgs 80-81, Figure 49
[122]Ibid, Pgs.99-111
[123]Ibid, Pgs.244-245

mainly because one mainstream expert summarily dismisses the accuracy of the Piri Re'is Map despite the obvious, and because Hapgood worked on an unrelated project with a psychic later in his life. Decide for yourself where his hypotheses are concerned but consider the following, for I find it rather interesting: Charles Hapgood earned his masters degree in medieval and modern history at Harvard and was working on his doctorate when circumstances of the Great Depression interrupted his studies. During World War Two, Hapgood was hired to serve in the Office of the Coordinator of Information which, in 1942, was renamed the Office of Strategic Services aka the OSS. It's possible that Hapgood's assignment with the Red Cross was a cover for intelligence collections. Lest one think the professor a mere foot soldier, Hapgood's duties included being liaison between The White House and the Secretary of War. As the reader likely knows, the OSS became the CIA in 1947.

If Hapgood was a flake, as some mainstream scientists insist, what might he have learned or seen as an OSS intelligence operative to inspire him to embrace hypotheses so unacceptable to the run-of-the-mill science technicians of modern academia? Could it have included knowledge or discoveries of evidence in favor of the hypothesis of a lost advanced civilization? Might Hapgood have come to his conclusions and hypotheses through exposure to real world intelligence supporting them? You decide that for yourself. I know what I think is possible.

Within the context of how Spain came to California and why, what relative factors of the lost advanced civilization hypothesis apply here? Unsurprisingly, I think we can refer to those two bugaboos who launch would-be debunkers into apoplexy, Joseph Farrell and David Hatcher Childress. They simply lay it out well. But I additionally point to other sources which I think serve the argument in favor of the idea.

On 19 March 2012, Scientific American posted an article about scientists working with data retrieved via NASA's Shuttle Radar Topography Mission which revealed substantial evidence expanding the magnitude of a known civilization, evidence dating back eight thousand years ago.[124] This is just one example of what scientists have been finding in the way of evidence of the lost expanse of known civilizations, demonstrating that these buried tracts of ancient civilizations are indeed there to find. But the question is of lost advanced civilizations, not merely settlements, essentially suburbs of known city centers.

While one may also point to a Scientific American article by Michael Shermer titled "*No, There Wasn't An Advanced Civilization 12,000 Years Ago*", posted 1 June 2017, when you actually read the article, it's basically about Shermer wielding his boner against Graham Hancock's ideas. However, what we're discussing here, cartography advanced beyond what is expected for its time, does not require anything science fiction in a primitive world. I am merely suggesting a maritime culture which may have been a few centuries or so ahead of the developers of various devices that became common and essential to seafarers of the 17th and 18th Centuries. The point in

[124]Virginia Gewin, *Satellites Expose 8,000 Years of Lost Civilization*, 19 March 2012 article from Nature Magazine, reposted by Scientific American and accessed Feb 2021.

citing articles from the modern scientific publishing world is to demonstrate that the existence of civilization where none was previously thought to be begs the question of what else might turn out to be true that was not previously thought to be so, especially where advanced civilization may be concerned?

Scientists have found a city under the Sahara Desert dating back three millennia where it was thought previously that there was only sand.[125] There is also the civilization dating back to 1800 BCE in China which disappeared and was unknown until the artifacts unlike any in the known history of the region were found.[126] There is, of course, Heinrich Schliemann and his discovery that Troy actually existed in the real world, not merely in literature.[127] What else might have actually existed that today remains shoved aside because 'it's only in literature' or its advocates stand outside the anointed circle-jerk of accepted academic society?

I have, in the second volume of this very series, presented the tale of the 'Liahona' as described in the controversial Book of Mormon, an object which functioned like a GPS device with user interface akin to the texting application we use on our cellphones today.[128] I present this within the context of a comparison between specific verses in the Book of Mormon

---

[125]Lizzie Wade, "Drones and Satellites Spot Lost Civilizations In Unlikely Places" (Science Mag 13 Feb 2015).

[126]Dirk Van Tuerenhout, PhD, "China's Lost Civilization: The Mystery of Sanxingdui" (Houston Museum of Natural Science)

[127]Alexandra Villing, "The Search For The Lost City of Troy" (The British Museum Blog, 18 June 2019)

[128]Joseph Smith, *The Book of Mormon*, 1 Nephi 16:28; Bosley, *Secret Missions 2: The Lost Expedition of Sir Richard Francis Burton* (Corvos/LCL Pgs 151-152

and description of a lost city in Manuscript 512 which Joseph Smith could not have been aware of at the time of the writing of his religious book. Admittedly, the Liahona device is a science fiction type of object but it's not alone among the stories out there about the advanced technological aptitude of the lost or even known ancient world. There is more.

David Hatcher Childress presents historical reports of this ancient technological aptitude in his various books. Childress presents batteries made in ancient Baghdad; accounts by Saint Augustine, 4th Century, and Pausanius, 2nd Century, of ever-burning electric lights; historical accounts of Archimedes' powerful solar mirror used by 3rd Century Greeks to burn invading fleets with the reflective power of the sun like a laser beam; and a lot more just in one book.[129] In another book, Childress presents evidence of Sumerian mining technology in Tiwanaku, Peru; ancient use of advanced architectural methods in Cuzco; possible aerial technology, such as gliders and balloons throughout Peru and in Bolivia long before practical application of these appeared in known history.[130]

The reader must resist interpreting these reports and claims within the context of our times. Ancient batteries were not encased in modern machined aluminum cells, as sold in packages at your local grocery store. They were made of primitive elements contained in clay jars. Archimedes' solar mirror weapon was not an electro-digital laser beam, it was literally a mirror and mirrors indeed reflect and bounce light. A

[129]David H Childress, *Technology of the Gods: The Incredible Sciences of the Ancients* (AUP 2000).
[130]Childress, *Ancient Technology In Peru & Bolivia (*AUP 2012)

mere handheld magnifying glass intensifies sunlight enough to kill insects, imagine what a large mirror could do with sunlight. Rudimentary gliders and hot air balloons are well within the accessible resources of ancient Peruvians and no one is arguing that these would be exactly like the ones we see today. The point is that evidence suggests ancient people had an aptitude beyond what is assumed by our smugly arrogant modern world. I cite these examples in order to argue that a sufficiently advanced understanding of navigation and cartography earlier than is generally believed is all that is necessary to back up the proposition that maps of an advanced nature existed during the medieval era.

Accepted human history tells us that the concept of longitude was developed in the 2nd Century BCE by Hipparchus, the father of trigonometry, and he placed the prime meridian through Alexandria, the very location of the ancient Library at the heart of our discussion on the Fourth Crusade. Following the fall of Rome, Muslim astronomer Abu al-Battānī determined the difference in longitude between Antakya and Raqqa with an error of less than 1°, using simultaneous observations of lunar eclipses. In the 12th Century AD, eclipses were again used, this time to establish longitudinal differences between France and England. The early 17th Century invention of the telescope followed by the invention of the pendulum clock, thrust astronomy and cartography forward. Determining longitude at sea was achieved in the same century greatly as a result of prizes offered by European nations to the first who could make the determination within 1 to .05 degree, as required by the British Longitude Act of 1714. John Harrison developed the game-changing chronometer through the mid part of that century. If this is the recognized history of development of this concept, why do we assume that a lost civilization which could easily have understood astronomical observation and the measurement of time did not apply these concepts to oceanic navigation?

When might seafaring have first brought explorers to the New World? It might have started with Egypt, for all intents and purposes. Joseph Farrell and Alexander Del Mar identify the Egyptian mining and slavery practices behind the role of gold in our story. Farrell identifies Egypt as likely the largest gold producing state in the world due to the Nile River.[131] Del Mar points out; "*Gold has been found in nearly every regional tributary to the Nile, from the Equator to the First Cataract.*"[132]

Del Mar and Farrell each associate the Bisharee Mines of Nubia with the heart of the Egyptian gold-mining industry, with only India being known to have possessed a larger one. Diodorus Siculus visited these mining operations and wrote of the slave labor used to work them. During his visit in 50BC, Diodorus witnessed the use of mercenary soldiers to work the slaves working the mines. This he explains as a tactic to avoid any sympathies between guards and slaves and prevent conspiracy to revolt.[133] Farrell sees an implication in the

[131]Farrell, *Babylon's Banksters: The Alchemy of Deep Physics, High Finance and Ancient Religion* (Feral House 2010) Pg.165.

[132]Del Mar, *A History of Money in Ancient Countries From the Earliest Times to the Present* (Kessinger reprint/Bell & Sons 1885) Pg.133.

[133]Diodorus Siculus, *The Historical Library of Diodorus the Sicilian* (Translated by G.Booth, 1814); Del Mar Pg.141; Farrell, *Babylon's Banksters* Pgs. 167-168.

existence of an international currency power behind the presence of a sufficient mercenary force to enforce the slavery imposed in the mining operations.[134] How might this Egyptian model of slavery and mining link to the secret cartographic tradition and the then hidden New World?

The Cham

Does it make sense that China, India, Persia and the Mesopotamian cultures can be traced through their histories back to 1000BC or even farther, yet Thailand, Cambodia, Malaysia, Sumatra, Java and the rest of Indonesia is a complete blank prior to 600AD? David Childress doesn't think it makes sense and he identifies these lands as part of a confederation of Hindu seafarers who identified their nation as the land of Champa. This confederation included black men, which implies Africans. That the Cham are alleged to have journeyed by sea throughout the Pacific, reaching the Philippines, New Guinea, Peru, Colombia and even Mexico,[135] suggests that they might be among the sources of the charts and maps of the 'secret cartographic tradition'. The Cham maps could very well have been among those in the Library of Alexandria that ended up in the Imperial Archives of Constantinople, sacked in 1204AD during the infamous Fourth Crusade. Childress spends two chapters of his book, *The Lost World of Cham,* laying out the likely Indian and African sources for the elephants they brought

---

[134]Farrell, *Babylon's Banksters,* Pgs.168-169.

[135]David Hatcher Childress, *The Lost World of Cham:The Transpacific Voyages of the Champa* (AUP 2017) Pgs.11-20.

to their Asian realm. Add the descriptions of Africans among their people and its likely that the Cham seafarers had journeyed to Egypt and other African shores. If that is the case, why is it hard to believe that Cham charts and maps could have ended up in Alexandria?

If the Cham seafarers did indeed reach the shores of South America, and even Mexico, and if their charts *could* be counted among the lost treasures of Alexandria's tragically destroyed library, we have a source of charted knowledge of the Americas long before 1492AD. If they reached Mexico, then what of California?

David Childress closes his book on the Cham seafarers with a chapter on the reported tale of discovery of what was described as a lost 'Egyptian' city in the Grand Canyon in 1909. Examining the details in the newspaper article of that year, Childress points out that the specifics on the artifacts and architectural design of said city is more Hindu and Indonesian than it ever was purely Egyptian, and if anything it may have been a blend of Indian with the Egyptian. That, Childress argues, could only have been a product of the Cham seafaring explorers. If Childress is correct, which would indicate that the newspaper account of 1909 is basically true, then that places the ancient Cham in what is now Arizona at a time long before Columbus ever sailed the ocean blue. And if the Cham had been to Arizona, why not California? In fact, I suggest the obvious: if the Cham sailed and ruled the Pacific for a time, California would be a given on their itinerary because, even if their alleged landing in Mexico led to an overland journey north to Arizona, it's not likely that Cham ships would not have made a coastal recon up the coast of California. A small mountain of conjecture, I admit, but if true it means that California would have been charted to some extent by the Cham.

If the Cham charted California, and the Cham charts ended up in the Library of Alexandria, then said charts could be the original source of knowledge of California that ended up in the hands of European knights during the Fourth Crusade sacking of the Imperial Archives of Constantinople, known repository of relics and surviving manuscripts from the ravaged Egyptian library. Thus can we hypothetically yet legitimately provide some idea of how 'California' came to Spain before 1492AD. And that's merely using the Cham as an example. There remain the possibilities that Phoenician seafarers from Carthage, King Solomon's fleet a century before the founding of Carthage, and whomever explains the legends of Quetzalcoatl, Viracocha and the Book of Mormon refugees in Latin America were all sources of mapping North America and California. Additionally, the Phoenicians, Trojans, Atlanteans and King Solomon are all popularly associated with theories of mining operations in the Americas in ancient times[136] There has been sufficient scholarship on pre-Columbian knowledge of the Americas to warrant the hypothesis of California having been charted and documented in remote ancient times.

---

[136]David Childress, *Lost Cities & Ancient Mysteries of South America* and *Lost Cities of North and Central America* (AUP 1986, 1992); Frank Joseph, *Atlantis In America* (Galde Press 1998); Harold T. Wilkins, *Mysteries of Ancient South America* (AUP 2000 Reprint of 1947 Edition). We can't neglect a possibility that the navigators of the massive ships of Zheng He's fleet during 14th-15th Centuries sailed the seas of the world with the aid of unknown charts handed down through the ages in China.

Now that we have considered the idea that California could have been on the charts and maps among the Alexandrian relics, how can we be reasonably certain that Montalvo had access to such information before writing *Las Sergas de Esplandian*? Not much is known about Garci Rodríguez de Montalvo except that relative to his translations and books, his offspring and their associations. But recall that he was part of the defense of a city, Alhama, specifically identified as part of a military force standing against the Moors. Was Montalvo himself a soldier? More to the point, was he a knight? Perhaps even *hidalgo de sangre*?

Having been a son of a wealthy and influential family, and alderman of his birthplace, Medina Del Campo, raises Montalvo's profile in favor of having been among the *hidalgo* (knightly) class. Being part of the defense of Alhama suggests military service, again suggesting *hidalgo* status, more literally. The strongest evidence for his knightly lineage is to be found in two historical documents: *De La Historia de Arevalo* written by an ancestor, Juan Jose de Montalvo in 1928. In the second volume of this book are listed several Montalvos dating back to the 14th Century, many of them with the *hidalgo* title 'Don'. One of them is identified by the rank of 'Capitan' and another is identified as 'Caballero de San Esteban'.[137] 'Caballero' means knight. In another historical source, *Genealogical and Heraldic History of the Spanish Monarchy*, the Montalvos are listed in the chapter on the House of Cordova relative to a marriage and

---

[137]Juan Jose de Montalvo, *History of Arevalo*, Volume II (1928) Pg.16.

genealogy.[138] The case for *hidalgo* status of *Esplandian* author Garci Montalvo just gets better.

It appears that many men of Montalvo's family were knights, in the post Templar sense, of course. But it gets even better than that, for Montalvo was of the Pollino line of the family. That's an Italian line, derived from the name 'Apollo' and often spelled Pollo – and is identified also as Polo.[139]

You read that right: Polo. Italian. If Montalvo was related to the Polo family of Italy, that's a big fat fingerprint of the secret cartographic tradition within his grasp. There may also be a tarot association as 'Pollino' also can mean 'fool'. That's perfectly OK and would serve the hermetical aspects of this whole California story. It so happens that in 2014 it was reported that a map was found which may prove that Marco Polo indeed reached the Americas via the Kamchatka Peninsula. It was found among documents originally compiled by Polo's daughter, by then in possession of an Italian immigrant living in San Jose, California in the 1930s, ending up in the Library of Congress. The map and accompanying documents were analyzed by the FBI and it may be that the map is a 14th or 15th Century copy of the original, placing the physical document within an era when the territory it charts was still supposedly unknown to Europeans. According to the map, Polo made it as far south as today's Seattle and Puget Sound. The 'holes' in the story, according to the author, are that Polo

---

[138]Francisco Fernandez de Bethancourt, *Historia genealógica y heráldica de la monarquía española,* Vol 6 (Enrique Teodoro Publishing Co, 1905) Pg.428.

[139]*Dictionary of American Family Names* (Oxford University Press 2013); Ancestry.com.

'told tall tales' and didn't mention the Americas in his famous *Travels.*[140]

At least the author admits to Polo's deathbed confession, that he had not written half of what he saw and did on his travels around the world. Fortunately we have Oderic of Pordenone whose own travels to Persia, India, Tibet, and China twenty five years or so after Polo's return greatly corroborated Marco Polo's alleged 'exaggerations'.[141] I would also point out the name of the author of the article, Michael Zennie. Interestingly close to the name Zeno of the Zeno brothers fame, the mapmakers who are found at the heart of the controversy over the secret cartographic tradition. But perhaps this is just one those 'coincidences', right?

Since Polo's famous journeys occurred almost a hundred years after the sacking of Constantinople, he may also have been a beneficiary of the secret maps captured there. Polo lived in the late 13th and early 14th Centuries. Supposing Montalvo truly was a descendant and had access to Polo's diaries and charts. I argue that the author of the *Esplandian* adventure would have known of any explorations Marco Polo may have made of California. But we need not rely solely upon this supposition, for another source of California was the Hadji Ahmed map nearly three centuries after Polo's journeys.

Hadji Ahmed's map of 1559AD is, according to Charles Hapgood, as astonishing as the Piri R'eis map of forty six years

---

[140]Michael Zennie, *The Incredible Map...*(Daily Mail Online, 25 Sep 2014, updated on 9 Oct 2015).

[141]Will Durant, *The Renaissance:A History of Civilization in Italy from 1304-1576 AD* (Simon & Schuster 1953) Pg 530.

prior. Hapgood cites that Ahmed had to have had access to some rather extraordinary source maps to create his own. Hapgood points out the 'modern' look of the American continents, in particular the *western* coasts. He writes that these coasts on the map look to be around *two hundred years ahead* of cartography of the era in which the map was made and drawn on a 'highly sophisticated projection'. Hapgood also points out that on the Ahmed map, there is 'a striking difference' between the eastern and western hemispheres of the world. The eastern hemisphere appears to have been drawn from commonly known geographical sources of Ahmed's time and is *significantly less accurate in our modern sense* than the mapping of the western hemisphere. Hapgood cannot explain how this was so during the middle of the 16th Century other than Ahmed, like Piri Reis before him and many others, had access to earlier charts of astounding accuracy.[142]

And the peninsula of what is today Baja California is right there on the astonishing Hadji Ahmed map, along with the rest of Alta California and territory north through Canada and turning westward toward Siberia.[143] Bear in mind that the Gulf of California was known before Cabrillo explored upper California, of course. Francisco de Ulloa had charted it in 1539AD, not long before Cabrillo was given command of the expedition to explore farther north. What is interesting to me about the Ahmed map is that it was drawn sixteen years following the Cabrillo expedition and presents an apparent

---

[142]Hapgood, Pg.99

[143]Ibid, Pg.100

assumption about the west coast of North America that could not have been known at that time, for it was at least twenty years following the date of Ahmed's map before Sir Francis Drake would make his secret exploration of the entire Pacific Northwest and Alaska, rounding the strait into the Arctic Circle – the first known journey by any European.[144] Now consider that the Ahmed map does not indicate anything like the bay of San Francisco, either backing up the popular assumption that Cabrillo never entered it – or that Cabrillo kept it *secret*, just as Drake was likely forced to by Elizabeth I after him.

The Ahmed map shows land connecting North America to Siberia, an area reportedly charted by Polo when a land bridge possibly still existed. Again, another corroboration of Marco Polo. Now consider the possibility of Montalvo as a family relation having access to Marco Polo's unpublished information and maps, as well as being *hidalgo de sangre* and having access to some of the same charts as Hadji Ahmed decades after. It may be that because Montalvo was *hidalgo de sangre* that he gained access to Marco Polo's secrets without needing a family connection – for Marco Polo provided the first copy of his *Travels* to the Templar Grand Master Thibault de Cepoy, leading many to suspect that Polo himself was a Templar.[145] The possible family connection comes into importance where specific information about 'California' may be hidden within Polo's secret papers and of this we cannot dismiss the potential veracity, but familial connection to Marco Polo is not required.

---

[144]Samuel Bawlf, *The Secret Voyage of Sir Francis Drake 1577-1580* (Penguin 2003)Pgs.185-327

[145]Farrell, *Thrice Great Hermetica*, Pg.144

Factor *hidalgo* privileges and a suggestive family connection to Polo into Montalvo writing his novel about the 'legendary' land of California and its Amazon queen, Califia. What of any secret inland explorations of what we know as California may have been included in Montalvo's source material?

There are real world features and facts of California that directly support themes and aspects of Montalvo's story and of others. We shall examine these shortly but, before we do, consider the possibility that Montalvo was privy to any possible observations of these things made by Polo and others, all of which were being kept secret during Montalvo's lifetime, especially when he wrote his addition to the *Amadis* saga. Take that consideration a step further and you can understand why Montalvo might have embedded secret information in the allegory of an adventure story.

Before we go into what is to be found in known California, and how it was known by Montalvo and others when the territory in question was greatly 'unknown', there remains another aspect of the whole California 'myth' to explore: the alchemical elements of the search for the land of the Amazon Queen, for there is more there than meets the eye. It turns out that one cannot look at the Spanish conquest of the New World without considering the esoteric purpose behind it.

For this we must return again to the work and ideas of Joseph Farrell, but there are others before him. Farrell is not alone in his perspectives (only where contrarians who never actually read his books are concerned).

Ego and fear are the answer. Every civilization thinks it's the smartest guy in the room. Fear of being bested, particularly fear of one's claim to supremacy being challenged, are powerful forces in the psyche of empire builders. We must resist being told to ignore that buffoon behind the curtain. We should refuse to bow before the artificial wizard of the technocratic Oz of modern times. I say there were indeed seafarers from civilizations with advanced maps and charts and portolans that existed prior to Medieval Europe. These were known in ancient times, I find reasonable to suggest, and housed by the Library of Alexandria until the idiotic sacking by those renowned maniacs of human history: religious zealots. I am also of that school of thought arguing that, among the repositories which received the lost resources of the destroyed library, was that similar establishment in Constantinople, and that said maps and charts of then forgotten civilizations were indeed among the treasures sought in the duplicitous Fourth Crusade. Further, I agree with those who propose that the Knights Templar and its associative and rival knightly orders were the captors and beneficiaries of said maps and charts and, additionally, that this led to discreet classified journeys to and explorations of the Americas well before Columbus.

And this, dear reader, is how the Spanish came to California.

I said earlier that Joseph Farrell puts it well. Here is his layout as essentially stated in 2010: There was in High Antiquity a maritime knowledge of the world commensurate with our own. This knowledge included awareness of North and South America which Columbus and those who followed him merely re-discovered for themselves. Said knowledge was recorded on charts and maps through the ages and was stored in repositories in multiple locations including the Library of Alexandria. Some of these charts and maps and related knowledge was rescued from the destruction of the Library and made it to the Eastern Roman Empire's imperial archives in Byzantium, specifically Constantinople.[146] I fail to see where this is a controversial summation but some will, based on their prejudice alone. How did Spain get to California as a result of these events?

It is very likely that the Knights Templar got their hands on the ancient charts showing the Americas which were then generally unknown to the European and Middle Eastern public. Several authors have already written of the theory that Templar knights, at the outset of their persecution in France, fled to Scotland, soon resulting in Henry Sinclair making a voyage to North America.[147] But there were Templars in Spain and Portugal, too. King Denis established the Order of Christ to shelter those Templars in Portugal, and subsequently Prince Henry 'the Navigator' was made administrator general of the order. Henry is credited with starting the European 'Age of Discovery' with the expeditions he sent out into the known and, some say, unknown world. Certainly one may reasonably suggest that Prince Henry and his explorers were privy to whatever charted knowledge of the Americas that Portuguese Templars may have possessed. Keep in mind that Juan Cabrillo, subject of the first book in this series, was Portuguese. In

[146]Farrell, *Financial Vipers*, Pg. 57

[147]Tim Wallace-Murphy & Marilyn Hopkins, William Mann, Joseph Farrell, Steven Sora, David Childress, Scott Wolter and others.

addition, the Templars in Spain at the time of the persecution were given refuge by King James II who took Denis of Portugal's lead and established the Order of Montesa for the Templars.[148] Whatever ancient charts of the Americas the Spanish Templars had in their possession at that time surely stayed in Spain for a time.

Not that they were naive and oblivious to the corrupt nature of power in any institution, the Templars got their first hint of what would lead to a rivalry with the very office they had served through the reprehensible Albigensian crusade in which the Church's loyal soldiers slaughtered Cathar men, women and children 'in the name of God'. The Pope insisted that Catholicism reign supreme, the King coveted dominance in the southern region of France, and crusaders returning from the Holy Land were available and in fighting condition,[149] thus was drummed up the claim that it was all to stamp out 'heresy'. The Templars did not participate in this particular crusade, it is suggested, because they had important business dealings with the Cathars of the Languedoc region of France. It is from this region they could supply their Spanish units participating in the Reconquista of Spain. It's likely that the leaders of the order saw in the Albigensian crusade what the Pope and the King of France had in store for them. Joseph Farrell argues that indeed the plan was to first take out the local Cathars and then, through

---

[148]Catholic Encyclopedia: Lamper, Montesa illustrata (Valencia, 1669); *Definiciones de la orden y cavalleria de Montesa* (Valencia, 1573); LAFUENTE, Hist. Ecl. de Espana (Madrid, 1874).

[149]Otto Rahn, *Lucifer's Court: A Heretic's Journey In Search of the Light Bringers* (Inner Traditions 2008 Edition of translation from 1936 original) Pg.13.

the issuance of classified instructions to local authorities, take out the larger corporate Templar order.[150]

So it was that in 1307AD, on Friday the 13th of October, multiple warrants were issued throughout France for the immediate arrest of all Knights Templar. The story is well known. The great majority of Templars based in France managed to escape the purge and their impressive fleet disappeared from the port of La Rochelle. Many of these knights fled to Scotland where they subsequently offered their services to Henry Sinclair and are rumored to have led explorations to the still secret Americas under his sponsorship, as well as participating in the resistance of Scotland to the English crown. Many others simply stayed put in those other places where the monarchs created new orders for them and shrugged off the warrants. There is also evidence that the age of piracy on the Atlantic and in the Caribbean actually started as a war between the ousted Templars setting their fleet against the ships of Catholic nations.[151]

Evidence of the possible presence of Knights Templar in the Americas before Columbus has been much proposed in our times. In the first volume of this series, published in 2014, I lay out my hypothesis that Knights Templar vaults were placed in various locations across North America. More specifically, new vaults were constructed in a westward direction as the continent was opened and the colonial population expanded.[152] I propose that Knights Templar established the first of these vaults while

---

[150]Farrell, *Thrice Great Hermetica* Pg.116

[151]Childress, *Pirates & The Lost Templar Fleet:The Secret Naval War Between the Templars and the Vatican* (AUP 2003)

accompanying Henry Sinclair to North America in the final decade of the 14th Century, very possibly on Nova Scotia at the infamous Oak Island site.[153] I further proposed, in that volume, that some time before Joan of Arc was burned at the stake, sixty-one years before Columbus' famous voyage, her very special and most coveted sword was secreted to the Templar vault in North America, wherever the vault was by that time.

Steven Sora has Henry Sinclair establishing a Templar colony on his alleged expedition to the Americas. In fact, Sora ties Sinclair family knowledge of the Americas to Columbus, via marriage connecting Henry's daughter to the an explorer named Drummond. It is their line which married into the Perestrellos family by the mid 15th Century and it was Felipa Perestrellos, whose father was a mariner, to whom Christopher Columbus would be married. From his mother-in-law, Columbus received all documents and charts owned by her husband – documents and charts which contained the combined knowledge of both families' regarding explorations westward, dating from the Viking age to the time of Columbus' marriage to Felipa and included Templar charts and maps.[154] Might this have been the source of secret maps and ancient charts which Columbus was rumored to possess?

Between the Westford Knight effigy in Massachusetts and Micmac stories of the foreign explorer 'Glooscap' and even the

---

[152]Bosley, *Secret Missions: The Hidden Legacy of Old California* (CORVOS 2014). Some people have read this book and claim they've never heard of it.

[153]Ibid, Chapter 3.

[154]Steven Sora, T*he Lost Colony of the Templars:Verrazano's Secret Mission To America* (Destiny Books 2004) Pgs: 1-3; 116-127

Prince Madoc tales as far south as Mobile, Alabama, we have tales of Knights Templar and their associates all over the eastern seaboard of North America – and that's just the Templars linked to Scotland. There is also the Portuguese Prince Henry the Navigator who in 1420, at 26 years old, established a clearing house of all nautical knowledge compiled by Jewish and Muslim astronomers in his employ, documenting accounts of sailors returning from distant seas.[155] Add to this the fact that Henry was also Administrator General of the Order of Christ, essentially making him the Grand Master of Knights Templar in Portugal.[156] One of Henry's ship captains was Bartolomeo Perestrello, the would-be father in law[157] of Christopher Columbus who would marry the captain's daughter. It was Bartolomeo's Templar charts and maps which Columbus would be given.[158] Will Durant said of Prince Henry: "*The discoveries begun by Henry the Navigator, advanced by Vasco da Gama, culminating in Columbus, and rounded out by Magellan effected the greatest commercial revolution in history before the coming of the airplane.*"[159]

What of the Templars in Spain following the persecution and disbanding of their order? They had been quite busy assisting the Spanish Crown with the Reconquista, as we learned with the Albigensian Crusade episode. It appears that the Templars involved with exploration prior to Columbus were those of

[155]Durant, *The Reformation: A History of European Civilization from Wyclif to Calvin, 1300-1564* (Simon & Schuster 1957) Pgs.192, 269

[156]Sora, Pg.177; Encyclopedia Britannica

[157]Bartolomeo Perestrello died two decades prior to his daughter's marriage.

[158]Sora, Pg180

[159]Durant, *Reformation* Pg.269

Scotland and Portugal, otherwise Spanish Templars were expanding Spain's interests in Africa, but despite what Spain was going through in their struggle with the Moors and then with each other, Spanish Templars were not ignoring what their brothers elsewhere were doing in the way of expanding the boundaries of the map, even if said maps didn't tell everything. It becomes clear, by the time Columbus emerges with the 1492 voyage, that Spanish Templars had been busy with their big move: The decision to open the Americas to European interests.

This is where I suggest that Templars operating with knowledge of the Americas prior to Columbus reached a point where they realized the New World could not be fully exploited by the few mariners and their crews who knew about these continents. The problem was that the banksters of Venice were all too happy to keep the Americas to themselves. The Templars had tasted insidious Venetian banker nature before. The Templars had a vision and that vision required a freedom unknown in Europe and elsewhere. Not only a political freedom of rights and civil laws but a literal freedom of movement. That would require an expansive horizon heretofore unavailable to the common person of the old world. Being cunning and as interested in commerce as anyone else, it's likely the Templars decided that the New World had to become known to all. This would provide the manpower to exploit the resources for centuries to come, but it would also offer a literal new world to the common men and women who could get themselves to these new lands. The New World had to be revealed.

This, of course, would piss off the banksters of Venice but the Templars were confident that a common interest in trade would be the middle ground upon which they could meet. Thus do I propose that the decision was made to open up the Americas. Naturally it would be a Templar, *hidalgo de sangre*, who would play the role of 'discoverer'. In Columbus, they had one. It's probably true that Columbus had been at least eyesight close to the Americas in the 1485 voyage so he would basically have known how to get there. But why a Spanish sponsored Genoese? Why not a Portuguese explorer?

One could interpret the choice of Genoese hidalgo Columbus as part of the Templar desire to keep Venice out of the event. Columbus being of a rival city would show a clear message to the Venetians. However, another reason for the choice of a Spanish expedition being given the honor might additionally pertain to hermetical considerations. It looks to me like the Templar plan rested upon Spain.

I contend that the Templars decided Spain would be their home base, perhaps even a place where they could re-emerge as the Knights Templar. This idea would require a book in itself but go with it for now. The idea is that the Iberian Peninsula has physical separation from France, the nation that betrayed the order. Yet it's even larger. The peninsula also comes with maritime powerhouse Portugal where the Templars had been functioning openly under a veneer of a new name, by the time in question. Having been active participants in the Reconquista, the people and the Crown of Spain would welcome the Templar refugees as permanent residents. It would also be a way to flub their noses at the rest of Europe (and England, for good measure).

Another benefit that I say the Templars were keen on was the ready availability of ports. Spain would also have been the perfect launching base for exploitation of New World shipping. The separation would allow the Templars the space to rebuild their fleet beyond previous limits – and the geography would give them the Atlantic and control of Gibraltar, and thus the Mediterranean. The order had a good relationship with Ferdinand and Isabella, particularly the queen. In order to establish themselves firmly in Spain, this is why I propose that the Templars presented Isabella with the New World.

The Templars selected Christopher Columbus, one of their own. He had been gifted his deceased father-in-law's charts and maps from his new wife's mother. It may have been these maps which led to the suspected 1485 voyage to the Americas that Columbus is thought by some to have successfully accomplished. If the Templars were going to pitch this gambit to the monarchs of Spain, they would do it in a way that would not reveal all their secret operations. Columbus, even as Templar, would not have to be involved with the most secret activities of Templar mariners in the New World if on his own (with help from those special maps) he had managed to get himself there once before. If that suspicion is true, Columbus keeping it a secret would certainly have impressed the Templars. Columbus was their man.

But *had* he indeed already been to the New World at the time he pitched the 1492 expedition?

One need only consider the *Capitulations* document signed by Christopher Columbus and Ferdinand and Isabella *prior* to his departure on the famous 1492 voyage. This document includes the statement: "*the things requested that Your Highnesses give and concede to don...Christopher Columbus as some compensation for what he* ***has discovered*** *in the ocean seas. And for the voyage which, with the aid of God, he is* ***now in the process of making*** *upon the said sea...*".[160] Ruggero Marino and Joseph Farrell each make the case that the use of past tense is key here – implying that Columbus had already seen the Americas in a prior secret voyage.[161] Again, Columbus is seriously suspected of having himself been a Templar, albeit of one of the orders established after their persecution. What are the clues? Among several are that mapmaker Giovanni Matteo Contarini referred to Columbus as 'Master', a term used only for men affiliated with knightly orders[162]and the curious fact that Columbus emblazoned the Templar Cross across the sails of of the trio of ships on the 1492 voyage, at a time when that was a rather bold association. Might he have done so in order that Templars in the Americas, upon his 1492 arrival, would recognize an ally in the approaching vessels?

Thus, I propose that the Knights Templar felt compelled to hide the location of California within a literary camouflage and, should the Church's explorers reach it anyway (which they did), to hide its properties from the Vatican for as long as possible.

---

[160]Ruggero Marino, *Christopher Columbus, The Last Templar* (Destiny Books 2005) Pg.205

[161]Farrell, *Thrice Great Hermetica,* Pgs.148-150

[162]Marino, Pg.237; Farrell, *Thrice Great Hermetica,* Pg.153.

Their new plan would result in the *Amadis of Gaul* sequel: *Las Sergas de Esplandian*.

Much is made of Knights Templar as bankers and that is indeed a major part of their story. But they were soldiers, don't forget. Similar to the US Marine Corps wherein every Marine, cook or combat, is a rifleman. Our examination here emphasizes the explorers among the Templar ranks. But they were also hermetical in their pursuits, many of them, and we mustn't neglect the alchemical thread running through these geographical pursuits, particularly where California was the objective. Clearly, from my perspective, the Knights Templar used literary camouflage to both find and keep hidden what they would ultimately reveal to Europe.

Alchemy has been embedded within literature for ages, from the Bible to Ovid's *Metamorphoses* and onward, alchemists have always believed that such texts alluded to a hidden physics[163]. I suggest the Templars framed their knowledge of New World secrets within alchemical context for two reasons: To hide it and to document the operative nature of some of the geomorphology found there.

Let's now get to the point. It's California we're talking about here and Edward Everett Hale provides an excellent overview of the *Amadis* sequel directly pertaining to this topic. In his 1885 book *His Level Best & Other Stories*, Hale includes a chapter titled "The Queen of California" in which he starts by citing *Las Sergas de Esplandian* as the original traceable use of the name 'California' in a 1510 edition of the book and the first

---

[163]Farrell, *Philosophers' Stone*, Pgs.69-70

application of the name to the North American territory being in a Mexican archival document dating first usage as 1526, though official history cites 1535. Hale references the Jesuit historian Miguel Venegas who doesn't confirm yet cites a proposed etymology of 'California' as *calida* and *fornax*, thus 'hot furnace'. Hale also rejects this idea based on Cortez having never been to the places in California to which it applies, because Cortez saw merely the Baja peninsula.[164]

Would a Jesuit be ignorant to the alchemical possibility in the phrase *calida fornax*? I sincerely doubt it. Members of the Jesuit order of the Roman Catholic church had been involved with alchemy for a while by that time, the German Jesuit Athanasius Kircher among them, and he died the year Venegas was born. Though Jesuits had the freedom to pursue alchemical studies, we are told that members of the order were not particularly enthused by such experimentation. We are told this because no Jesuit ever wrote a book on alchemy and because Kircher published a criticism on the subject yet applied alchemy in some of his own works. While we are told of Kircher's expressed contempt for the egos of alchemists, Jesuit historians also tell us that members of the order embedded their alchemical experiments within general scientific papers and pursuits, thus admitting that Jesuits indeed practiced alchemy.[165] Methinks Kircher does protest too much.

---

[164]Edward Everett Hale, "The Queen of California" (From the book *His Level Best*, Roberts, 1885) Pgs.234-236

[165]Martha Baldwin, *Alchemy in The Society of Jesus* (Alchemy Revisited by Von Martels, Brill Archive 1990). But trust them with your immortal soul, of course, they would never lie about that.

I also suspect that Venegas sought to downplay the alchemy theme, where the naming of California was concerned, to divert the reader's attention away from possibilities such as *calida fornax* referring to an *athanor*, a furnace used in alchemy[166]. Perhaps as Philostratus used 'athanor' to describe an 'occult hill',[167] *calida fornax* was given to the California territory because it, too, is a furnace for alchemical activity, on a massive scale. I further suspect that Jesuit scientists recognized the role alchemy played in the whole California adventure and were diligently studying source material from such a perspective in order to decode geographical and mineral details. At the time when the New World was still a secret between Templars and other close-mouthed mariners, the secrets still looked like an adventure story to most Catholic priests – but those familiar with alchemy would have seen through the camouflage and, in the church, that would have been the Jesuits.

California as alchemical furnace is an important detail for, as Joseph Farrell in his analysis of the Biblical Golden Calf tale identifies: "*High heat was involved in its confection*" and "*Some sort of sequence of colors – from white to red – was the signal of a successful operation*".[168] Interestingly, this reference to colors will specifically relate to the idea of California the physical place being the athanor at the heart of my hypothesis.

Let's proceed further into the alchemy embedded within *Esplandian*. Hale continues in his overview of the story with its reference to California being located near the Terrestrial

---

[166]Merriam-Webster Dictionary

[167]Philostratus, *The Life of Apollonius of Tyana,* Trans. By F. C. Moneybeare 1912

[168]Farrell, *Philosophers' Stone* Pg.71

Paradise, itself a known theme in alchemy, representative of the perfect state of an element or combination thereof. Might Hale have been oblivious to this reference? Probably. I suggest the use of 'Terrestrial Paradise' in *Esplandian*'s reference to California is alluding to the physical territory itself holding special properties conducive to natural alchemy on a massive geographical scale and thus amenable to manipulation through scientific alchemy or metaphysical sorcery (which we shall revisit shortly).

Hale points out where *Esplandian* follows a reference to Terrestrial Paradise with an immediate reference to colors: the 'Amazonian' women of California are described as black and their armor as gold, the only metal to be found in their mythical land. Isn't that a bit obvious to us now? Black is a very important color in alchemy as it appears at some stage in *every* alchemical operation. Some might argue that reference to 'black women' means Africans and thus could not possibly be California, but that would be exposing a typically foolish prejudice by seeing the past through the limited and vain perspective of the present.[169] In fact, the term 'black' was used for other non-white races, for example 'black wife' in 19th Century reference to Richard Francis Burton's domestic mate during his assignment in India.[170] Describing the women of the mythical California as 'black' does not necessarily make them Africans, rather it could just as likely refers to their non-white feature further deepened by the sun of their 'hot furnace'

[169]Such idiocy is quite popular in our times, especially with the identity politics mob. This is how histories are devastated to serve the objective of cultural tyranny.
[170]Bosley, *SM2: Burton.*

homeland. However, they *still* could indeed have been Africans who came to the Americas ages ago, perhaps with King Solomon's miners. My point is that the description of the Amazons as black, Africans or not, further emphasizes an alchemical reference which I believe is the purpose.

The reference to gold is obvious, especially since 1849. In *Esplandian*, through an *hidalgo de sangre* author Montalvo, the Templars were communicating that gold was to be found in this California territory – and I suggest in a literal alchemy context a la that which I propose at Puma Punku in *Secret Missions 2:The Lost Expedition of Sir Richard Francis Burton*[171]: California, geomorphologically, is a gold-producing machine, in this case *naturally*. This will come up again later in the conflict between Templars and the Vatican agents. Meanwhile, we will continue for, aside from black and gold, we must cite that the stages of colors, though they vary from one experiment to another, usually go from white to red. As stated earlier, this I think offers a dual suggestion. Templar robes are traditionally white with red crosses, but over three hundred years following the publication of *Esplandian*, we will see these become the prominent colors of the US State of California and I suspect not accidentally no matter what the official story insists.

We very soon learn that the queen of the mythical land is named 'Califia'. Scholars have proposed that this name, along with California, references the Caliphate simply because of the Reconquista ie Caliphs were on the minds of Spaniards. Perhaps. But even more interestingly we soon learn that she has

---

[171] Ibid Pgs 271-286

led her army of women to Constantinople to join forces with the sultan intent on sacking the great city.

Sound familiar? I think this is a direct reference to the Fourth Crusade and *Esplandian*'s use of Constantinople is telling the informed reader that Califia coming to the city is code for how the actual territory of 'California', aka *calida fornax,* came into the hands of the Knights Templar. How can I make this 'leap'? Because in the story, Califia is defeated (conquered?) and gives herself in marriage to a knight in Esplandian's court. If indeed knowledge of New World geography was captured with the documents and maps seized from the Imperial Archives then I suggest that this included information relative to California.

Of *Esplandian*'s California itself, we learn of mountains and steep cliffs. Since the story was written over two centuries before any Europeans were alleged to have explored the interior of California, how did the author know about the impressive mountain ranges there? This suggests somebody went there prior to Columbus' 1492 voyage. We are also told by Montalvo via *Esplandian* that California is known for its steep rock cliffs into which were dug caves within which lived Califia and her Amazons.[172] Are these Amazonian caves what Cabrillo was looking for when he so dangerously hugged the coastline cliffs during his 1542-43 expedition?[173]

---

[172]Montalvo, *Las Sergas de Esplandian* (1508); Hale, Pg. 246

[173]Bosley, *SM1:California*, Chapter 14; It should also be noted that Bourke Lee in *Death Valley Men* (1930) tells of miners who allege to have found caves hewn in high cliffs. This account describes these caves as mooring docks for the ancient ships that sailed the waters once covering the now desert expanse. Death Valley as ancient seabed is a major part of the theory that California may indeed have been an island as described in *Esplandian* which also says that the Amazonians of California indeed

Esplandian also tells us that this mythical California is home to griffins, those legendary winged creatures, mostly bird, large enough for humans to ride. These griffins of California are used in battle at the Constantinople setting and are fierce and bloodthirsty. Yet another possible allusion to actual California, for the largest land bird in all of North America is the California Condor, of which known specimens have measured eleven feet in wingspan. The condor has been confused for airplanes in modern times.[174] *Esplandian* specifically describes the griffins as tearing apart the enemy soldiers at Constantinople, and the California Condor's talons indeed are akin to other predator birds around the world. The condor, being a vulture, is a flesh eater and therefore as 'bloodthirsty' as the griffins in *Esplandian*. Again, is it merely coincidence that Montalvo associated huge flesh-eating birds with California? And who knows how big condors surviving from the prehistoric era may have been when any secret Templar exploration might have occurred after the Fourth Crusade?

Yet another clue to the novel *Esplandian* communicating information about actual California is to be found in the queen herself for, as Cabrillo and those who followed would learn, the Chumash were led by a female chief. The similarity doesn't end there for the Chumash were also a sea-going tribe.[175] Might this be a native hold-over from ancient times? It's doubtful that the

---

possessed a large fleet of sea-crossing ships.

[174]Wikipedia.

[175]The Chumash would journey as far as San Bernardino Valley to build their ceremonial pearl canoes known as *tomols*. Source: *Empire of the Wheel* Volume 1 by Bosley & Spence, Corvos Books 2011.

Chumash are the same culture as that depicted in *Esplandian* and suggested by other clues of some ancient presence in California for the Chumash do not live without men and their women are not warriors. More likely is that this revered California tribe was influenced by the now lost civilization which inspired *Las Sergas de Esplandian*. In the story, Califia tells her captors: "*My lineage is very old, — for it comes from royal blood so far back that there is no memory of the beginnings of it...*"

In that statement, we can rightfully be reminded of the goddess Hekate, herself a chthonic deity whose true origin is unknown, despite all the subsequent appropriations claiming her as their own (including modern day witches). I argue that this is no mistake. As I shall address in a later chapter, the presence of Hekate in California may indeed reveal a lost civilization that once flourished here. If the Templar explorers knew this, Montalvo could very well have consciously made reference to Hekate with that one statement of Califia's dialogue.

Perhaps one of the most intriguing points about Califia herself is that the novel Esplandian describes her as "very large in person" and "strong of limb".[176] Having been written in the late 15th Century, it's interesting that Montalvo's narrative precedes the reported discovery of giant skeletons in various California sites centuries later. Reportedly, in July 1895 a group of miners found the tomb of a woman whose skeleton was 6 feet and 8 inches tall and unidentified 'Los Angeles scientists' determined

---

[176]Kevin Starr, *California: A History* (Modern Library 2005) Pg.5

she would have stood seven feet tall in life. Her tomb was found to be sealed with an advanced skill in masonry.[177] There are of course other reported discoveries of giant skeletons, including the 1833 report of soldiers finding the remains of a twelve foot tall man with double rows of teeth, and another giant male skeleton with extra teeth found on Santa Rosa Island.[178]

It is my position that Montalvo wrote *Las Sergas de Esplandian* on commission. I propose that Templar mariners sought to put down their knowledge of California in a form that would communicate to those who understood its real meaning, while camouflaging said knowledge from those whom they preferred to not know it. Thus do I suggest that the real California was intended to be kept from the Templars' rivals in the exploitation of the New World they were promoting. I shall take it a step further and suggest that the novel *Esplandian* was perhaps intended to be part of the Templar plan for opening up the New World as a gift of secrets to their chosen monarch, Queen Isabella of Spain – but ended up being a pierced veil instead of shrouding the rich territory of California when things turned the wrong direction and the queen threw a wrench into the Templar plan.

So what happened?

Enter The Pope

[177]Brad Steiger, *Montezuma's Serpent and Other True Supernatural Tales of the Southwest* (Paragon House 1992); Childress, *Lost Cities...Southwest* (AUP 2009), Pgs 501-502.

[178]Childress, *Lost Cities...Southwest,* Pgs 502-503; Frank Edwards *Stranger Than Science* (Stuart 1983).

We come to what I personally think was to prove an unfortunate turn of events for the European exploitation of the New World, second only to the bad decision to bring slavery here. The New World could have been the place with which Europeans colonizers might have set a precedent and prohibited the institution of human slavery, but they didn't. It was business as usual, in that regard. After that, I find the influence of the Roman Catholic church to have been a mixed bag, specifically the influence of Vatican ideology in the long run.[179] Essentially, Queen Isabella made a pious error.

In a time when the secular influence of the papacy was on the rise, and even many Christians saw it and were concerned, Queen Isabella began to have reservations about what she observed as immorality of the popes, specifically the display of nepotism which Rodrigo Borgia aka Pope Alexander VI was presenting. Despite this and other issues with the Pope's mercenary streak, Isabella sincerely hoped to bring the good of Christianity to the New World and thus set forth to present a deal to Alexander VI. The queen's righteous ideals were not without practicality for she also sought to secure a monopoly over the discoveries that Columbus was reporting during the 1492 expedition.[180]

---

[179]I do mean 'big picture' and 'long run'. There will certainly be instances of charity, sincere good will, and much helping of one's fellow man where individual cases and particular priests are concerned. The Roman Catholic church is not staffed entirely by degenerate villains, but just enough to taint its reputation. For the record: I have never been a member of the Roman Catholic church. I come to my critical view via study of history and personal observation. WB

[180]Downey, Pgs. 264-267

Isabella sent the report from Columbus directly to the pope before the explorer could even appear before her at court. She was putting into Alexander VI's hands the power to decide ownership of the lands claimed by Columbus. The pope was no fool. King Ferdinand and Spain had been quite instrumental in his rise to the papacy and, he knew, fast claim had to be made on these new territories before the rest of Europe went to plant their flags. His response to Isabella's request was to issue four papal bulls acquiescing to every one of the queen's requests. In fact, it is regarded that Alexander VI simply let the Spanish monarchy write the documents for the pope's signature – with one bit thrown in by the pope himself: the *Inter Caetera* of 4 May 1493 stipulated that religious evangelization was the first and foremost purpose of the conquest of the New World, specifically that "*the Catholic faith and the Christian religion,* ***particularly in our times****, shall be exalted and everywhere amplified and spread, that the salvation of souls may be provided for and barbarous nations subjugated and brought to the very true faith.*"[181]

Isabella was more than pleased to promote Vatican requirements in the New World ventures henceforth, for she believed they would be carried out in the spirit of honor and morality.[182] Thus was the infamous line drawn that would piss off Portugal, giving the New World discoveries specifically to Queen Isabella, as the grant specified the 'rulers of Castile and Leon', which meant the discoveries would belong to her, not

[181]Downey, Pgs 267-269, emphasis mine. Pope Alexander VI wanted to make sure the benefit and its power were his to enjoy.

[182]Bless her little heart.

Ferdinand. Subsequently, Portugal and Spain would agree to a revision of the line that resulted in Brazil for Portugal. The bottom line here is that Isabel got what she wanted and the price was to give the Vatican what it wanted: a new world to dominate, in both the population and the geographical treasures.[183]

Columbus and the Templars must have been flabbergasted at this turn of events. Here the Templars had decided to hand the New World, which they had known about and explored for over a century, to Spain in a neat package, and the queen who had been so accommodating went and shared those accommodations with the very institution complicit in the Templar order's persecution. The Templars and any other explorers sponsored not just by Spain but any Catholic nation would now have to cooperate with the Vatican's representatives in the field.[184] This would lead to competing forces vying for New World control. In my opinion, it ultimately led to a struggle over California between the knights and their old betrayers. I suggest this is why *Las Sergas de Esplandian* was written shortly after Columbus' departure on the 1492 expedition, being an attempt to encode California into a work of literature that could be distributed to as many potential explorers as possible, both to delay Vatican attempts to claim California and to better ensure as much non-Catholic claim to

[183]Downey Pgs 268-270

[184]This had to be every bit as malodorous as Communist party 'political officers' assigned to every Russian military vessel and unit during the days of the Soviet Union, as well as our present day Marxist inclined social gestapo in the US. WB

the still secret territory as necessary to make papal domination difficult, if not impossible.

Following Columbus' 1492 voyage, Spain took the lead in the exploration of the Americas, though by 1500AD Portugal had taken advantage of the line-adjusting Treaty of Tordesillas and claimed Brazil at the hand of Pedro Cabral, whom the reader will remember I propose was the father of Juan Cabrillo, per the first volume of this series. Spain was yet two decades from conquering Mexico, having established a few colonies in the Caribbean Indies. Pizarro would not conquer Peru until 1537AD. But California was on their minds, for *Amadis of Gaul* had been around for a presently unknown number of years and was first known to be formally published in 1508AD, followed by sequels, the fifth of which was the aforementioned *Las Sergas de Esplandian*, wherein California is first mentioned. Credited with initial publication in 1510AD, it is believed to have been previously printed in 1496AD, and having been written shortly after Columbus departed for the New World in 1492. That its author, Montalvo, translated *Amadis* from its original Portuguese into Spanish is very interesting within the context of Spanish and Portuguese rivalry during this age of exploration.

This raises the question of what Portuguese Templars who were embedded within the Order of Christ knew about California in 1492AD, and how involved they may have been in the proposed revelation of the New World through fellow knight Columbus. Might this knowledge have been the impetus of the beef resulting in the Treaty of Tordesillas? Did Juan

Cabrillo learn what he knew of the mysterious legends of California through exposure to the Spanish versions of the sagas of *Amadis* and *Esplandian*? Or might he have been privy to a Portuguese knowledge of California separate from that of Spain?

It could have been both, actually, as the stories of *Amadis* were written long before Columbus' 1492 voyage, likely before his proposed secret 1485 voyage and long before Montalvo wrote and published the *Esplandian* sequel (in Spanish) between 1492 and Isabella's death in 1504. Only if California was known to the mystery cartographers whose charts and portolans were captured during the Fourth Crusade sacking of Constantinople in 1204AD could it be even suggested that reaching California was always a part of Spain's objective in the New World. Since I do agree that such materials were indeed captured by Templar associated knights and used for clandestine pre-Columbian voyages to the Americas by European explorers, I'm going to commit to the idea, with the caveat that the true California objective was held as a close secret by all who pursued it.

Why do I think this is the case? Because California appears, in my opinion, to have been embedded into an existing fantasy tale for the very purpose of camouflage. Complete secrecy would have been out of the question out of mere practicality. Any explorer seeking the legendary land had to rely upon other people. Worse, he had to *trust* other people. By some point in any expedition, the cat would most certainly slip out of the bag, that someone was looking for something more than fresh colonial territory would get out. Better to hide it in plain sight and take a good-natured ribbing about one's choice in reading material than to try and maintain a secrecy that simply would not last. For it wasn't simply the land one would be looking for in the pursuit of California, it was the land's secrets. The common soldier or sailor could walk all over the terrain called California and not see what those in the know were looking for, offering a new perspective on Cabrillo's odd obsession with the coastal cliffs and his alleged ignorance of the bay of San Francisco.

I argue that Cabrillo understood what was encoded in *Esplandian* but his men did not, no matter how familiar they may have been with the literary sagas of *Amadis* and *Esplandian*. Before we go to Cabrillo and what he could have been looking for in northern California, we must return to Oviedo and consider further what may have been revealed in his book. Recall that several sections were missing for three hundred years, pretty much spanning the age of Spanish exploration and conquest of the Americas. Was there something in Oviedo's books that someone did not want out there? If not exactly what is depicted, could what was written still have spilled the frijoles on the specifics of a clandestine pursuit by the Crown and its representative explorers? Might the offending material have been related to specifics of geography and resources, in particular *mineral* resources?

It is well-documented history that Spain was seeking sources of gold in the New World. The activities of Hernan Cortez, Francisco Pizarro, and other conquistadors are at the heart of

Spain's quest for gold, silver and other treasures. Aside from what was plundered from the Aztecs and Inca in their respective cities and palaces, might some Spanish participants of the quest have known where to look before setting sail from the Iberian Peninsula? The possible answer to this question has its roots in both the sacking of Constantinople and the alchemy of money.

It could take an entire book to explain this thoroughly and, fortunately, others have done that for me. I will cover the pertinent highlights of how the alchemy of money and sympathetic magic may have fueled Spain's quest for California. First, I propose that certain participants were aware and in possession of the ancient charts showing lands that were supposed to have been undiscovered prior to the Age of Discovery; that popular literature of the time was encoded with specifics of the 'unknown' lands along with clues as to what one would find there; that agents of the Vatican imposed themselves upon the conquest of the New World and used sorcery in pursuit of their objectives. I have further speculations, but we'll start with these.[185]

Who among the explorers would have possessed any of the legendary charts believed to have been captured during the Fourth Crusade? More specifically, who among the explorers of the Iberian Peninsula? I agree with the hypothesis that Columbus did. I suspect Vasco da Gama did, as well, and

[185]If it bothers you when I refer to the ideas and works of Joseph Farrell and Sesh Heri, 'tough titty' as they say. I am not only friends with these gentlemen but I have done much research and investigation with Sesh Heri, and equally much analysis and discussion with Dr. Farrell. Our association as researchers is a natural consequence of chasing somewhat the same tiger. WB

shared them with his protege Pedro Cabral. One could suppose that any of the explorers who were members of knightly orders might have entered the conquest armed with such knowledge as the charts offered. Because this chapter deals specifically with California, I will keep the focus here and include Juan Cabrillo among said informed conquistadors, as his reported actions and demeanor reflected such knowledge, in my estimation. Additionally, if I am correct about Cabrillo's parentage, Cabral may have passed on charts and the like to Juan, as Vasco da Gama certainly shared what he knew with Cabral. Further, I would suggest that any of the inside players involved with the serious quest for California would have been equipped with the same knowledge, including Spain's agents of Rome via the church, which could explain Cabrillo's discreet behavior on his expedition.

How do we know Cabrillo had knowledge, if not charts and the pertinent, and possibly encoded, literature? He may have gained some advantage with intelligence from the first inland foray into Alta California by Alarcon and Diaz two years prior,[186] but the episode of the cliffs along what is today Monterey on to south of Big Sur is the best indicator. Recall from the first volume of this series that members of the expedition reported Cabrillo had frightened everyone aboard his ship when he insisted upon sailing tight along the coastline, hazarding collision with the cliff wall. He explained to no one why he was doing this.[187] Clearly, Cabrillo was looking for

[186]Kevin Starr, *California: A History* (Modern Library 2005) Pg.22

[187]Bosley, *Secret Missions: The Hidden Legacy of Old California* (CORVOS 2014), 'The Cliffs', Chapter 14.

something very specific. Was this particular thing merely an examination of natural features in pursuit of a personal suspicion about the terrain? Or was Cabrillo indeed looking for some specific thing he believed was there by virtue of a secret chart or document, or encoded literature, stating or suggesting that it was there? Perhaps the cavern dwellings of the Amazons?

What about the ludicrous assumption that Cabrillo missed the opening to the bay at today's San Francisco not once but *twice* – an assumption made because there was nothing in the ship's log about it. A log which the very same assumptive historians admit was incomplete.[188] We are to believe that a man who would hug the dangerous cliffs of the coastline, a man who didn't miss the mouth of the Russian River, lets fog deter him from noticing that the land makes an eastern curve into open waters but he just sails on northward – and then makes the same mistake coming south when again the land makes an eastward turn. The technically accurate term for this assumption is 'bullshit'. I argue in the first volume that Cabrillo would not have 'missed' the opening of the bay and that he likely entered and had a look around. Why would such a significant find go unreported in the log and then denied? I say Cabrillo was looking for something in particular and I suspect that said something was of interest to the cadre of explorers in possession of the secret knowledge. Or perhaps Cabrillo alone had his reasons for keeping it undocumented. Personally, I

---

[188]Ibid, 'San Francisco Bay' Chapter 14.

don't believe that the mouth of San Francisco Bay was first European-discovered in 1775 as historians believe.[189]

What of Point Conception or Catalina Island? Cabrillo anchored his ships twice alone on the journey northward, between Goleta and the Point, which was a sacred location for the Chumash. Point Conception juts out prominently, actually facing south from an otherwise westward facing coastline. The Chumash call this spot a '*humqaq*' and believe it serves as a gateway between our realm and the land of the dead. Of all the Channel Islands, Cabrillo seemed especially interested in the island we know today as Catalina. The Chumash had their ancient religious center there and some called the island '*Limu*' – suspiciously close to Lemuria, in many opinions.[190] What might Cabrillo have been looking for in these places? Despite the temptation to discuss any possibility of interdimensional travel at Point Conception, we must recognize the more practical connection between these two locations: The Chumash. And this brings us back to *Las Sergas de Esplandian* and what may have been encoded within this popular adventure romance saga of the late 15th Century.

Earlier I identified some of what I think is encoded in the tale of *Esplandian*. Similarly to historical mapmakers adding phony islands to their charts as a means of copyright protection

---

[189]Kevin Starr, *California: A History* (Modern Library 2005) Pgs 35-36; Various.

[190]Bosley SM1, Point Conception & Chapter 14. An AP sourced article I found, which unfortunately offers no identification of date or the newspaper that printed it, claims archaeologists found evidence of child sacrifice on Catalina associated with a temple of Chiningchininch, yet the contents provide no clear support for the headline. See illustrations. WB

Renaissance style[191], I propose that Montalvo wrote the sequel to *Amadis de Gaul* when he did, right after Columbus returned from his historical 1492 voyage, to communicate key facts about 'California' for the explorers in on the secret cartographic tradition. Said key facts would have been drawn from information captured during the Fourth Crusade, verified and documented by secret Templar explorations and then passed down to select readers associated with the various knightly orders. My suspicion is that Juan Cabrillo was in possession of a copy of the Montalvo novel during his expedition to Alta California, at the very least intimately familiar with it. I also think there was more than merely geographical information to be gleaned from this.

Within such a context as we are discussing here, it's not out of the question to suggest that certain explorers and their benefactors may also have been aware of geological conditions conducive to the natural process of the creation of gold. Since we know that Spain did not come away with as much gold as they had hoped[192] in spite of the nearly two hundred tons they got their hands on over the course of a century and a half. I have already discussed the possible role of alchemy in the very naming of California. Could this be at the heart of the issue? Is California literally that alchemical furnace, a naturally magical ground ripe for large scale hermetical manipulation?

Suppose the lure of gold revealed other knowledge about certain landscapes. As I suggested in the Burton volume of this

[191]Sam Roberts, *The Story of Ireland's 'Phantom Island'*... (Irish Mirror 14 Feb 21), courtesy of Olav Phillips & Richard Clements.
[192]Bosley, *SM2:Burton*, Pgs 286-289

series, that Tihuanaco and its associated site Puma Punku were where the pre-Inca civilization actually manufactured gold via an advanced understanding of the geophysics there, suppose California possessed the same qualities. If one controlled the territory, one could take advantage of the resources in such a way to literally possess a gold factory – a natural gold manufacturing machine. One would need only to know how to read the terrain and that's where geomorphology comes into play. As we have learned in several of my previous books, this is also how one may find telluric currents and gravity anomalies laid out across the land and sometimes in interesting patterns. California is a land covered in these curious lines of energy and I have found them to be at the heart of two other mysteries.[193]

Sesh Heri finds telluric energy/gravity anomalies at the heart of the natural process of the making of gold. In his analysis, California is a land mass uniquely created by tectonic force. In Chapter Two of Heri's study of this phenomenon, *The Handprint of Atlas*, he explains his theory behind the physical formation of California in terms of geomorphology. Heri specifically identifies continental drift as the main force creating the conditions wherein various elements come together for a curious result. He suggests that straight-line gravity anomalies moved by the continental drift of tectonic plates cause interesting results. Paranormal phenomena are frequently linked to sites of increased gravity. Said anomalies appear to interact with patterns in the so called 'world grid' of energy as to allow manifestations of increased phenomena, be it

[193]*Latitude 33: Key to the Kingdom* and the *Empire of the Wheel* trilogy.

hauntings, UFOs or what have you.[194] In his analysis of California, he finds something very interesting and more relative to our examination here.

Using Indian Rock in Berkeley as an example, Heri demonstrates his hypothesis that California's geography works like a machine to produce gold. Heri proposes that Indian Rock's positional movement over thousands of years has shifted it from it's original location at the center of what is today a traffic circle mere yards away. The roads leading into this traffic circle are actually built upon natural folds of the land leading to its center. This was done by design, suggests Heri. The flow of the traffic into and around the circle is immersed in and draws out the natural energy forces found there. Heri also discovered that the energy is fed by a major straight-line gravity anomaly flowing with telluric current and runs roughly southwest-northeast through the traffic circle – intersecting perpendicularly with another straight-line gravity anomaly running roughly northwest-southeast.[195] This southwest-northeast line continues on eastward to intersect with another northwest-southeast straight-line gravity anomaly which itself intersects with yet another southwest-northeast straight-line gravity anomaly farther north. This intersection which is farther north frames the Sutter Buttes within a 90-degree angle and that, dear reader, is where it becomes even more interesting to our examination.

---

[194]Sesh Heri, *The Handprint of Atlas* (CORVOS Books 2010), Pgs 27-31.
[195] Heri, Pgs 32-34

The Sutter Buttes is the smallest mountain range in the world and it also has a very special meaning to the Maidu people as the place where the dying go to ascend into the afterlife.[196] It is a place also associated with the Kuksu cult of pre-Columbian tribal males of the region who would gather in underground lodges and perform rituals in re-enactment of ancient mythological events. The location of this mountain range is smack dab in the corner of the aforementioned 90 degree angle formed by straight-line gravity anomalies – and it is linked directly to California's gold. Before we can get there, we must first fill in the gap between Cabrillo and John C. Fremont for therein we find the handprint of Vatican agents and their designs on California.

Following the reported death of Juan Cabrillo, which I deem a disappearance because his remains have never turned up in over 478 years, it was as if Spain wanted to forget California. Even fifty-six years after Spain claimed California, it went unattended enough for Sir Francis Drake to freely make his journey up the coastline and leave his mark uncontested on the history of the future state. There is much conjecture surrounding Drake's alleged interest in today's San Francisco Bay. Some say he found the bay which everyone says Cabrillo missed twice, some say Drake actually made his historic landfall up in Oregon.[197] I propose that Drake landed in both territories for I no more believe Drake missed the future San

---

[196]Don Knapp, 'A Chance To Hike California's Hidden Buttes', NY Times, 16 March 2007; Wikipedia.

[197]Melissa Darby, *Thunder Go North: The Hunt for Sir Francis Drake's Fair and Good Bay* (University of Utah Press 2019)

Francisco Bay than I believe Cabrillo did. So why the apparent secrecy? Why was this too large to miss bay the most denied discovery in the Age of Discovery?

The question might be answered better by the question: What was there? What might these men have been looking for – within a context of a land charted by an ancient civilization's suppressed charts? What might have been so special about this particular bay within the context of secret knowledge and very possible Templar interest or even awareness? The answer lies in the geomorphological analyses we have from Sesh Heri. If the reader is willing to take the leap that the Templar explorers were aware of such phenomena of earthly terrain as telluric current, plate tectonics, and straight-line gravity anomalies, then what Heri has posited about such phenomena at Indian Rock and Sutter Buttes, relative to these geophysical properties, must be part of the answer. If you will allow, for the sake of speculation, that the Templars knew this about the greater San Francisco Bay area, then knowing of the *hidalgo de sangre* lineage of Juan Cabrillo that I have laid out in this series should render the suggestion that Cabrillo knowing this information is a reasonable proposition. And I say if Cabrillo possessed such knowledge, so was it likely that Sir Francis Drake knew it, for the English explorer had visited Patagonia in the footsteps of Magellan whose journey was edited from the narrative for three hundred years. How can we presume Drake knew it?

Because that arch occultist and spymaster John Dee was behind the secret aspects of the design of England's foray into exploration of the Americas, specifically the Spanish territories on the Pacific coasts of both New World continents, and Drake was recruited to lead it.[198] Dee personally produced maps depicting an accuracy of New World territories that only Drake's voyage could have backed up, but before Drake ever made that voyage, Dee was already the number one geographer and navigational scientist in England – and the explorer captain is believed to have been briefed and educated on the issues relative to the expedition not long before departing.[199] I strongly suggest that John Dee was as much aware of geophysical phenomena embedded within the secret sea charts tradition as anyone of his time. There is no way that he did not inform Drake of these things to the extent that the captain was assigned to search for evidence and data. So again what were Cabrillo and then Drake looking for?

Sources of gold, of course. Heri suggests that the 1849 gold strike at Sutter's Mill was a staged event because US authorities already knew that gold was there, and he believes they knew it because of the geomorphology.[200] The same geomorphology that I say the Templar explorers were aware of via the secret sea charts captured at Constantinople during the Fourth Crusade, and the same geomorphological secrets that would have been passed down through Templar descendants after the order was disbanded publicly. That's how Cabrillo would have known it and that's how Dee likely knew it enough to inform Drake.

I propose that certain characteristics of terrain and geology were sought by Cabrillo and then by Drake several decades

[198]Bawlf, Pgs. 51-53
[199]Bawlf, Pgs 69-70.
[200]Heri, *The Handprint of Atlas*, Pgs 66-67

after him. This might have been known by benefit of an actual ancient chart of the bay or calculated by a pre-Columbian Templar exploration based on ancient information, and would likely have been some of the same information provided to the author of *Las Sergas de Esplandian.* It was apparently enough that these men confirmed the existence of San Francisco Bay to their respective masters for nothing else seems to have been done about it for a very long time. Perhaps they didn't know exactly what to do with it initially, at least it wasn't until after Cabrillo and Drake that Spain started the galleons running between the Philippines and North America.

We are led to believe that Spain cared nothing for further exploration of California, except the Manila Galleons making landings on the coast for resupply, until the 1602 expedition of Sebastian Vizcaino, who followed Cabrillo's route very closely yet supposedly *also* missed the San Francisco Bay![201] And we are also led to believe that Spain still did nothing with California for an additional 167 years all due to the poor decision of one short-sighted man, the Viceroy Marques de Montesclaros, who forbade it.[202] This I find impossible to believe, that one man would have deterred all players in Spain from development of a large potential bonanza of wealth, therefore I don't believe it. Why?

Because that is a ridiculous number of years for a nation like Spain to ignore a vast and potentially rich territory simply because of one man's reported folly. That and because, in 1591,

---

[201]Corle, *The Royal Highway*, Pgs. 36-37.

[202]Ibid Pg.39

Montesclaros was made a Knight of the Order of Santiago of Portugal,[203] one of the kingdoms that told the persecutors of the Knights Templar to go take a hike. Knights of the Order of Santiago fought alongside Templars during the Reconquista and they were among the existing orders of the Iberian Peninsula when the Templars were disbanded and many were absorbed into other orders. Montesclaros was in fact *hidalgo*, very possibly *hidalgo de sangre*, a descended Templar. If anyone was involved in keeping California off limits to the conquistadors so that Templar sponsored exploration could continue, it would have been this Viceroy of New Spain and Peru, Marques de Montesclaros.

I suspect that clandestine exploration and documentation of the secrets of California occurred between 1602AD and 1769AD years during which our next players entered the stage. However, before we introduce them, what might the *hidalgo* agents of Spain been looking for during this 167 year period?

We are told of an historical record dating to 1574AD in Guadalajara, Mexico, which tells of an official inquiry into the reported sighting of eight foreign ships sailing as a fleet northward in the Gulf of California. They were allegedly described as resembling Galician caravels adorned with pelican shaped figureheads. Not being affiliated with the Spanish, these foreign ships were of concern to the officials of New Spain. Their investigation reportedly turned up credible witnesses including soldiers, natives, and even a Franciscan friar with past experience in European seaports and their common vessels.

---

[203]Wikipedia

Said friar claimed to not recognize the style of these ships.[204] Were these ships in the style of those vessels of Queen Califia's fleet as portrayed in *Las Sergas de Esplandian*? Might Spanish agents have been seeking contact with a kingdom they suspected was somewhere in Alta California?

The discussion of Viking expeditions to the Americas is a popular topic in recent decades. Interestingly, the Seri tribe of Tiburon Island in the Gulf of California has a story of blond blue eyed men and a woman who came to their waters in a long boat 'with the head of a snake'.[205] The original source of this tale is from the 1939 book *Last of the Seris* by anthropologists Dane and Mary Roberts Coolidge, documented during their six week stay with the tribe. In the book, Mary states her belief that the Baja Seris had encountered Norwegians. David Childress suggests that pre-Columbian Viking explorers may have had the opportunity to pass through the Arctic and make their way south via the Bering Strait to the west coast of North America when in 900-1100 AD high temperatures in the Northern Hemisphere melted away a large area of arctic ice.[206] This is an interesting episode when you consider stories of lost ships have been told in and around Southern California for a long time. Did *hidalgo* explorers find any evidence of this during those 167 dark years?

There is the 1939 claim of Petra Tucker whose husband Santiago claimed to have found an odd ship partially buried in

---

[204]Choral Pepper, *Desert Lore of Southern California* (Sunbelt 1993); Childress, *Lost Cities and Ancient Mysteries of the Southwest* (AUP 2009) Pg 534

[205]Childress, *Lost Cities & Ancient Mysteries of the Southwest*, Pg.535.

[206]Ibid

the sand of a deep canyon in the desert outside Tecate, California.[207] Santiago described the vessel as having a bow shaped like a curved neck with the head of a bird. He told his wife of strange markings on the wall of the canyon in a language he didn't recognize and also brought home one of the 'round discs' attached to the side of the ship. Was this a Viking shield? We may never know because it was subsequently lost, according to Petra. This ship may have been associated with another report made in 1933 of a similar ancient vessel protruding from the wall of another canyon at Agua Caliente Springs in the Anza-Borrego desert west of the Salton Sea.[208] These 20th Century reports are quite interesting but is there anything of the period 1602-1769 AD to possibly lend credence to such tales?

Juan de Iturbe of the 1615AD expedition[209] is said to have sailed north through a channel in the Gulf of California at high tide and found himself in a different sea. But when the tide reversed, he was forced to abandon his ship, laden with pearls.[210] Interestingly, sources say that the lakes of Southern California started to evaporate more as recently as 1600AD and the modern Salton Sea is 236 feet below sea level[211] so at one time the Gulf of California waters could indeed have reached much farther north. Stories such as these recounted here do lend

---

[207]Alexander Nazaryan, *Searching for California's Lost Viking Treasure Ship* (Newsweek 2 Feb 2017); Childress, *Lost...Southwest* Pg 534

[208]Williams & Pepper, *The Mysterious West* (World Publishing 1967); Childress, Lost...Southwest, Pgs 536-537

[209]Stanford Libraries, "California As An Island in Maps".

[210]Childress, *Southwest*, Pg. 538

[211]US Geological Survey.

some consideration to the idea of California having been an island in the remote past, which allows for further consideration of the ancient fleet of the Amazons in *Esplandian*. But what of the suggestion of clandestine explorations during the period between the alleged moratorium and the arrival of the church missionaries?

During this 167 years of apparent inactivity, it would seem that Alta California was important to Spain only in its support of the Manila Galleon, which made the trek to the Philippines and back to New Spain (Mexico) once every year.[212] Providing temporary safe haven and refurbishment, California was indeed serving some known but limited purpose. We are told that the interior was being neglected where Spanish exploitation was concerned, but was that truly the case?

Think about it. The Manila Galleon made the trek from the Philippines back to New Spain by way of the California coast every year. How easy it would have been for a small contingent of select soldiers and explorers to have been delivered onto California's shores by the Manila Galleon and left there to make their way into the interior. How much easier still would it have been for a single agent to be picked up *after* his mission in the interior and ride back to New Spain aboard the Manila Galleon. Either way works, operationally. Soldiers heading across the Pacific to the Philippines raises no suspicions about their interest in California. An undocumented operative hitching a ride out of Monterey or the Channel Islands, upon return to Mexico, would likely be assumed to have come from the

[212]Corle; Starr; Various

Philippines with the rest of the crew. Therefore, courtesy of the Manila Galleons, Spain was actually providing the perfect delivery and pickup service for undercover explorers of the interior of California the entire 167 years of reported inactivity, but they never took advantage of it?

While one is hard pressed to find stories that might suggest secret Spanish exploration of California between 1602 and 1769, it should be noted that plans for establishing a colony in Alta California were being drafted and presented during the 1740s.[213] This still leaves about 140 years wide open. What makes it difficult to prove is that such classified expeditions could have been small, thus leaving a smaller footprint if at all. It's like looking for that needle in the haystack. Factor in the possibility that such expeditions might have been commissioned to independent explorers, somewhat like privateer captains on the seas, and that needle just got even harder to find. And to add another layer of insurmountable odds against finding evidence of such expeditions, consider that the *hidalgo* Montesclaros and his *hidalgo* successors would have commissioned only *hidalgo* explorers and the secret might be kept forever. Unable offer neither proof nor firm evidence, I simply contend that such secret expeditions could have been carried out by virtue of available resources and what we do know about the men most likely to make it happen.

With post-persecution *hidalgo de sangre* Templar descendants numbering in every Spanish order, and so many of

[213]Thomas Scharf, *Plans for the Occupation of Upper California: A New Look At The "Dark Age" From 1602 to 1769* (San Diego Historical Society Quarterly – Winter '78, Vol 24, No. 1).

them soldiers or in other New World positions of authority, 140 years of relative freedom would mean pre-Columbian Templar freedom throughout California, as many suspect the same through all the Americas. It seems, however, that no one offered California to the Spanish crown the way I suspect those Templars offered their New World package to Isabella. But just as Isabella went and brought the Pope in on the deal in 1492, the papal throne would extend its grip to California and this time its agents did not intend to let go.

The Jesuits

The Society of Jesus was founded by Ignatius Loyola, a Spanish Basque priest.[214] Called Jesuits, the order has quite a history. One might call them the 'counter-Templars' of the Catholic church for they are papal loyalists and are known to be experts across a wide range of fields from finance to technology and science. Their history in the Americas places them within the spotlight of this examination for they were there during that period when California was allegedly disregarded. In fact, California appears to have been an objective of the Jesuit order from the day they issued orders to newly inducted member Eusebio Kuhn, aka Father Kino.

Kino is discussed in the first volume of this series[215]. He began as a student in the Society of Jesus in 1665 and would become a priest twelve years later. An Austrian born in Italy, Kino was educated at Innsbruck but went on to teach

[214] Durant, *Rousseau and Revolution...Europe from 1715 to 1789*, Pg 283.
[215] Bosley, SM1, Chapter 4.

mathematics, astronomy and natural sciences at Freiburg, Landsberg and Ingolstadt, legendary territory of Frankenstein repute, and the heart of alchemical education in Bavaria. His first assignment upon acceptance as a priest in the Jesuit order?

To lead an expedition through Baja California. Isn't that interesting? As discussed in the first volume of this series, Kino also explored a particular corner of Arizona. This included a keen interest in what he named 'Casa Grande', now believed to have been an astronomical observatory and usually credited to the Hohokam civilization. As posed in the first volume, what if Kino had been sent to Arizona specifically because this alleged Hohokam observatory was already known to his superiors? Kino's first writing in New Spain (Mexico) was an article on a comet. He taught astronomy in Bavaria. I say he was sent to Arizona, to what we know today as Tucson, to investigate what the Jesuit order possibly already knew was there. How did they know? Likely through intelligence collections on secret Templar reports or some such report from a previous clandestine exploration. Kino may have been sent to the North American southwest specifically to investigate whatever the Jesuit order knew of Templar activities there.

It so happens that Kino was also an expert cartographer as well.[216] If there was anyone serving as an agent of the Jesuits to follow through on possible Templar explorations of the Americas, motivated by possession of ancient charts and maps, it was Father Kino, and indeed there he was, and his first

[216]Ernest J. Burrus, *Kino and the Cartography of Northwestern New Spain* (excerpt at the Kino Heritage Society; 1965)

mission to explore California, the very land of mystery we are discussing. I do not think we have been told the true mission of Father Kino, at least not where California is concerned. He would recruit two additional Jesuit priests to his mission: Juan Maria Salvatierra and Juan Ugarte. Together, these three enterprising representatives of the pope established the Pious Fund of the Californias, essentially a spiritual extortion scheme through which noble and wealthy Catholics could buy their way into salvation by literally paying for it. This is how these 'good priests' raised the expeditionary funds that the Spanish government denied them.[217] The fund hauled in enough booty to finance Jesuit industry, raise an army of Jesuit mercenaries, and to establish the church as state in California territories.

Starting to see the picture yet? Three Jesuits, under orders to Kino from their Society masters in Rome, took advantage of what Spain was apparently neglecting. As I say here about California having been an objective long before Columbus, knowledge of it gleaned from ancient charts and other texts captured during the Fourth Crusade, the Jesuits had their eye on the legendary territory and its legendary resources from early on in their involvement with the New World. I propose that the Jesuits sought to control California before the Templar influenced powers could do so. It worked for a while, too. California's first real step toward modern development was due to the efforts and accomplishments which these priests set into motion. They were literally given a license to develop California how they saw fit, issued by the Spanish government

[217]Corle, Pgs 41-43

on the 5th of February 1697 and they ran with it.[218] Salvatierra and Ugarte established the Mission Trail with sites up and down Baja and this was, of course, continued in Alta California. It was Kino who first envisioned an actual California road[219] and this would be laid mostly along the course of previous expeditions, connecting the missions already built to provide rest and refurbishment for Spanish travelers official or otherwise. Known as the Royal Road, or El Camino Real, the route and the missions built along it were also a statement of possession, clearly that of the church.

But none of it north of Baja would be built by the Jesuits as they were banished from the Americas in the spring of 1767 by decree of King Charles who charged the order with conspiracy to assassinate Joseph I of Portugal, encouraging insurrection in the colonies, and evading taxes through corrupt trade practices.[220] Though it is said the King did not provide evidence, still the Jesuits had been doing essentially the same things that a previous king and pope had accused the Templars of doing, building their own power base separate and unaccountable to authority. The establishment of El Camino Real in Alta California would fall to the Franciscans.

Sentiment had grown against the Jesuits and their disbandment had been ordered following their arrest and expulsion from Spanish America. In that same year, Gaspar de Portola was commissioned to explore the route for the proposed road. Jose de Galvez was sent by Charles III to pursue Spanish interests

[218]Corle, Pg 41
[219]Ibid, Pg 44
[220]Durant, *Rousseau and Revolution*, Pgs 283-285

more aggressively in California and Galvez did just that. It was he who encouraged Kino's original vision for El Camino Real – but not in the interests of the church. Galvez was adamant that Spanish California not be controlled by the Jesuits but rather by Spain, ie the royal government, not the church.[221]

It may be here that the struggle between the Templar faction and the Jesuits for control of California was ignited in earnest, for Galvez was born *hidalgo (*likely *de sangre)* by virtue of his ancestor Anton who had served as a knight during the Reconquista.[222] Members of the Galvez family were knights of the Order of Calatrava which had been established after taking over property passed to them by the Knights Templar, approved by papal decree in September of 1164AD. Jose de Galvez, in my opinion, was the first to fire a shot across the Jesuit bow over the issue of California. Being the oldest order on the Iberian Peninsula, this order was based in Castile where Templar properties were not turned over to the Hospitallers after the 1307 disbandment.[223] The Order of Calatrava and its associate Order of Montesa,[224] previously discussed, indeed absorbed refugee Templar knights, thus Galvez was a Templar by association if not blood. As such, Galvez' adamant position against Jesuit control in Spanish America would have been interpreted as Templar resistance by them.

---

[221] Herbert I Priestley, *Jose de Galvez: Visitor-General of New Spain 1765-1771* (University of California 1916); Corle, Pg 45

[222] Ibid, Pgs 1-2.

[223] Wikipedia, various

[224] Catholic Encyclopedia, Lamper, Montesa illustrata (Valencia, 1669); *Definiciones de la orden y cavalleria de Montesa* (Valencia, 1573); LAFUENTE, Hist. Ecl. de Espana (Madrid, 1874).

So with the Jesuits officially removed from Spanish America, the development of Spanish California fell to the Franciscans who took on the establishment of El Camino Real and the missions which are today such a substantial symbol of the state. The city of San Diego was founded in 1769, then simply an outpost which is today's tourist area called Old Town. It was nearby on a hilltop that Father Junipero Serra founded the Mission San Diego de Alcala, the first of California's famous 'Mission Trail'.[225] Serra, it should be noted, sought to preserve the work of the Jesuits. He was also educated in theology at Llullian University on Palma de Mallorca, a place where the Jesuits also had an academic presence. Despite a history of alleged rivalry between the orders, the Jesuits were founded upon a heavy Franciscan influence.[226] I propose that the Jesuits found sympathetic and agreeable Franciscans to carry on their particular vision by proxy despite any differences between their respective organizational cultures. Especially suggestive when you consider what esotericism Serra may have been exposed to at the Llullian University,[227] its namesake a likely influence upon my hypothesis here.

Though across centuries Father Serra has been presented to school children in California as a benevolent founder of

---

[225]Corle, Pgs 51-53; The author was born in San Diego and educated there and has visited again recently on research for this book, including the Mission itself. WB

[226]Adam Sorrels, "Lecture Discusses Franciscan Roots of Jesuit Spirituality" (The Torch 27 Nov 2019) derived from Franco Mormando, Professor, Boston College.

[227]Ramon Llull was a 13th/14th Century Christian mystic who discovered a metaphysical algebra inherent in the three monotheistic religions. Lllull was deeply influenced by Moorish ideas. Also refer to Farrell, *Thrice Great Hermetica*, Pgs 180-183.

California's greatness, the man enslaved local natives and used severe corporal punishment on them if they tried to escape the mission property. Serra and his fellow missionaries used the natives as slave labor to build their churches and zanjas. These natives would be put into chains if they were caught fleeing. The native women raped by Spanish soldiers were also forced to stick around and endure further abuse. This was as much the legacy of the Franciscan development of California as anything else.[228] Galvez had a different vision of how the Franciscans and Spanish soldiers were to treat the natives. To explorer Gaspar de Portola, he had instructed:

> "*To prevent difficulties and disaster in the outcome, the most prudent supervision must be exercised. Therefore,* ***I charge you with zeal and vigilance to maintain the most exact discipline over the soldiers of the expedition*** *as well as over the muleteers, especially from the frontier on,* ***so that the Indians will be well treated. The soldiers are to be punished as in the case of an irremissible crime if they offer any affront or violence to the women*** *because, besides being offenses against God, such excesses committed by them could also bring disaster to the entire expedition*."[229]

How is it that men of God see fit to ignore the humane orders of the secular superiors of their venture and instead advocate brutality? This is the same church from which the cruel excesses of the Inquisition had sprung. In fact, it was the Franciscans and the Dominican Order that were assigned to

[228] The Guardian, "Junípero Serra's Brutal Story in Spotlight as Pope Prepares for Canonisation" (2015); Editors, 'Junipero Serra' (Biography.com 13 Aug 2019);

[229] Maynard Geiger. *The Life and Times of Fray Junípero Serra (*Academy of American Franciscan History, 1959) Vol. 1, p. 209; Emphasis mine.

facilitate the edicts of the Inquisition. Both orders carried it to Mexico. Essentially, the self-flagellating Serra and his fellow missionaries thought they knew better than everyone else. The 'benevolent' Padre Serra is here described following his arrival in Mexico by the accomplished expert California chronicler Kevin Starr, University Professor of History, University of Southern California, as follows:

"*...the diminutive friar* ***relished physical suffering*** *and mortification as part of the ferocious asceticism* ***that would characterize the rest of his life***. *Serra slept on a board bed,* ***scourged himself, and lacerated his flesh with stones in the course of highly emotional sermons***. *As such, he represented a paradox: a priest formed by an almost medieval piety given a crucial assignment to an enterprise intended, in some measure, to establish a civil society in California.* ***The tension involved in such a paradox would soon surface***."[230] (Emphasis mine)

Ya think? Serra believed in spreading his relish for masochism around the native community enslaved by he and his pious colleagues.[231] Yet this was the man entrusted with the 'abandoned' Jesuit mission to impose the interests of the church onto the native peoples of the California territory. He may have been the only one among the missionaries with an addiction to a deviant fetish, but he was the one in charge and the one credited with 'civilizing' California, and the one recently sainted by the

[230]Starr, *California: A History* (Modern Library 2005) Pgs.33-34

[231]I'll have to check my sources but this may additionally qualify Serra as a sadist. At the very least, Junipero Serra qualifies as a masochist, according to *Masochism: A Jungian View* by analyst Lyn Cowan (Spring Pubs 1982) Pgs 98-102.

pope. As regards the establishment of the missionary vision along El Camino Royal, Serra accordingly carried out his duties to his masters, whom I say were the banished Jesuits back in the Vatican.

Jesuits were certainly the influential order back in Spain for they served as confessors to royalty and they dominated education in the Spanish world, all during the period of the Inquisition, which the Dominicans, who soon joined the Franciscans on their venture in the Americas, controlled. It is said that in Spain there were less books printed in the 18th Century than in the 16th Century thanks to Inquisition suppression.[232] Such was imbalance between secular and religious Spanish culture.

The Mission Trail, as it's called, was established from San Diego northward along the coastline to the Mission San Francisco de Solano, twenty-one in all built in the span of fifty-four years. Of major significance here is that all but one of these missions is located upon major straight-line gravity anomalies and/or their curvilinear counterparts, flowing with telluric current, aka the 'world grid system' as identified by my associate Sesh Heri on the map provided to me over a decade prior to this writing. That exception is Mission San Luis Obispo, founded in 1772 and named after a member of the House of Anjou, a dynasty present in the Joan of Arc and Rennes le Chateau sagas. Interestingly, the architecture of Mission San Luis Obispo is unlike all the other mission churches, being L-shaped. It would also be used by John C.

---

[232]Durant, *Rousseau and Revolution*, Pgs 275-276

Fremont during the Bear Flag Rebellion which we shall discuss shortly.

I find it very significant that the Spanish missions were built along the gravity anomaly/telluric current grid. One might argue it a coincidence but I raise the issue of the context of this very examination. I have laid out what I think is a compelling argument that California was being explored and developed by knightly and religious orders which were operating with the benefit of information captured during the Fourth Crusade, specifically information of interest to those among those orders with an understanding of alchemy and other special knowledge and including ancient maps and charts. My suspicion is that El Camino Real and its accompanying missions were consciously constructed upon these lines of planetary energy. I further suggest that this was done to better facilitate whatever sorcery was being conducted by members of the ecclesiastical orders in question, namely the Franciscans and Dominicans, with likely guidance from Jesuits who, though banished, could have easily continued to have their hand in California. In fact, I say that it is this very phenomenon of gravity-line anomaly energy that Jesuits and Templars alike were looking to exploit in the territory.

A curious exception in the process of establishing the mission trail is to be found in today's Pasadena. In July of 1769, Catalan born soldier Gaspar de Portola departed north from San Diego with the alumnus Serra student, Father Crespi, in his company. Their expedition followed a more inland course which would serve to identify the future location of Mission San Juan

Capistrano and also give a name to the river they would follow, the Santa Ana. In his diary, not translated until 1927, Father Crespi would write of "a spacious valley" with a plain which he describes as "very extensive" and "good land for planting all kinds of grains and seeds". What's more is that Crespi described this location like so: "*...the **most suitable site of all that we have seen** for a mission, for it has all the requisites of a large mission.*" And yet, no mission was built there. The location is today identified as the Arroyo Seco and is the site of the Devil's Gate Dam.[233] So why didn't they build the mission there?

It is true that Gaspar de Portola described the Arroyo Seco as the canyon with the least water in this area, but there was plenty enough water otherwise to create the abundantly desirable scene which Father Crespi described. We are told that Portola wanted to head toward the sea and thus would they subsequently establish the mission in what would become Los Angeles. But might there have been another reason the Arroyo Seco was not desirable?

Today, this area is known for being the site of NASA's Jet Propulsion Laboratory and that opens up a volume of Pasadena history which might explain why Portola led his expedition away. JPL was famously founded by legendary and somewhat infamous (depending upon who you talk to) Jack Parsons who was long familiar with the Arroyo Seco where he and his associates would test the rocket engines they had invented. It should be no surprise to also find strange tales of a paranormal

---

[233]Corle, Pgs 56-57; *Fray Juan Crespi,* Translation by Herbert Bolton, 1927.

and occult nature linked to the place, specifically the park at Devil's Gate Dam.[234] Parsons had also been a well known practitioner of high black magic and even considered himself (and L Ron Hubbard) the cause for what he believed to be an interdimensional event, not a UFO, at Roswell, New Mexico in 1947. Parson's mentor was Aleister Crowley and all that goes with that. It is therefore no surprise to me that Portola did not allow the mission to be established there.

That the Catholic priest documented the area as ideal for the mission might come as a surprise to the average person, if a no-nonsense soldier liked Portola sensed something off about the place, but the very context of what we're discussing here suggests to me that the priest perhaps was *supposed* to identify such sites where the church's own brand of magic might be conducted. It's a curious thing that an area described as ideal by the priest establishing a mission was rejected so clearly by the commander of the expedition, a soldier. I find it interesting, but historians will point out that Los Angeles site was closer to the sea anyway, so we must move on.

Through what is today's Sepulveda Pass they would continue, northward toward and along the coast, to Ventura, Santa Barbara, Gaviota[235], Refugio, Point Conception and then the aforementioned San Luis Obispo where we have an interesting association with that figure whom I have proposed a link to

[234]David Paulides, *The Devil's In The Detail* (2014); WB: I have conducted personal research and investigation on multiple occasions in this very park including the Devil's Gate Dam itself. I experienced firsthand some curious phenomena on my first trip there, a blind visit. I didn't know I was going there until we arrived. My opinion is that something in the location is hypernatural.

[235]Site of an early Zodiac Killer double murder.

Cabrillo in the first book of this series, Joan of Arc. Named for Bishop Louis of Toulouse, an Angevin by birth who gave up his inheritance to dedicate himself to the church. It may have been no mere act of admiration by the Franciscans that this site in California was named after this particular bishop.

The House of Anjou was a major dynasty in medieval European history, originally a Frankish line. Their family expanded and their influence spread throughout much of Europe, including King Denis of Portugal, he who gave sanctuary to the persecuted Knights Templar, creating the Order of Christ for them after their own was dismantled and outlawed. As I propose in the first volume of this series, this act of King Denis plays an important role in the very exploration of the Americas and particularly in the *hidalgo de sangre* status which I claim for Juan Cabrillo via the man I am convinced was very likely his father, Pedro Cabral, the Portuguese explorer who claimed Brazil for Portugal and was a knight of the Order of Christ. That I also suspect Juan Cabrillo could have been seeking the sword of Joan of Arc, which I propose was brought to the Americas by the Knights Templar after they went underground, makes this mission site in California all the more interesting. Was there any more to the dedication of San Luis Obispo than mere veneration on the part of Franciscans involved in the establishment of California's Mission Trail?

Unlike the Jesuits, the Franciscans were not so interested in scientific pursuits and it shows in their administration of the Mission Trail.[236] But that doesn't mean there wasn't anything

[236]Starr, *California: A History*, Pgs.36-37.

about the site to meet criteria more esoteric in nature than they cared to pursue. Referring to the map Sesh Heri provided to me years ago, the one which identifies telluric current gravity anomaly configurations across the continental United States, I could see that San Luis Obispo is in the center of three nearby configurations. One is north at Paso Robles, another south at Lompoc-Point Conception, and the third is east at the north end of the Carrizo Plain National Monument. This does not mean San Luis Obispo is not affected at all by these energy flows, nor does it mean that nothing of special interest within our context is present there. There's a Dinosaur Caves Park at nearby Pismo Beach. These caves were once known as Caverns of Mystery in the early 20th Century. They collapsed and washed away decades ago but might have been there when Juan Cabrillo sailed the coastline and could certainly have been known to the Portola expedition. But caves alone aren't quite enough.

Though Cabrillo famously hugged the coastline during his expedition, clearly looking for something (caves being a reasonable proposition), I can't shake the notion of a French connection, so to speak, to this area. Since I proposed that Joan of Arc's sword may very well have been the artifact which I speculate Cabrillo found in California, it seems reasonable to consider the French connection whether connected to this relic or at least to the Templars. We could be looking at something as simple as the Vatican having intelligence of a previous Templar site at this place and thus the Franciscans were instructed to name it after the French bishop as a means of communicating this knowledge to select others in the know. Perhaps the priest and clerical retinue on the 16th Century Alta California expedition reported to the Vatican on Cabrillo's keen interest in the coastline features. The subsequent 18th Century Portola expedition Franciscan could have been instructed to establish a mission at the site and label it in honor of the sainted French bishop to meet the previously suggested circumstances. If this proposition was true, this further suggests that the Vatican could have had reason to think that Joan of Arc's sword was hidden in California by that time and may have thought they had found it at San Luis Obispo.

In the first volume of this series, I hypothesize that Joan's sword was much farther south, in today's Mount Rubidoux in Riverside. But I could be wrong about that. Cabrillo could have obtained the sword from, or had reason to believe it was located in the caves that once existed at what would become San Luis Obispo, specifically today's Pismo Beach. Perhaps Vatican agents thought they would at least find a Templar vault there and the church mission would provide a base from which to operate during the search. The choice of Louis the Bishop, the Angevin saint, as the namesake of the site would, in my opinion, serve to specifically identify its link to Joan of Arc via Rene d'Anjou, the duke who was a major supporter of the maiden from Orleans and even went to battle with her.[237] Some sources say Joan was of the nobility, that the crown knew it, and she was actually of the House of Anjou.[238] It is my

[237]Goldstone, *The Maid and the Queen*, Pg 194; Durant, The Renaissance, Pgs 349 7 353; 'Priory of Sion' article at crusaderhistory.wordpress.com

[238]Eric Christian Hansen, wildlife biologist and forester by education, claims that Joan's father Jacques d'Arc was actually the father of Charles VII who did quickly

suspicion that the mystery of Rennes le Chateau, long associated with the maid's benefactor Rene d'Anjou, likely has every bit as much to do with Joan as it does the Magdalene. My point is that San Luis Obispo may indeed be a clue that the Joan of Arc sword hypothesis in the first book of this series has some merit.

Within the context of my hypothesis that the Jesuits had an interest in both seeking the telluric current/gravity anomaly sites, as well as seeking suspected Templar sites, specifically vaults, if they were there, I suggest that their banishment before being able to commence the Mission Trail into Alta California frustrated these efforts. That they had to work through the Franciscans and Dominicans would have made the objectives much less transparent. The clerics to whom the Mission Trail foundation fell to would have been taking orders with the true objectives embedded within or working with orders they might not understand the function of, yet had to simply follow. If such circumstances of a distant Vatican hand at the helm of the Mission Trail endeavor indeed existed, there is no reason to dismiss the possibility that undercover Jesuit agents would have been placed discreetly among the personnel and been present throughout the Portola expedition. Such an operational tactic would have been the most practical way for the Jesuits to ensure the greatest degree of success in their clandestine aims.

---

ennobled the family during Joan's saga. Hansen also claims Joan was a relative of Queen Sibilla of Jerusalem, herself of the House of Anjou. He also cites the modern Knights Templar Order as claiming Joan was indeed *hidalgo de sangre*, which I agree with. Yet another source claims Joan was descended in the same line as Fulk the Black, a dark figure for reasons more than his name.

It is a fact that, among those first missions established, San Luis Obispo wasn't built like any of the other missions. It was L-shaped, for one thing. Does that mean anything? It's one more notable item other than being named for a sainted French bishop, but since the mission doesn't appear to sit directly upon telluric current/gravity anomaly, I can't feel confident in applying any speculation of it being a temple used as a communication device a la Farrell and DeHart's *Grid of the Gods* hypothesis.[239] I am confident with the suggestion that Mission San Luis Obispo could have been established with the function of archaeological base camp in mind. The caves at Pismo Beach weren't the only ones, for there were other caves along the entire local coastline up to Avila Beach. Whatever other implications remain are for another book.

Continuing north, it is my suspicion that whatever Cabrillo was looking for in today's San Francisco Bay that compelled him to such secrecy was related to telluric energy/gravity anomaly nodes linked to the geomorphological system so instrumental to the gold deposits of California. I propose that California was charted in ancient times and said charting was among the documents captured during the Fourth Crusade, as alluded to earlier. Cabrillo's reconnaissance of the bay would have been part of his clandestine mission. The Portola

[239] I struggled with laying out my very thinly supported proposition that there was such a technological communications system built into the California missions, and if anyone involved here would have attempted such a thing, it would have been the Jesuits. But they lost the mission of establishing the trail and its facilities and wouldn't likely have revealed knowledge of such things, as would happen had they trusted the Franciscans or Dominicans to operate it. I may approach this possibility in a future volume after I have done more research.

expedition over two centuries later approached the bay by land but purveyors of mainstream history try to convince us that the commander wasn't impressed and never saw the mouth to the sea anyway.[240] I don't buy it. It's more likely that Portola kept a classified log and expressed 'disappointment' and 'failure' in his standard log. It's also possible that my suspected Vatican agent would have been the one on the secret mission and maintained the classified log on the side patrol to search for what was really drawing them to San Francisco Bay.

So what were they looking for?

For the record, I suggest Sir Francis Drake was seeking the same thing when he secretly explored the bay a few decades after Cabrillo. If my suspicion about ancient charts of California and explorers covertly looking for gold deposits bears fruit, I would propose that they would have been looking for geological features which could have been measured by tools of the day, ie simple magnetic signature, basic soil sample analysis, topography such as it was. They might have been looking for such features relative to the telluric current/gravity anomalies without even knowing of said currents. These features would eventually have led someone like a trail of bread crumbs to the heart of the gold deposits in California – if they knew how to recognize those crumbs. What I propose was found in San Francisco Bay was likely a feature in an eastern point, near today's Berkeley.

In *The Handprint of Atlas,* Sesh Heri details his hypothesis on the telluric current/gravity anomalies of the San Francisco Bay

---

[240]Corle, Pgs 61-63; Starr, Pg.35

area and its effects upon the geomorphology of the region. Heri specifically identifies with this the aforementioned Circle in Kensington, a community formerly associated with Berkeley. Now a literal traffic circle, this feature is just down the street from Indian Rock, a large rhyolite boulder about six hundred feet north of the Circle. Heri explains in the book how Indian Rock started in the Circle and through time shifted to its present position. Heri also identifies an intersection at the Circle of two main lines of gravity anomaly telluric current that are part of the so called 'World Grid' of natural energy. One of these lines continues northeast to present day Sacramento and on through Auburn and Donner Summit, all the way to Pyramid Lake, Nevada. The Circle marks the spot where the stresses from multiple land masses converge in a single point, intensified by the telluric energy and in turn intensifying the energy itself. Heri proposes that Pyramid Lake is a node upon which several large land masses turn and is a spot of great gravity stress and compression.

Sesh Heri suggests that the line of energy running through The Circle in the East Bay of San Francisco, and on northeast beyond Sacramento, would lead anyone with the knowledge of how to read the geomorphology of the terrain directly to the gold deposits to be found there. Heri believes that an immense volcano once occupied the region and Lake Tahoe now fills its eroded crater. He explains further:

"*This suggests the possibility to me that land masses subjected to a balanced stress in a gravitational field-- in essence subjected to a scalar-type of standing wave stress-- would absorb a great deal of kinetic stress energy over a long period of time. A mass that cumulatively absorbs a great deal of gravitational stress may eventually become so unstable that it reconfigures into another element. An extremely unstable atomic structure-- one that is "ripe" to use an old alchemical term-- may reconfigure by a low energy trigger, such as the chemical explosion of gunpowder or a similar kind of explosion in the magma of an erupting volcano.*

This would explain the natural transmutation of elements within the earth, especially the formation of gold within the caldera of large volcanoes formed from the cumulative stress of a faint gravity anomaly line, and it would confirm the old alchemical idea that gold "grows" in the earth. It would also explain the presence of the Mother Lode in the Sierra Nevada Mountains west of Lake Tahoe. The gold would have erupted from the giant volcano that eventually became Lake Tahoe. The pattern of the ejected magma was to the west of the volcano. This became folded into the earth in veins when the land was uplifted and folded into mountains." (The Handprint of Atlas, Pgs 122-123)

Could an application of this natural process of the manufacture of gold, the alchemical 'dry method', factor into a Templar recapture of California? But before that could happen, I suspect that San Francisco Bay had to be explored and charted so that specific geomorphological features could be identified. The Templar plan would likely have started with Cabrillo's secret recon of the bay. All of this could have been a big part of why Drake's actual voyage remained secret for four hundred years. I think this geomorphological identification objective continued with the Portola expedition, specifically assigned to Pedro Fages and his cartographer Miguel Costanso, who is credited as the first European to see the bay. I do not believe that is true, as you know, but Costanso may indeed have been the first known European to have seen that spot now called The Circle. Being the cartographer on an Alta California expedition, particularly because of the context in which I argue these expeditions were carried out, ie with classified objectives, Miguel Costanso would likely have been approved by those involved with the secret arcane pursuits.

Does this suggest that Costanso, or Fages even, were linked to the parties possessing knowledge captured during the Fourth Crusade? I have not yet been able to find any direct links but it should be noted that Costanso is a name derived from the Italian Costanzo and very quickly one finds Giovanni Battista Costanzo listed among a list of architects, engineers and military officers involved with charting a Ligurian region of Italy in the 16th and 17th Centuries.[241] Finding much beyond that is difficult thus far, but with the historical relations between Italy and Spain, each having controlled the other in ancient and Medieval times, there naturally was migration between the two. It's possible to suggest a relation between the Italian Costanzo cited in the cartographic history and the cartographer Costanso of Spain. One possible clue is that Costanzo is mentioned among military officers. Usually the word 'soldier' is used in the general sense, thus when I see 'military officer' specified I wonder if *hidalgo* status came with that. At present it's a thin

---

[241] David Woodward, *The History of Cartography, Volume 3: Cartography in the European Renaissance, Part 1* (Univ of Chicago Press 2007) Page 868.

suggestion but at least there's that in Costanso's case, a thread to be pulled is better than none at all.

Whether Costanso or Fages were specifically in the know on any arcane mission to find particular geomorphological landmarks of the terrain in San Francisco Bay, Costanso was the cartographer and whatever he documented and turned in to superiors would have served those who were involved. I propose that features such as Sesh Heri identifies with The Circle in the east bay town of Kensington is exactly what was being looked for in San Francisco Bay. I propose that such phenomena of geography was anticipated by the Vatican scientists and their associates in the Spanish court as well as by Juan Cabrillo and Francis Drake before them. Because this nodal point near Berkeley identifies a point on a world grid telluric energy/gravity anomaly line leading to the gold deposits, the European discovery of San Francisco Bay was the prime reason for the search for California to begin with, in my opinion. The problem for Spain and the Vatican, from my perspective, is that the Templars knew about it long before they did.

Even though Fages and Costanso of the Portola expedition likely discovered the nodal point in the east bay, Cabrillo, Drake and Templars before them had also been there, I am convinced. Cabrillo and Drake were probably aware of the nodal point in a more vague context than the Templars who might have been to the area, but the Templars weren't able to do much with the information beyond noting it. Sesh Heri has an hypothesis that Pyramid Lake is the site of an ancient vault hiding secret information not found until the 19th Century. He argues that California may have been one of many ancient 'lands of Ophir' and implies that Phoenicians built the pyramid shaped 'rock' in Pyramid Lake.[242] Hypothetical Templar explorers of California would likely have recognized this or even known it to be the case. Again, not much was apparently done with this information beyond noting it, until the 19th Century.

Heri suggests that the Spanish and the Vatican were aware of the geomorphological significance of the Twin Peaks in San Francisco and its connection via the world grid line across the bay, through Sacramento, and directly to the 600 foot tall pyramid in Pyramid Lake.[243] He also thinks they eventually suspected or even knew where the mother lode of gold was generally located but their plan to exploit it came too late. I argue that the Templars beat them to it, robbing Spain and the Church entirely of the dream of possessing the lost Amazon kingdom of Califia...for a time.

From this point forward to our present day, it is my opinion that the battle for essential control of California between the Vatican/Jesuits and the Knights Templar was conducted via political influences filtered through the church and Freemasonry, respectively. That is to say, the Templars got control of California when it became a territory and then a state in the Union, and the Vatican/Jesuits set about a long term campaign to get back control via stacking the political deck.

[242]Heri, *Handprint of Atlas*, Pgs 125-126.
[243]Ibid Pgs 126-127.

Being that a critical number of the founding fathers were freemasons and much clandestine activity of the rebellion was conducted through masonic lodges, the United States is a Templar nation. I say this was never lost on the Vatican/Jesuit players in the California game. And behind all this was the knowledge both sides had of the geomorphological secrets and their relation to the gold desposits.

John C. Fremont is a colorful and checkered figure in California and US history. He was opposed to slavery but not to murdering natives on sight while in California, defying an order to leave that independent republic because of his revolutionary pot-stirring. Fremont's deeds were done before war had been declared on Mexico by the United States so his encouragement of American resident insurgence in California was simply illegal and essentially uncalled for. However, he was encouraged by private dispatches, hand delivered by US Marine Corp officer Archibald Gillespie, from Senators Thomas Hart Benton and James Buchanan, tipping Fremont off that war with Mexico would definitely be declared. Benton was a major expansionist also involved in the Texas rebellion. This was all Fremont needed to justify further military operations on California territory.[244]

Much of California was taken without resistance, including Santa Barbara and Los Angeles. Ultimately, the Treaty of Cahuenga ended the war in California, the Californios agreeing to surrender their artillery. Fremont represented the United

[244]Allan Nevins, *Fremont:Pathmarker of the West* (Bison Books, Feb 1992); J.M. Guinn, 'California Under the Rule of Spain and Mexico' (Historical Society of Southern California); Starr, *California: A History*; Various.

States in the drafting and signing of this treaty. The Californios were told to return to their homes and agreed to obey US law but were not required to sign a loyalty pledge. Subsequently, the Treaty of Guadalupe Hidalgo was signed between the United States and Mexico, ceding much territory to the United States. Californios were given US citizenship and some were elected to state government. Many Californios preferred that their homeland become part of the United States in contrast to Mexico having centralized governance under its control, sending governors from Mexico instead of from election by the local population. It could actually be said that the first volley in the secret war for control of California was fired by Mexico.

Under the *Decree for the Secularisation of the Missions of the Californias* of 1833, the Spanish missions lost much of their property and could no longer enslave natives to do the labor. The motivation for independent Mexico was that the missions were loyal to the Spanish crown, not to Mexico. Their land was handed over to the Californio citizens who established the ranchos, some of the very same Californios who would side with the United States in the following decade. Spanish padres were replaced with Mexican priests and the missions were reduced to the church itself and the accompanying structures. Spaniards under 60 years of age were banished from the territory. This certainly didn't make the Vatican Jesuits happy, as their own vision of state had defined much of Spanish colonization in North American Spanish territories and stood as a barrier to settlement by anyone but the Jesuits aka ‘the church’.[245]

Despite an intention to establish a colony based on the principles of a free republic (inspired by the United States), including freedom from the rule of the Catholic church, Mexico did no better than Spain in two distinct ways: their social caste system got in the way of the common citizen and the natives were still denied the return of their lands seized by the Jesuit missions.[246] These two realities plus the Enlightenment values spreading throughout the western world sparked the Californio embrace of the United States. Between the earlier banishment of the Jesuits, the loss of the mission properties and local power under Mexican secularization, and the subsequent acquisition by the United States, the Vatican/Jesuits had lost the realm of Amazons to that old enemy of the church – and that meant they had also lost the very reason for venturing forth in Columbus’ wake to begin with: the secrets of gold and the very power of the Earth. It may be that the California state flag still flaunts a Templar association.

This brings us back to what John Fremont knew and what he was really doing during his second expedition. As an officer of the US Army Corps of Topographical Engineers, Fremont was distinctly qualified to read the terrain and understand what he was looking at. More specifically, Fremont would likely have been able to read the geomorphology and recognize the very special signs and features associated with the world grid and

[245]Starr, Pg 28.
[246]Starr.

telluric/gravity anomaly influences, including sighting likely gold deposit areas. But lest the reader wonder if Fremont actually did possess such knowledge on his own, his explorations involved sponsors who instructed his objectives and likely guided him in the more arcane aspects of his expedition – and to whom he was loyal: Senators Benton and Buchanan.

It appears to Sesh Heri that Fremont was operating with prior knowledge of the gold deposits, the possible mother lode source of the old Amazon realm legends of California, I would add. Looking at it from the perspective that Knights Templar explorers, especially post persecution in the 14th Century, had been on expeditions across North America, such information would have started for them in whatever documents in their possession were seized during the Fourth Crusade. Once analyzed by their own cartographers, scientists and alchemists, the documents would have given up secrets of the New World. Whatever the Templars learned of California gold would have been investigated and whatever was learned from that effort would certainly have found its way through the centuries to their colleagues in the English colonies for whom freemasonry played a role in their independence and national vision. Some scholars agree that the United States is a masonic nation, maybe the first one, thus a Templar stake in the wealth and strength of the new country led to sharing the order's secrets with select leaders in Congress and in the President's Cabinet. Senator Benton was a Freemason and James Buchanan, who would subseqently become President of the United States, served as Deputy Grand Master of the Pennsylvania State Lodge.[247]

With Benton and Buchanan calling the shots for the second Fremont expedition, we must consider what they knew about what Fremont was looking at and for. Again, I advocate looking more closely at the Louisiana Territory for I am in that school of thought that suspects something arcane was embedded within the landscape and factored into the deal with Napoleon. It is my suspicion that what Fremont found on his second expedition, according to Sesh Heri, was, at the very least, part of a secret objective in obtaining the Louisiana Territory, but not found until later. Benton had gone head to head against the central bankers with Andrew Jackson so it is doubtful he got close enough to Nicholas Biddle to learn any insider bits on the Lewis and Clark expedition. What I suspect about Biddle, as discussed in Volume 4, is that while conducting the audit and the rewriting of the journals of the famous expedition, he learned something about the archaeological secrets that could at that time be confirmed in the Louisiana Territory and used this information to his own benefit.[248] But Buchanan wasn't so distant.

In the volume on Napoleon, I suggest that Biddle used secret knowledge from the Lewis and Clark expedition to buy his career in the banking oligarchy and very well may have been conspiring with international banking figures in a backroom deal relative to potential discovery of the gold deposits

[247]Steven L Harrison, *Tales From The Craft* (Softworks Inc 2014) Pg 129; LaPorte York Rite Commandery #12 KT; Today in Masonic History, masonrytoday.com
[248]Bosley, *The Esoteric Napoleon*, Pgs 298-300.

embedded within centuries old tales of the Amazon queen and further identified via Lewis and Clark. It is my suspicion that Napoleon knew something of the arcane secrets of the territory when he sold it to the United States and, if my wild hypothesis is correct (and I am not nearly the first to suspect it is), the former emperor planned and bankrolled private expeditions in the Americas after adopting his new identity, looking for more of the same. There is an interesting connection between Biddle, Bonaparte and James Buchanan.

'Joseph' Bonaparte was a member of the American Philosophical Society with James Buchanan[249] and Nicholas Biddle. This organization was a scientific research foundation much like the Royal Society of England and, much like that society in England, included men interested quite a bit in arcane science. If any group of prominent men in the United States of that time would have been involved in esoteric archaeology, such as Phoenicians in the Louisiana Territory or Templar explorations of California before (and after) Columbus, it would have been the American Philosophical Society. And since the Society's founders, as well as Buchanan and 'Joseph' Bonaparte and several other members, were Freemasons, it was likely a Templar friendly organization.[250] Biddle had been a friendly associate of 'Joseph' Bonaparte but by 1835 had turned against him.[251] It should be noted that Biddle was among the

---

[249]List of Members of the American Philosophical Society (1846)

[250]American Philosophical Society website; Deanna Spingola, *A Study in Imperialism, Genocide and Emancipation* (Trafford 2011) Pg 153; Wikipedia; Various

[251]Shannon Selin, 'Nicholas Biddle, Proud American' (shannonselin.com; Nicholas B Wainwright, 'Glimpses of Napoleon in 1804' *Pennsylvania Magazine of History and*

few Freemasons acceptable to and admired by Anti-Masons of the day, certainly no friends to any Templars who may have been on the scene.[252]

So what did Senators Benton and Buchanan know when they backed and directed Fremont's second expedition? Sesh Heri has an idea and visits that possibility in his nonfiction study, *The Handprint of Atlas*. Essentially, Heri believes that knowledge of how the planet manufactures gold via the aforementioned natural dry method led parties in the US government, which included Buchanan and Benton, to send Fremont on the expedition to ostensibly chart Oregon territory, but Fremont also did other things. Those 'in the know' in leadership of the United States, Heri proposes, specifically wanted California for what they believed about the gold deposits and employed westward expansionists like Benton to get it done. Fremont was an expansionist with ambitions beyond a military career and he was Benton's son-in-law. He was willing to do what was necessary. Where the arcane aspects of Fremont's second expedition come into play is when he discovered the 600-foot tall rock which juts out from what is now Pyramid Lake in Nevada.

Also known as Fremont's Pyramid, Heri believes this three-sided rock is indeed a man-made object. He proposes that Fremont may have been armed with an ancient map of the Pacific Northwest and the pyramid shaped rock in the lake in Nevada was a relic of Phoenician mining explorers. In short,

---

Biography, Vol 2 No. 1 (Jan 1978, Pgs 106-107.

[252]Jonathan Punkin, *Downfall of Freemasonry* (Unction Room 1838), Pg.129. This dubious honor could be due to duplicity on Biddle's part.

Heri suggests that this region from Pyramid Lake running southwest along the telluric current/gravity anomaly world grid line all the way to the Twin Peaks in San Francisco is one of many 'lands of Ophir' identified in ancient times as one location of the mines of Solomon. The discovery of the pyramid rock was, according to Heri, proof of whatever the ancient map would have said was there and that in turn was proof that this area spanning from Nevada into California was possibly the source of gold for the Phoenician explorers. Heri also thinks this discovery explains the mysterious purchase of a cannon.[253]

John Fremont purchased an M1835 Cyrus Alger mountain Howitzer[254] and trailed it along for several difficult miles of the journey yet never fired it once. Heri suggests that Fremont used the cannon as a means of hiding something valuable. The idea is that this something isn't what Fremont would have wanted to have on his person for possible fear of his life. Keep in mind that Meriwether Lewis had died under very strange and questionable circumstances nearly forty years prior. Was Lewis murdered over something related to this very territory Fremont was now exploring? Could Lewis have been murdered over something he learned from ancient documentation or something he and Clark discovered during their expedition? If Fremont and others suspected this was so, that could explain Fremont's unconventional decision to drag a cannon along on a scientific expedition over rugged territory. Heri suggests that no thief or assassin would think to look in a cannon. He also proposes that

[253]Heri, *Handprint of Atlas*, Pgs 106-109
[254]Dennis Cassinelli, *Ely Times* 10 Feb 17; Nevada State Museum

some sort of ‘key’ to what was being looked for could have been camouflaged as a cannonball or some such other paraphernalia.

The problem with Heri’s cannon hypothesis is that it’s just not practical. The difficulty of dealing with the cannon would have drawn much attention to it and that would have defeated its purpose as a hiding place. I suggest that the cannon was a misguided notion involved with a desire to stir up the rebellious activities Fremont would later foment among American residents of Mexican California. The cannon was abandoned within a hundred miles south of Pyramid Lake. Heri says that was because it had served a purpose relative to whatever Fremont may actually have discovered in the pyramid rock. I suggest it was abandoned due to the increasing impracticality of having it along. I could be wrong.

Heri suggests that Fremont and his scouts Kit Carson and Charles Preuss[255] slipped away from camp in the night and used whatever the previously mentioned key may have been to open a vault within Pyramid Rock where they may have found scrolls, charts or other ancient documents revealing the locations of lost gold mines. A very intriguing idea which I think has a degree of credibility. I might also suggest the possibility that, instead of Phoenicians, the pyramid in the lake and the vault’s contents could have been fashioned by mining

[255]Preuss arrived in the US in 1834 and worked for Ferdinand Hassler who was head of the Coast Survey and the US Bureau of Weights & Measures. Consider the importance of that within the context of the lost technology of the forgotten civilization as discussed in *SM2:Burton*, Pgs 17-20; *Civilization One*, Knight & Butler, Pg 108.

explorers of the Cham empire or whomever else Califia's empire could have been. One must not dismiss yet another alternative that it was Templar explorers who could have secreted Heri's proposed charts and scrolls inside the speculative vault. Therein we have reason to suspect that Pyramid Rock, aka Fremont's Pyramid, could have been used as a hiding place for valuable information *about* the gold deposits in California territory and this secret was conveyed to Fremont via Freemasons Buchanan and Benton who themselves could have received it through masonic affiliation, especially those within the American Philosophical Society. Who knows?

It is a curious thing that once Fremont's expedition was in California, coincidentally following the telluric current/gravity anomaly world grid line, a few members of the party got separated from the main group, including scout and cartographer Charles Preuss who somehow found himself in Coloma, a native village. Qualified to read the terrain in the special way we have been discussing here, isn't it interesting that Preuss the cartographer would happen to wander off to the future site of Sutter's Mill which would be the site where gold was 'first discovered' in California? Heri believes the Sutter's Mill gold discovery event was staged, that Fremont and his benefactors Benton and Buchanan and their associates and masters already knew gold would be found.

Whatever was found inside Pyramid Rock might have revealed the exact location of the lode and the Sutter's Mill event could have been staged to not reveal it. According to Heri's analysis, the mother lode was likely located to the north on the telluric current/gravity anomaly world grid line. Heri suggests the Sutter's Mill gold strike was also staged to additionally spark a mass of American immigration into California. I would add that an American making the public discovery at Sutter's Mill served to further reinforce an American claim to the territory, as the 'discovery' of the gold there was not yet known to the signers of the Treaty of Guadalupe Hidalgo a week later, ceding California to the United States.[256]

It's all very interesting, if true. I think it resonates with the context of my Templar-Vatican war over control of California so let's proceed. Whatever the case, the United States got control of California in February of 1848 and the first public confirmation of the 'discovery' of gold at Sutter's Mill was in March. Heri goes on in his thesis with the details about the whys and wherefores of the Sutter's Mill plan, but for my purpose here I say it was through Fremont's second expedition, and the chicanery around the 'discovery' of gold in California, that the Templar faction gained control of California through its masonic agency nation, the United States. Even the state flag would come to flaunt a possible Templar role: Sutter was Swiss, the flag's designer borrowed the bear from the Bern, Switzerland, city coat of arms,[257] and some scholars advocate that the Templars have a history with Switzerland, especially

[256]The earlier Treaty of Cahuenga merely ended the military actions between US and Californio forces. Mexico still owned California when Marshall, a New Jersey native, 'discovered' gold at Sutter's Mill.
[257]California State Flag, Wikipedia.

post persecution.[258] Not to mention that the flag is mostly white with a red stripe and a red star, famously the colors of Templar tunics.

All of this, in my opinion, would have royally pissed off the Vatican/Jesuit faction in Rome overseeing its interests in the territory.

But the Jesuits did not give up the ship. They opted for a form of magick, specifically a socio-political alchemy, if you will. Through this, I propose, they have pursued to regain control of their once lost territory. Here's how I see it:

With the United States in possession of California, all the gold and other resources which Rome had certainly envisioned as its own now belonged to the proxy Templar nation which was openly not a Catholic state. Secular Templarism, you could call it, had manifested itself boldly onto the world stage and would, as we know, cause all manner of problems for oligarchies everywhere. The advantage the Vatican had was that their empire crossed many boundaries of politics. It mattered not who the regime was if the people were Catholic, the church would remain and exhibit its influence through one governmental body after another. I propose this is what Rome did, where California is concerned.

With the missions losing their control of large properties in California by 1833 and the much of the rest of their power there by 1847, we have a little over a century to examine the Vatican's shift in strategy. Make no mistake, I'm saying that

---

[258]Patrick von Stutenzee, The Knights Templar In Switzerland, (https://stutenzeehistoryblog.blogspot.com/)

they wanted California back. Was it really just about gold? Let's examine what California actually meant in terms of resources.

In the first five years of the California gold rush, 375 tons of the stuff were extracted, which equals $16 billion today. Between 1853, when hydraulic mining began, and around 1885, an additional $15 billion in today's value was mined. After 1890, when dredging became practical, an additional value of $28 billion in today's dollars was extracted. Over $100 billion of today's dollars in gold has been mined from California since the beginning of the Gold Rush. [259] Some of that went to the US government to support the Union Army during the Civil War and US industry was certainly a prime beneficiary of the resource. As California rapidly developed under the United States, machinery and tool making saw a boom. Railroads advanced in development. Foreign manufacturers contributed to the sudden new market of American California. And that was at first to support primarily the gold mining industry but exploded as other industries such as service (hotels, restaurants, etc), clothing, and the like, grew up around the mining population. Agriculture offered another option to the enterprising Californian and the state became a major national, and eventually global, provider of produce.[260] California became the envy of the world.

---

[259]Mining History and Geology of the Motherlode (http://virtual.yosemite.cc.ca.us/ghayes/goldrush.htm); US Geological Survey; Various.

[260]Norwich University Online, *Historical Impact of the California Gold Rush* (2 Oct 2017)

Asses were certainly burning in Rome. Since the Vatican/Jesuits had felt all of this California wealth wrenched from its hands by the rising tide of Enlightenment values, the church had to watch as the proxy Templar secularists built their lucrative new empire. But the church had a plan. Through the 19th Century, California Catholic bishops had to appeal to European Catholics for material assistance. The church focused on steady operations during this time. But the Jesuits didn't waste any time. In 1850, Jesuits from Italy established a college in San Francisco and the following year Jesuits founded Santa Clara College and there followed several more Catholic colleges throughout the state. There are today four Jesuit universities in California. With the arrival and participation of various convents in California, the Catholic church became involved in healthcare. Politics was another route for Catholic influence, the first elected governor being a Catholic himself proved that, despite some anti-Catholic sentiment in the state, that avenue was not kept from them. With education, healthcare and politics on their chessboard, it was only natural that the church exhibit its presence and influence in journalism. 1858 saw the establishment of the first Catholic newspaper in California and others followed, serving to promote the Catholic identity among citizens throughout the state. And there was always the charitable angle to be applied. Between education, welfare, healthcare, politics and journalism, the Vatican's representatives in California had endured despite the setback, its talons dug in just enough.[261]

Understand that the sort of plotting I am insinuating need not involve even the awareness of the majority of those whose otherwise altruistic intentions result in truly objective good works. What I am suggesting is that certain players at higher levels used the results of such good works, accomplished by local priests and nuns and their congregations, for nefarious purpose. Religion is a strong bond for many people, naturally so in the 19th Century. Education influences and forms social philosophy which in turn influences and forms political philosophy. The Jesuits first got the church into education in California, and then politics and journalism followed. Newspapers were very influential in those days and a pro-Catholic newspaper, of which there were a few, was no exception. They may have lost administrative control of the ancient Amazonian land of gold, but the Vatican/Jesuit faction was extending its tentacles throughout the social capillaries of American California and would eventually capture political control indirectly.[262]

Until that day, the Vatican's representatives in California provided spiritual leadership and charity to their devoted members and the public at large for over a century. For much of the late 19th Century and first half of the 20th, the church found itself competing with protestant churches and the rise of

---

[261]New Catholic Encyclopedia, 'The Catholic Church in California' (Encyclopedia.com 1 June 2021)

[262]Ibid; William Issel, *Church and State in The City: Catholics and Politics in Twentieth Century San Francisco* (Temple Univ Press 2013).

Marxism. These were its two main concerns as to any real opposition to their influence in California. But somewhere mid-century, shortly before Vatican II in 1962, the church seems to have found a way to work with the Marxist influence.

While California under the American flag was growing and becoming the agricultural, industrial and technological force that it would be by the 1950s, the Catholic church in California was taking advantage of the prosperity. Healthcare has been a service of the Catholic church for centuries, with 200 hospitals established in the Americas by the 16th Century under stewardship of the Order of St John of God. In 19th Century California, orders of nuns were a driving force in Catholic healthcare, leading to the many church affiliated hospitals in the state. Today, Catholic healthcare is the largest nonprofit healthcare provider in the United States and has been in California even longer.[263] That's a respectable piece of the current $3.8 trillion pie spent on healthcare in the US.[264] In California it's a $400 billion industry.[265] When executives in the non-profit Catholic healthcare system make over $1 million in salary, non-profit doesn't mean non-lucrative.[266] Based on available statistics, the Catholic healthcare system pays its executives in the high six figures and seven figures salaries.[267] Catholic non-profit hospitals are 501C corporations – tax

[263]Catholic Healthcare Association of the United States, statistics as of March 2021.
[264]Peterson-KFF Health System Tracker as of 23 Dec 2020.
[265]California Health Care Foundation
[266]Tracey Drury, "Meet The Top Paid Hospital Executives in Western New York" (Buffalo Business First, 21 Jan 2021)
[267]Anne Paddock, "Executive Compensation At St Joseph Health (CA)" (Paddock Post, 13 October 2020)

exempt. Non-profit hospitals are considered by some to be the worst abuse of tax exemption ever.[268] Business activity of Catholic healthcare is subject to approval by the Vatican, of course.[269]

In agriculture in California, the Catholic church has had a close association to (mostly Catholic) labor since the 19th Century. The church has even involved itself in labor negotiations within the immense agricultural industry[270] of the state, an industry which presently produces $50 billion a year. They ought to be close to labor because it was their missions which essentially started California agriculture back when they forced local natives into the labor force.[271] The irony is staggering but there they are influencing a major industry worth billions, capable of bringing it to a screeching halt, should they advise it.

As liberal as the modern Catholic church can be, it still isn't exempt from troubles with the California state legislature. In recent years the state lawmakers have tried to revoke the right to keep confessions private, tried to force the church hospitals to perform abortions, and even attempted to lump Catholics in with hate criminals. [272] Still, there are numerous Catholics in state level politics, and they made up roughly 58% of the

---

[268]Marni Jameson Carey, "How Non-Profit Hospitals Get Away With The Biggest Ripoff in America" (Medical Economic, 17 Jan 2020)

[269] "CHI-Dignity merger cleared by Vatican". Modern Healthcare. 2018-10-16. Retrieved 2020-08-07. "Catholic Healthcare West becomes Dignity Health" SFGate. 2012-01-25. Retrieved 2020-08-07.

[270] "Higgins and Chavez: The UFW and the Church" (Catholic University of America)

[271]Corle Pgs 71, 89-90; Starr Pgs 36-38, 40-41; Various.

[272]SB360, SB379, SB655

legislature between 1967-1995[273], a crucial period in my hypothesis. It isn't that Catholics don't do good, it's that the Vatican and its representatives are often involved in questionable or even nefarious activities. It is specifically a Vatican agenda, likely administered through Jesuits, that I propose has now ruined California.

Much has been written and reported about the ruination of the once golden state. It is such a prevalent story that California has become the butt of jokes and target of derision in our times not out of regional jealousy of our weather, our beaches, and health nuts and surfers and movie stars, but because not many Americans want to live here anymore – due to the lousy schools, weakened economy, foolish social idealism, (and foolish movie stars). It's a pretty sad state of affairs when an article published over ten years ago is still relative and things look like they have actually worsened since, as Joel Kotkin wrote in Forbes Magazine in July of 2009:

"Right now California's economy is moribund, and the prospects for a quick turnaround are not good. Unable to pay its bills, the state is issuing IOUs; its once strong credit rating has collapsed. The state that once boasted the seventh-largest gross domestic product in the world is looking less like a celebrated global innovator and more like a fiscal basket case along the lines of Argentina or Latvia...It took some amazing incompetence to toss this best-endowed of places down into the dustbin of history... But the fundamental problem remains. California's economy--once wondrously diverse with aerospace, high-tech, agriculture and international trade--has run aground.

---

[273]Karol & Thurston, "From Personal To Partisan: Abortion, Party & Religion Among California State Legislators" (Cambridge Univ Press 2020) Pg 19

Burdened by taxes and ever-growing regulation, the state is routinely rated by executives as having among the worst business climates in the nation. No surprise, then, that California's jobs engine has sputtered..."[274]

Kotkin blames five perpetrators: Arnold Schwarzenegger, public sector pensions and salaries, environmentalists, corporate apathy, and Californians themselves for letting it happen. Most of us agree on the Schwarzenegger indictment. Talk about the biggest and most aggravating political disappointment of a lifetime, enough said about that guy. Public sector issues are also pretty universally recognized as a problem here and they reached criminal status in some municipalities since Kotkin's article. Evironmentalists have ruined the good name and tradition of California conservationalists – as well as destroying over a half a million acres of what once was some of the most productive agricultural fields in the world (much of it gone to dirt for a goddamned fish). Corporate apathy can likely be in part blamed on corporate fear of radical activists, who are completely out of control as of this writing. But in fairness to 'Californians', the demographics have changed even more noticeably since Kotkin's article and that has seen the one culprit Kotkin doesn't mention stay in power: the political philosophy of the California state legislature. All the crap above is a product of direct influence of state politicians or the sociopolitical environment they have created and nurtured.

Governor Gavin Newsom is only half jokingly referred to as 'Real Estate Salesman of the Year' because he's driven more

[274]Joel Kotkin, "Who Killed California's Economy?" (Forbes 7 July 2009)

Californians to sell their homes and flee than any other reason, thus Newsom has been great for home investment everywhere else. He is presently under recall threat as I write this. What might Newsom and California's sociopolitical condition have to do with any Vatican/Jesuit skullduggery?

Consider the above perpetrators identified by Kotkin. Environmentalists are Eco-Socialsists and their philosophy demands the dismantling of capitalism. That alone can describe the destruction of California. Ruin fields, ruin agriculture, ruin a major element of California's commercial base. When before they criticized him, Eco-Socialists 'thinkers' now praise Karl Marx for his early 'green' ideas regarding the planet and nature.[275] With the detrimental effect this has on employment of migrant workers, most of them Catholic, you'd think the church would be opposed to socialism. But not the Vatican. The Pope stated in 2019 that 'ecological sin' is an act against God and future generations,[276] aping essentially what Karl Marx said in the 19th Century: Society must "hand it [the planet] down to succeeding generations in an improved condition".[277] Superficially not a bad sentiment but in practical socialist terms a politically subtle tactic of destruction.

Pope Francis advocates climate change crisis philosophy and speaks of nature in essentially New Age terms. There are several articles on the Pope's statements which, of themselves, are rather tame and not unreasonable to the average person, if

[275]John Bellamy Foster, Paul Burkett.
[276]Pope Francis 21 Nov 2019, E&E News, article by Maya Earls "Pope Might Make Environmental destruction A Sin".
[277]*Das Kapital* Vol 3, Chapter 46.

not strong enough for the activist.[278] But the Vatican has been pushing eco-socialism from this gentle spiritual angle before Francis came along. With the Rerum Novarum in 1891, Pope Leo XIII moved the Vatican away from its perceived tacit acceptance of capitalism.[279] Whereas Pope John Paul II was considerate and diplomatic in his thoughts and statements on capitalism, admitting that it's a complex issue where economic philosophy choices are made, subsequent Vatican opinions began to display certain buzzwords of the socialist-globalist playbook. Pope Benedict said, "*...the social doctrine of the Church has unceasingly highlighted the importance of* ***distributive justice*** *and* ***social justice*** *for the market economy…*"[280]

'Distribution' and 'social justice' for the market economy. What exactly did Benedict mean? The Jesuit scholars make it a little more clear here: *"It is "the political community" which has responsibility for directing economic activity towards the common good. Grave imbalances are produced, he writes, "when economic action, conceived merely as an engine for wealth creation, is* ***detached from political action, conceived as a means for pursuing justice through redistribution****"*[281]

[278]National Geographic, "Nature Never Forgives: 7 of Pope Francis's Greenest Quotes" (Sep 2015); "Vatican Was Going Green Long Before Pope's Climate Decree" (June 2015); "How Green Was the 'Green Pope?" (Feb 2013)

[279] Fred Kammer, SJ, "Catholic Social Doctrine Is Not A Surrogate For Capitalism." [Blessed John Paul II] (Jesuit Social Research Institute, Loyala Univ New Orleans, 19 Feb 2012)

[280]Ibid

[281]Ibid

Jesuit author Fred Kammer additionally clarifies the Vatican's vision in the following excerpt, lest you not yet comprehend the implication: "*Benedict further acknowledges that, "the State finds itself having to address the* ***limitations to its sovereignty imposed by the new context of international trade and finance,*** *which is characterized by increasing mobility both of financial capital and means of production, material and immaterial". This has altered the political power of States and* ***calls for a reevaluation of the role of the States****. Rather than "being too precipitous in declaring the demise of the State," however, Benedict suggests that in the current world economic crisis the State's role seems destined to grow in working towards resolution of this crisis. In addition, he argues that* ***governments must commit themselves to greater collaboration*** *with one another* ***to deal with a transnational integrated economy****, as well as a* ***stronger and reformed United Nations*** *and other* ***international economic institutions and international finance****.*"[282]

It's all about acceptance of a globalist authority and submission to a globalist system and its demands, or your nation's role will be 'reevaluated'. Now it may be easier to see how the Vatican can tacitly motivate Eco-Socialist activism to use politics to destroy the agricultural industry of California and put migrant Catholic out of work despite the local diocese priests trying to help them. The Vatican is willing to sacrifice Catholics for its own aims because its industry will never be decimated. Roman Catholicism may go (and good riddance, I say), but the Vatican is already bucking for relevance in the global religion some say it advocates through Pope Francis. In 2019, Francis signed "*A Document on Human Fraternity for*

---

[282]Ibid

World Peace and Living Together" along with grand imam Sheikh Ahmad el-Tayeb while in the United Arab Emirates. In itself, the document calls for peace and unity and acceptance between the world's religions. However, not everyone sees it that way.

Rabbi Yeshayahu Hollander says, "*This meeting between the Pope and the Imam is the Vatican abdicating to Islam. The Vatican has realized that they cannot convert the Muslims so they are announcing that they will no longer try. The Catholic Church would like the Muslims to reciprocate in kind but in truth, the Imam did nothing of the sort.*"[283]

Muslims converted to Roman Catholicism may see this 'acceptance' and 'tolerance' of Islam as the Vatican intention to say or do nothing about Quran edicts regarding conversion to Islam, among many reasons why those Muslims converted to Christianity, to be sure. Once again, Vatican diplomacy serving the Vatican, Catholics be damned, if need be. When the pope is a South American leftist making deals with China which a Catholic expert on the situation, Cardinal Joseph Zen, says will destroy the church there[284], what can Catholics do? The Vatican will do as the Vatican sees fit and the Vatican will survive.

Now bring it back to California from the perspective I have proposed. Is it really all that surprising that Pope Leo XIII brought about the Vatican's turning away from capitalism in 1891 when the socialist movement was picking up speed by the

---

[283]Adam E Berkowitz, "Pope Meets With Muslim Leader, Rabbi Says "Esau Sending Ishmael To Complete The Holocaust" (Israel365 News 17 Nov 19)

[284]Sainsbury, Michael "Cardinal Zen Targets Vatican Silence On China, Hong Kong – La Croix International" (La Croix 9 Dec 2019).

1870s? Reformist movements became active in California throughout the 1890s. By 1901, the Socialist Party of America was founded and the Socialist Party of California represented its interests and objectives shortly after. In the Golden State, Northern California was all about the labor movement Reds, with Southern California representing Fabian Socialist bourgeoisie, the kind of people who would praise the Nazis and offer advice on which gas to use to kill 'unworthies'.[285] Socialism was becoming the vogue back then and disenchanted or aloof Californians, ever the cultural outlier, were ripe to embrace it. Here at last was a way to strike back at those clever Templars who had taken California away from the Vatican.

It is my speculative hypothesis that, while the California dioceses and priests were competing with socialists for recruits during the first half of the 20th Century, the Vatican was shifting its support to Marxist ideals, in a diplomatic manner, of course. I suspect that Vatican Jesuits with interest in California saw this move as a favorable condition to plant the seeds of the destruction of California, that is the Templar-United States capitalist California. It is my suggestion that this is what happened to the Golden State throughout the 20th Century, seeds planted through several decades, the actual signs of ruination beginning to show in the late 1980s. Vatican agents watched as Marxist thought took root in California, for as Cardinal Reinhard Marx of Germany says of Roman Catholicism: "*We*

---

[285]George Bernard Shaw, Interview in BBC Magazine 1933, lecture at the Eugenic Education Society in 1910; *Empire of the Wheel 1* Pg 382.

are all on the shoulders of Karl Marx. ***Without Karl Marx, there would be no Catholic social teaching.***"[286]

The Jesuit rejection of capitalism and its embrace of Marxism is well discussed and documented on both sides.[287] The Jesuits don't deny this. So how might they have damaged California?

This is where that socio-political alchemy comes in.

Through their influence. As already pointed out, California is presently is a place where the media openly ridicule the current governor for being 'Real Estate Agent of the Year' because his policies and management were responsible for a record number of people leaving the state, selling their home and/or buying homes in other states. Almost half the residents of San Francisco have blamed their departure or plans to leave the city on the increasing urban ruination, human defecation in the streets, official encouragement of drug abuse, physical assaults and epic shoplifting that is forcing many stores to move to shorter hours, closing their doors at the previously unheard of hour of six pm. The radical wave rolling through the metropolitan areas and the apathy of sitting legislators and the promotion of the political wilding by newly elected members to the state house are driving even self-described liberals from the state. All of the woes of a once great place can be traced to the

[286]Marcin Rzegocki, Cardinal Marx quoted from *Frankfurter Allgemeine Sonntagszeitung*, on bicentennial of Karl Marx. Acton Univ Online, Transatlantic Blog 16 May 2018

[287]Chris Fleming, David Rigamer, Walter Block, *The Jesuits: The Jesuits: From Markets To Marxism; From Property Protection To Social Progressivism,* (Romanian Economic Business Review, Romanian-American University, vol. 7(2), pages 7-22, June); Kammer, "Catholicism and Capitalism", Jesuit Social Research Institute; Damian Thompson, "Why Are America's Jesuits Going To Bat For Communism?" New York Post 29 July 2019;

radical or grievously misguided political left – the side of the spectrum which the Roman Catholic church champions, especially the Jesuits.

It is noteworthy that the current governor and the one before him are both products of Santa Clara University, a private Jesuit institution.[288] Gavin Newsom has a long history with Gordon Getty, a son of J Paul Getty, the wealthy oilman. Gordon has been an investor in Newsom's business ventures and those acquainted with the association between them say Newsom is essentially a Getty family member. As did Newsom, Gordon Getty received a Jesuit education, himself an attendee of the historic St Ignatius Preparatory College in San Francisco and his politics are in line with them, being a major donor to candidates Nancy Pelosi, John Kerry, Gavin Newsom and other Democrats. Though not raised Catholic, J Paul Getty seemed to have a proclivity for stern leftist idealism as he was known for admiring Adolf Hitler and Josef Stalin *during* the WW2 era, which got him into some trouble with the FBI for a while.[289] However, he was a Christian Scientist so perhaps founder Mary Baker Eddy's uncertain past in Spiritualism made up for a lack of direct Jesuit influence?

Not likely, for Eddy advocated neutrality on political expression of Christian Scientists. She had started out as a Jacksonian Democrat but became a Republican with the

---

[288]Gavin Newsom and Jerry Brown.

[289]Gary Langer, 'Biographer: FBI Investigated Getty as a Nazi Sympathizer' (AP News 22 Dec 1985); Top Stories: Culture, 'Oil Baron Getty Revealed as Hitler Fan' (Deutsche Welle aka DW, accessed 6 July 21); Wikipedia bio ignores J Paul Getty's WW2 controversy.

election of Abraham Lincoln whom she greatly admired.[290] J Paul Getty likely came to his positive reviews of Hitler and Stalin on his own which possibly pleased some Jesuits, according to a variety of researchers over the years who have linked members of the order to Nazi activities.[291] Gordon Getty, graduate of St Ignatius, most probably does please the Jesuits, especially in his avid support and influence upon fellow Jesuit academic alumnus Gavin Newsom. But perhaps I'm being too heavy-handed on the Society?

Consider the words of Avro Manhattan in *The Catholic Church Against the Twentieth Century*[292]. In his chapter on the religious orders of the church and their role in promoting and securing the power and influence of Rome, Manhattan describes the Jesuits as supreme among the Catholic orders "*whose task is primarily that of consolidating and penetrating every stratum of society in all parts of the world, the dominion of the Catholic Church.*"[293] Manhattan focuses upon the Jesuits because, he says, their order is specifically dedicated to Papal authority around the world: "*Indeed, the primary cause for the creation of the Order was the need for special soldiers and defenders of the absolute theocracy of the* ***Papacy****.*"[294] (Emphasis mine – WB).

---

[290]Mary Baker Eddy Library, 'What Were Eddy's Political Views?' (22 Feb 13); Mary Baker Eddy bio, Wikipedia.

[291]I refer the reader to enthusiastic anti-Catholic author Edmond Paris and another author, officially detested by the church, Viktor Novak.

[292]London Watts & Co, 1947.

[293]Avro Manhattan, Pg53.

[294]Ibid

Ignatius Loyola, former flamboyant soldier and philanderer, experienced a conversion during recovery from a cannonball injury to his leg and subsequently pursued his clerical career after suffering hallucinations of a serpentine entity while undergoing painful medical treatment. Manhattan points out the militaristic influence which Ignatius brought to the foundation of the Society of Jesus. Manhattan writes: "*Of the various vows, that of obedience was considered the most important: complete, absolute, unquestionable, blind...In a letter to his followers at Coimbra, Loyola declared that the General of the Order stands in the place of God, without reference to his personal wisdom, piety, or discretion...(T)hat going beyond the letter of command, even in things abstractly good and praiseworthy, is disobedience...*"[295]

Manhattan further emphasizes this blind obedience by presenting the Order's own words to the Pope: "*Thus, in the order of the Jesuits, obedience takes the place of every motive or affection; obedience, absolute and unconditional, without one thought or question* ***as to its objects or consequences****.*"[296] (Emphasis Manhattan's)

Think about that. I can personally vouch that such unquestioning obedience is not expected in the US military, as the right to refuse to carry out an unlawful order is instructed during initial training and mandated by the UCMJ, Article 90 2(a). With the Jesuit order accountable directly to the Pope, not to a Congress of civilian representatives nor a free press,

---

[295]Ibid, Pgs53-54

[296]Ibid Pg54; Leopold von Ranke, *History of the Popes: Their Church and State* (Collier & Sons 1901)

consider the latitude with which a Superior General of the Society of Jesus acts when his subordinates question not the objectives nor consequences of his orders. What manner of nefarious skullduggery might the Jesuit Order have proliferated through the centuries in the interest of securing the power of specifically the Papacy?

Let us look again at Manhattan's words: "*Thus the Company (Society) of Jesus became, and still is, a theocracy within a theocracy. It's rigid machinery was created to assist in the achievement of the Company (Society)'s goal – the strengthening of the Church's (specifically Papal) authority through* ***educating youth****, preaching and missionary work; It* ***began by founding colleges in many countries****...* ***Over the Portuguese colonies, the Jesuits exercised almost complete mastery****...*

"Ever since, ***throughout the centuries and in all countries,*** *the Jesuits have gone on with their work of consolidating the religious and* ***political power of the Catholic Church****. They have* ***reached an extraordinary perfection and skill in training young people for high offices*** *either in the Catholic Church itself or* ***in civil governments****. As a Jesuit historian wrote: 'Many are now shining in the purple of the Hierarchy* ***whom we had but lately on the benches of our schools****;* ***others are engaged in the government of States and cities.'***

"This training of the spiritual and temporal ruling classes has made the Jesuits inclined to meddle in religious and political events. ***Their activities in the political spheres of all countries have been innumerable****, and that is the main cause of their*

having been continually persecuted, expelled, or banished by kings, emperors, and Governments of all kinds, including the most devout Catholic kings and countries. Indeed, ***owing to their continuous interference and intrigues in the politics of many countries in Europe, as well as in that of the Catholic Church, the Pope himself was forced to suppress the Order altogether.***

"That was in 1773, and the Pope concerned was Clement XIV, who for many years had received ***complaints from the sovereigns and Governments of Europe regarding the interference in public matters (by) the Jesuits, who were accused of being 'disturbers of public peace'***

"However, in 1814 the Order was universally restored. Since that date, they have continued to spread, and ***in many countries they still retain the quasi-monopoly of education...They are to be found behind high educational institutions, the Press, radio, political parties, and Governments****..."*[297]

I think it is evident what has happened to California since the return of the Society of Jesus to the shores of the 'new world' in 1814. Avro Manhattan is just one author who has laid out the determined agenda of the Jesuits to manipulate directly or control through more subtle influence the states and cities over which they have no legal authority. Manhattan's research and perspective illustrates exactly the point I am hoping to make here, that the Society of Jesus, having once intended to get their roots into California but being foiled by their own misdeeds, resulting in their banishment from the Americas, found their

[297]Manhattan Pgs 55-56; bold emphases mine.

way back in to the Golden State: through the minds of youth, the propaganda power of the Press and eventually the electronic media, political philosophy, and ultimately the actual seats of government power.

The 20th Century saw the emergence of leftism in California and leftism is the preferred political weapon of the modern Jesuit Order over a free society. Even California native Democrat liberals acknowledge that leftism has gone awry and is destroying cities. California has gone from a powerhouse in its golden age to a dreadful mess in merely half a century, thanks largely in recent years to the most recent governors: the political weather vane opportunist Schwarzenegger, and those two products of Jesuit higher education, Jerry Brown and Gavin Newsom. The rise of Marxist ideals in the state dating back to before World War 2, from seeds planted in the days of Jack London before that, gave the Jesuits their fertile ground for the Order's particular brand of manipulation. I have no doubt that they were likely manipulating the political right where necessary to counter whatever resistant influence the Templars mustered, but that is only my opinion.

The sociopolitical alchemy which I propose the Jesuits have used has proven a clever choice. Their return to the Americas and specifically to California coincided with the emergence of the Industrial Revolution and a rise in materialist thought. They didn't need to use literally arcane hocus-pocus because political movements provided the method. The alchemy was achieved purely in the psychological realm, using the common elements of human needs and aspirations, stirring up fears and emotions.

It is very similar to what I think has has happened to the United States in general since 9/11. This is where the ideas of Ramon Llull must be considered.

Llull, the Christian mystic, is credited with contributions to election theory and his influence on the United States electoral college is obvious. [298] When you dive deep into the subject of the historical development of elections, especially where Llull and successors Condorcet and Borda are concerned, you see the enthusiastic application of these thinkers' ideas in the Roman Catholic bishop ranks. The sources are noted but the basic gist is that the bishops liked using an electoral system to their benefit, ie manipulation. In other words, if the bishops don't like what the masses vote, they can assume a self-bestowed mantle of 'truth and honesty' and cast their votes how they see fit, since they are the electors.[299] Though Llull influenced Condorcet and Borda, they and others altered his original theory and certainly applied it in a manner not intended by Llull, ie the Vatican bishops.[300] Where this links the Jesuits to my speculative hypothesis of gaming the politics of California to their will is when Llull et al lead to 'social choice theory' which is a mathematecizing, if you will, how people/the public, make choices, primarily applied to the political arena. See the potential for the magick?

---

[298]McLean & London, "Ramon Llull and the Theory of Voting" (Studia Llulliana 32, 1992); Christian List, "Social Choice Theory" (Stanford Encyclopedia of Philosophy 18 Dec 2013); Josep Colomer, "Ramon Llull: From Ars Electionis to Social Choice Theory" (Social Choice and Welfare Vol 40, No 2, Feb 2013); Wikipedia.

[299]Ibid.

[300]Ibid; Noel Blanco Mourelle, "Every Knowable Thing: The Art of Ramon Llull and the Construction of Knowledge" (Thesis, Columbia University 2017);

With social choice theory, one may divine better understanding of how people think when made to choose, in this case between candidates. If you can understand this function, you may better predict what those choices will be. And if you're able to predict, the next step might be to influence those choices, more specifically you might be able to manipulate which choices are made. A dive into this subject of social choice theory shows it to be a product of and certainly a tool used by purveyors of concepts such as social justice and a bevy of buzzwords popular with the progressive left – again, the political field in which the Jesuits like to play. Thus do I propose that herein lies the political alchemy used to destroy American/Templar California: a mutated form of Llull via Condorcet and Borda applied by the Jesuits in California to stir up, through sentiment and fear, manipulative social forces such as virtue signaling and character assassination in order to transform public sentiment and social choice to a model of their own liking. This was the Jesuit alchemy, I propose, and the unwitting masses were the prima matera manipulated in a crucible of lies, with emotion and ignorance the active ingredients.

This is my hypothesis. Whatever the truth may be, something along these lines has been at play by someone. I haven't even begun to cover what treacheries those driving the other side's wagon have likely engaged in, save for a glimpse presented here of the inglorious acts of John C. Fremont and his associates. As stated previously, I see the perfidious actions of particular Jesuits and Vatican players as an unfortunate reflection of otherwise good Catholics. Likewise do I see the unsavory behavior of certain players on the American/Templar California team as a bad stain on their otherwise worthy number.

Clearly an entire volume could be dedicated to presenting this idea of mine in a properly thorough hypothesis and I may have to do so eventually. For now, I have merely tried to present the reader with the historical context of the visionary ideal of California, the possible ancient veracity behind that ideal, a basic understanding of the pertinent historical factors behind California's esoteric and alchemical role in this series of books, and my very speculative hypothesis as to the forces wrestling over control of one of the most intriguing territories on Earth. There is so much more to tell but I must stop right here and leave the reader's head full of the questions unanswered.

It may be that the true story of California hasn't even begun to be told. I suspect when it is, at the center of it all will be the mysterious visitors who came to our world long ago.

Which brings us to our next chapter…

Chapter Eight

The Back of Beyond

From the very beginning, with my first nonfiction book, *Latitude 33: Key to the Kingdom*, my work has involved the association between telluric current, geomorphology, gravity anomalies, the popular concept of ley lines and the hypothetical effects these phenomena exhibit upon the landscapes, the objects, and human activity in those places which have been identified to me as connected directly to this so called 'world grid' of energy. This has been especially evident where these forces are multiplied by their intersections. The more dramatic possibilities are admittedly speculative yet repeatedly have I found a correlation between whatever I am investigating and this web of energy lines identified to me by my associate Sesh Heri. Amid all this is always a connection of synchronicity, as it is popularly defined today, ie the meaningful connection. Too many times has this happened for me to dismiss it.

One of the most stark correlations I noticed came a few years ago when I first became acquainted with the work of David Paulides. In his *Missing 411* series, Paulides presents numerous cases of disappearance of adults and children from wilderness areas, specifically US National Parks. I have discussed for several years now the maps made for me by Sesh Heri in 2008-2009 and since, specifically a map of the continental US showing the telluric current/gravity anomaly lines as Heri identified them from studying topographical maps and applying principles of geomorphology and plate tectonics to the data. I was stunned, though not surprised, when I first saw Paulides' map relative to his research as published in his 2011 book *Missing 411: Western United States & Canada*. The maps are almost identical.

Where Paulides shows the clusters of missing persons relative to wilderness areas, my Sesh Heri map shows major intersections and configurations of the telluric energy/gravity anomalies across the nation. I cannot help but think there is a correlation between these intensified spots of world grid energy and the disappearances of the people documented in Paulides' books.[301]What's more is Paulides' observation of a prominent presence of granite where these disappearances occur. I think he's really onto something here.

As I discussed in *Empire of the Wheel 3: The Nameless Ones*, granite is a significant storehouse of natural energy as a paramagnetic substance.[302] Somehow this presence of granite has something to do with these disappearances, I am convinced, and I have no doubt that Paulides sees this, too. It is my suspicion that the telluric energy stored in the granite, at the very least, disoriented the individuals who became lost, possibly misdirecting even the searchers. That Paulides also

---

[301]When I first saw the correlation, I contacted Paulides to no avail. He is notoriously resistant to any suggestion that anyone else's research might resonate with his own. The similarity between his cluster map and my telluric current/gravity anomaly map is so startling that there must be an association of phenomena between the two.
[302]EOTW3 Pg 41.

notes the presence of stormy weather during these incidents is no surprise to Heri or myself. There is something between Heri's map and Paulides' work that will ultimately prove to link the missing to these gravity anomaly hot spots.

Take Yosemite National Park. In *Missing 411: Western United States & Canada*, Paulides presents the cases of Walter Gordon (26) and Orvar Von Laass (30), both of whom disappeared from Yosemite Valley not far from the Ahwahnee Hotel.[303] Gordon disappeared on 20 July 1954 after departing from Camp Curry to hike to Glacier Point, both locations south of the grand hotel. Von Laass disappeared on 9 October 1954 after departing the Ahwahnee Hotel to go on a two hour hike. Paulides reports that dogs searching for Von Laass hit on his scent twice at the base of the Royal Arches Cliff not even a half a mile from the hotel, a spot which is not very secluded. Neither men were ever found. Interestingly, the families of both men wrote a letter to President Eisenhower a few weeks after Von Laass disappeared, beseeching the president to activate 'special warfare troops' to search for their sons. Paulides relates that no explanation was offered regarding a particular statement in the letter: "*The men's fates may exist in remote corners of the national preserve.*"

What did that mean? It sounds like a statement made by someone who might possibly know something more. As this is all the information available to Paulides, we are left to ponder the implications. Where these cases are relative to this book is that Sesh Heri provided me with a telluric current/gravity

---

[303]Paulides, Pgs 130-131; 154-156.

anomaly map of Yosemite Valley. According to Heri's geomorphological analysis based on topographical maps, there is an impressive intersection of four curvilinear gravity anomaly lines at the base of Royal Arches Cliff. The central vertical curvilinear Heri map line goes south of the intersection point, right through Camp Curry, splitting in two, and both continue on to Glacier Point, essentially the path of Walter Gordon's intended hike. And that's not where it ends.

The horizontal curvilinear Heri map line crossing the three verticals at the major intersection of these energy lines extends east by northeast and passes right through the area where fourteen year old Stacey Arras disappeared on a hike to Sunrise Lakes on 17 July 1981.[304] As Paulides points out throughout his book, there is a prominent amount of granite in all the areas associated with these disappearances. As stated previously, granite is a paramagnetic stone, a storehouse of natural energy. There are 33 unsolved cases[305] of people who disappeared in Yosemite National Park. Some were found alive, some were found dead, and others were never found at all. I suggest that they all have at least one thing in common: Something in Yosemite disorients people who find themselves in spots strong with natural energy and Sesh Heri's analysis may provide important data.

Whether the disoriented person walks off a cliff, or is attacked by an animal, or falls into a crevasse, or ends up dragged into an animal den never to be found, I suspect something affected the

---

[304]Ibid, Pgs 119-121.

[305]That number!

faculties of human senses of these victims, primarily sight and hearing. In the cases where some are found, it is usually because said individual stopped walking and laid down. The only 'real world' possibilities are that the missing fell into a very deep hole or were dragged into an animal den and consumed thoroughly, the bones somewhere deep in a cavern. There is, of course, the possibility of human treachery; that a criminal abduction took place and that the missing became murder victims, their remains taken out of the park or disposed in some untraceable manner.

There is another possibility. Something of an extraordinary nature could have happened, especially in the cases of those who were never found. Such a possibility deserves a book all its own. Some readers think Paulides suspects something along these lines, specifically that Bigfoot is abducting people, and even UFOs have been discussed along with suggestions of other related phenomena.[306] But Paulides isn't saying and perhaps that's wise. However, Sesh Heri and I have never stopped ourselves at that line and we aren't stopping now. We certainly suspect extraordinary phenomena in the cases linked directly to the lines, from a possible disorienting effect to the very outrageous suggestion of spectral dimensionality as I have discussed in *Latitude 33* relative to the enigmatic Alfred, and as proposed in the cases of the mysterious deaths in San Bernardino in 1915 in the *Empire of the Wheel* books. Some of those who remain missing may have experienced a wider

[306] *Where Did The Road Go?* 20 Dec 2018.

context of our physical spectrum. Might they be still on our plane but just out of sight?

The suggestion implies a tragic end for, unless they were fortunate enough to be found, as some were, one could wander unseen until exposure, madness or starvation leads to death. This is definitely a subject worthy of its own dedicated examination but I have other points to make within our context here. Since I have demonstrated the resonance between Paulides' work on the Yosemite cases and mine and Sesh Heri's research and analyses, where the telluric current/gravity anomaly world grid is concerned, what else hints at a connection?

One interesting point between the Yosemite disappearances and my research is that Yosemite sits on the southeastern side of Tuolumne County and is a mere few miles from the legendary home base of the curious Sonora Aero Club.

This group allegedly designed, built and flew small rudimentary craft called 'aeros' forty years before the great 1890s airship mystery that started in Northern California. I have proposed in *Empire of the Wheel 2: Friends From Sonora* that the aeros and the mystery airships of the 1890s could have used the world grid telluric current/gravity anomaly lines as a ship uses ocean currents. I even provide the correlating links between the lines of energy on the Heri map and the reported sightings from newspapers in the late 19th Century incidents. Sesh Heri's analysis of the Tuolumne County area illustrates that it's a place rich with telluric current and gravity anomaly energy. He suspects, as I do, that relative phenomena are highly present in the area. In fact, one intense intersection of energy lines there creates a nodal point on the original residential property of the Rosasco family, where Frank Rosasco, prominent in the *Empire of the Wheel* mystery, spent almost sixty years surveying an unidentified something on the ranch and obsessively working out mathematical equations and making astronomical observations. His family may have been among the ranchers working with the Sonora Aero Club.[307]

If there is indeed some functional utilization of the world grid telluric current/gravity anomalies in what appears to be 'antigravity' flight, is it therefore any surprise that the members of the Sonora Aero Club selected this landscape right next door to Yosemite Valley where there would be numerous strange disappearances in spots heavy with paramagnetic granite (no pun intended) and rich with extraordinary natural phenomena? That there have been numerous odd disappearances in Yosemite National Park has been demonstrated, but what about any disappearances prior to the opening of the Yosemite Valley to outdoor tourism?

Paulides writes of the Miwok or Me-Wuk tribe who lived there before the national park was opened. They had been there for 8,000 years and to them the valley was sacred.[308] There is one theorist whose controversial claim is that the Miwok arrived by sea as Siberians a mere 3,000 years ago.[309] The Miwok are known for harvesting mussels and diving for

---

[307] *EOTW2:Friends From Sonora* (Corvos) 2013

[308] Paulides, Pg 111.

[309] Billiter, Los Angeles Times 28 Nov 2014; Otto Van Sadovsky, *The Discovery of California: A Cal-Ugrian Comparative Study* (Akadémiai Kiadó 1996).

abalone on the coast of California so perhaps there is something to that idea, though I might suggest ancestral connection to the Cham empire explorers.[310] Miwok spirituality recognizes the presence of spirits around us and they treat these spirits respectfully, otherwise some bad things can happen. They believe.

Isn't that interesting?

It so happens that in Miwok mythology some very interesting ideas are indeed found to resonate with what David Paulides has reported about Yosemite. The Miwok believed that Yosemite Valley was sacred. One particular spot west of the Ahwahnee Hotel and Royal Arches Cliff area, where Gordon and Von Laass disappeared, is the famous El Capitan. According to Miwok mythology, El Capitan was a small rock nearer the ground upon which a bear family fell asleep one night. They awoke to find themselves in the sky, for El Capitan had suddenly sprouted up to its present elevation of 3,000 feet. By the time they could be reached, the bears had died of starvation and only their bones were brought down.[311] In this tale we have elements of some Yosemite incidents discussed in Paulides' *Missing 411* in which only bones are found after the disappearance. I have already pointed out that starvation could be a very real factor for some victims. But this bear family myth isn't where it ends.

---

[310]I have discussed the ancient Cham reaching California in previous books and I refer the reader to David Childress' *The Lost World of Cham.*

[311] S.A. Barrett, 'Myths of the Southern Sierra Miwok' *American Archaeology and Ethnology* Vol. 16, No. 1, pp. 1-2, March 27, 1919, (University of California Publications) Pg 22.

Let S. A. Barrett tell it from his 1919 work:

"*In the waters just below Yosemite Falls live the po'lotī, a group of dangerous spirit women. The incident related in the following story issaid to have been the work of these spirits.*

There was, in olden times, a village a short distance from the foot of Yosemite Falls. A maiden from this village went to the stream for a basket of water. She dipped the basket into the stream as usual but brought it up full of snakes. She went farther up stream and tried again, but with the same result. She tried repeatedly, each time a little farther up stream, but always drew a basketful of snakes. Finally she reached the pool at the foot of Yosemite Falls and a sudden, violent wind blew her into it.

During the night she gave birth to a child which she wrapped in a blanket and brought home the next morning. The girl's mother was very curious and soon took the blanket off the baby in order to see it. Immediately a violent gale arose and blew the entire village and its inhabitants into this same pool. Nothing has ever been seen or heard of them since."[312]

And there is yet more that Barrett shares:

"*The Spirits above Bridal Veil Falls.—A short distance above Bridal Veil Falls is a lake somewhat like Mirror lake. Here live certain beautiful maidens whose tresses hang down to their feet. They have a* ***very sharp sense of smell and can detect easily the approach of a human being. They cause a violent wind in an endeavor to blow the victim into the lake and drown him. These maidens then devour him. The victim's spirit remains forever in the depths of the lake.*** *Very little is known of the personal appearance of these women except that they are very beautiful, are pure white, with blue eyes, and have very long hair.* ***That so little is known of them is due to the***

[312]Barrett, Pg.23

fact that they are greatly feared and anyone who is so unfortunate as to come in sight of one of them takes no time for observations but makes off, if possible, at top speed. *Similar women are in the waters above Yosemite Falls.*" (Emphases mine - WB)

And still more:

"*The Spirits at the foot of Bridal Veil Falls.—Another class of these supernatural beings are* ***the pū'hūnū, who formerly lived in the pool at the foot of Bridal Veil Falls.*** *Informants could not give very definite accounts of these beings but knew that* ***they were harmless except in that they always caused the water of the fall to blow out and wet anyone who approached too close to its foot***." (Emphases mine – WB)

Isn't that delightful. Granite that sprouts monstrously high in the night in a place where granite is always present in disappearance cases isn't enough. Here are additionally frightening spirit beings possessed of great beauty, perhaps so stunning as to render their victims docile, and who possess superior physical senses and feed on those who wander into their territory. Causing a wind to blow the victim over the edge suggests a supernatural command of nature or perhaps an understanding of the presence of telluric current and how to use its related phenomena. That these spirits eat their victims reminds us again of the cases in Paulides' book in which bones were found. The extra bit that the souls of the victims spend eternity locked in some dreadful underworld at the site of their grisly end just makes it all the more resonant with the context of this book for here we have a thematic association with our ever prevalent Hekate, a goddess of the underworld land of the dead.

The curious similarities to the Miwok myths of Yosemite and the cases of missing persons in the national park are frankly rather creepy. Consider the story of the bears on the suddenly shifting and mountainous rock, El Capitan. Then consider how many times Paulides points out the cases wherein a victim, especially a child, has been found at an elevation that was simply impossible for them to have reached in the elapsed time and prevalent conditions. This happened in Yosemite and we're talking thousands of feet. Also consider the cases in which Paulides points out that the victim was found wedged into a tight crevasse. I ask the reader: Are these instances of a sudden or near immediate shift in massive boulders (or plates) of the granite so prevalent in Yosemite Valley?

A sudden and admittedly uncanny shift of a mountain or granite ridgeline could conceivably thrust one of these missing children hundreds or a thousand or more feet higher than they were moments before. Could such a sudden shift additionally cause some sort of magnetic-gravity effect which further disorients the victim?

Over half of the cases in Yosemite involve bodies of water, be it lakes, reservoirs, rivers or creeks. Yes this is a wilderness area and of course many people go there because of these very features. But not all the cases feature a victim's intent to go to a lake nor emphasize that the last place they were seen was a river or creek. Then there are those victims found in pools at the foot of waterfalls, right out of the Miwok myth of the spirit beings who cause their victims to be blown over the falls. One case in particular is just too resonant with this mythology.

One of the two most gruesome cases is that of Evelyn Rosemann who in 1968 was found at the base of Nevada Falls in Yosemite. Her body had been severely battered, her sweater pulled up over her head and her pants pulled down to her ankles. Part of her brain was found fifty feet away at the presumed point of impact after the nearly 600 foot fall. Her vagina showed evidence of sexual assault which investigators think occurred *after* her death from the fall. And it doesn't even end there for recall the Miwok myth and that the spirit beings cause a wind which blows their victim over the edge to their death. Investigators on the Rosemann case insist that she could not have simply floated over the edge of the falls via the creek as the flow was minimal, rather she was "launched off the top", forensics indicating that Evelyn had been "thrown a distance off the cliff".[313]

Like by a strong sudden wind…?

Another horrific Yosemite case reflective of the Miwok legend is that of David Huckins, a park employee who in February1986 disappeared while jogging. Between July and October, his arm was found near a river campground, his torso and other pieces were found two miles away in the Merced River, and his scapula and humerus were found a couple of miles from that. Experts ruled out bears because, when Huckins disappeared, bears were hibernating.[314] In the Miwok myth, those beautiful lady spirits eat their victims, devour them. What the exact brand of hell is going on here?

---

[313]Paulides, Pgs 148-149.

[314]Ibid Pg 138

What was going on in Yosemite Valley for thousands of years that the Miwok have horrific myths about it? If you only read Paulides book about 20th Century cases, you would reasonably assume that the cause might be some human terror indicative of our times. But the existence of these myths so nearly identical to these missing persons cases, and significantly predating them, suggests the obvious: Something terrible has been going on in the Yosemite Valley for thousands of years. We are just now hearing about it in more direct terms. How many such tragic disappearances and deaths happened to the Miwok before 1850 when the first American explorer is said to have seen the valley for the first time?

What gave me goosebumps when I read Barrett's 1919 telling of these myths is the description of the spirit ladies: *pure white, with blue eyes*. This immediately reminded me of the Erl King's pale daughters who come to steal a child from his frightened father racing through the woods to save him. Those pale fey ghouls ultimately succeed, presumably carrying the child's spirit to the land of the dead. But it also made me think of many other such fairy world beings of fair color and bright eyes, and the numerous tales of them abducting humans to their dimension. Still there is an even more sinister and closer similarity in the '*yakshas*' found in Hinduism, Buddhist and Jainist texts; some of them demonic fairies of the wilderness who haunt mountains and forests and lure their human prey in order to eat them. In this alone may we find evidence that the Miwoks indeed have some ancestral link to the Cham empire, for the Cham were made up of Hindus, Buddhists and Jainists.[315]

But one cannot mention pale blue eyed spirit beings, or especially fairies, and not acknowledge those beings of great significance to this book and everything else I have investigated in all my works: the Tuatha de Danann. And it is a bit disturbing, honestly. We will be discussing the Tuatha connection to this series in the next chapter so for right now we will stick to their relevance here.

It is my contention that the beings called the Tuatha de Danann by the ancient Irish are indeed from another world. I have proposed in other works that these beings came to our world to escape a conflict of their own civilization, a civil war. They don't likely call themselves by the popular Irish name we all know, but in that name is a clue as to their influence in our world as well as the conflict in their own. Tuatha de Danann means 'children of Anu' and this logically links them to the Anunnaki, in the minds of most people. The description of them is quite similar enough to descriptions of the Anunnaki that they must certainly be of the same race of beings, yet there seems to be a difference between the two in that the Tuatha have a reputation for being benevolent conquerors who bring Earth people up to a higher technological level, while the Anunnaki tend to lord it over humans who encounter them. I suggest in

---

[315]Childress, *Lost World of Cham*; George Cœdès, *The Making of South East Asia*, (University of California Press 1966); Will Durant, *The Story of Civilization Part I: Our Oriental Heritage* (Simon & Schuster 1954); Georges Maspéro, *The Champa Kingdom: The History of an Extinct Vietnamese Culture* (White Lotus Press 2002); Wikipedia.

other works that there are **the** 'Anunnaki' but they and the Tuatha are '*anunnaki*' the way we on Earth are all 'humans'.

The Anunnaki were supposed to have worn an unidentified substance called 'melam' which served to simultaneously captivate and terrify humans looking upon them. This 'melam' is the same thing as 'glamory' which comes from glamour, defined by Merriam-Webster as an 'alluring yet illusory beauty' and a 'magic spell'. Glamory is associated with the fairy beings, including the Tuatha de Danann. The ultimate effect on the human psyche is to be stunned into inaction, thus making it easier to prey upon us. Good fairies are said to use this power merely to flee once they are seen by a human, and hiding their true nature is part of its use. Could the true nature of some of these flesh-devouring spirits in the Miwok myth be hidden behind a camouflage of beautiful pale ladies with bright shining blue eyes?

Could the Yosemite Valley be the territory of these demonic spirits, said racial '*anunnaki*' cousins of the Tuatha de Danann who are themselves described as 'pale' or white with blonde or red hair and blue or green eyes? My research has never turned up such demonically monstrous behavior on the part of the Tuatha, yet these Miwok legend spirit ladies of the falls in Yosemite Valley look just like them. It gives me some comfort that I see a schism between the '*anunnaki*' beings, suggesting to me that the Tuatha do not hunt, murder and devour the flesh of human victims who wander into their landscape. I hope I'm right, *if* all this is real. But that would suggest that we have the the others called Anunnaki with which to contend.

Speaking of 'dark figures', what about Hekate? I will be discussing her in the next chapter, but relative to this examination of Yosemite Valley I will remind the reader that I have previously proposed the intersections of telluric current/gravity anomaly lines to be the domain of this 'Goddess of the Crossroads'. I strongly suspect her presence in Yosemite as well. I have become convinced over the years that she is among the original Tuatha who arrived in ancient Ireland from their other world. Might Hekate actually help keep her ravenous lady cousins at bay as much as possible?

This is all fanciful speculation, of course[316], but we must consider such lore embedded so deeply within the human psyche as a possible source of a madness that could drive human beings to horrendous acts which become the stuff of legends. If that's the case, that homicidal maniacs are responsible for pushing people over cliffs and then eating their flesh, where did these pale white, blue eyed maniacs come from?

Were these alleged spirit-demon ladies actually a forgotten colony of the legendary California Amazons discussed previously? Were they remnants of ancient seafarer explorers from Europe? Who knows? It's even less comforting that David Paulides has written multiple volumes laying out the hundreds of cases of people gone missing inside our national wilderness areas and under much the same circumstances as those in the

---

[316]Unless it isn't.

Yosemite cases. His research even traces the mystery to the San Bernardino Mountains in the heart of the *Empire of the Wheel.*

Two strange disappearances occurred in Big Bear Lake, just a forty-five minute drive up the mountain from my home. One was on 5 July 1947[317] when a three year old son of a US Marine stationed at Barstow disappeared during a family vacation. Search dogs followed the boy's scent trail for four miles to no avail. Fifty-six hours later, the boy was found not far south of the east end of Big Bear Lake where the terrain geomorphologically suggests that a curvilinear line of telluric energy/gravity anomaly runs through a shallow canyon. He was alive, sleeping beside a log in an area that had been previously searched.[318] Interestingly, the case before this one which has personal significance for me.

In the middle of the day on 11 May 1938, two-year old David Baumgarten disappeared from the vicinity of a country store on the north side of Big Bear Lake. His father was a sales representative for a food company and had stopped at the store. The authorities were alerted and Sheriff Emmett L. Shay deployed several deputies and search dogs, going all night and well into the following day. Not until thirty hours after disappearing was young David found by his father a distance of four miles from the store where he disappeared. David was unconscious and face down in the snow, but very much alive, with only three deep scratches on his face to indicate any

[317]Note to reader: This was within a day or two of events in Roswell NM the same year.
[318]Paulides, Pg 165.

harm.[319] The question is: Where was David for thirty hours? Is it reasonable that a nonstop search involving several deputies and dogs could actually have missed an area a mere four miles from the disappearance spot? How did a two year old get that far away in a snowy hilly area?

Here's where it's weird for me. The Sheriff at the time was Emmett Shay, the son of Walter Shay, the sheriff investigating the Cora Stanton mystery chronicled in *Empire of the Wheel*. There is a telluric line/gravity anomaly line running through the town of Big Bear Lake, just south of the lake itself, with curvilinears sprouting off from that. That main line running through the town continues on through what used to be Baldwin Lake where years before another member of the Shay family had tried to rescue one of the seven victims featured in *Empire of the Wheel*. And finally, certainly not least, I happen to be acquainted with David Baumgarten for many years but never knew about the disappearance until reading Paulides' book.

My father knew David Baumgarten through business. They had known each other for thirty years, by the time of my dad's death. David attended his funeral in 2008. I decided to call Baumgarten and he agreed to discuss his disappearance with me,[320] explaining that, when the incident occurred, he was so young that he doesn't recall anything about his disappearance. That doesn't eliminate an extraordinary aspect to his disappearance because the two year old David survived for

---

[319]Paulides Pgs 164-165

[320]Per telephone conversation on Tuesday, June 22nd 2021.

thirty hours before he was found. Presently, I think there is something odd about this incident.[321]

It doesn't surprise me that mysterious disappearances as presented by David Paulides also happened in the San Bernardino Mountains, certainly not after my experience investigating for the *Empire of the Wheel* books. It is also my experience with those seven years of investigation that keep me open to the possibility of some extraordinary phenomenon at play with these disappearances. I see it as likelihood more than a mere possibility, but that's just my perspective. I can't help but wonder if something akin to the things of Miwok legends in Yosemite could be lurking in these mountains just above my home.

That 1915 victim who died in Baldwin Lake drowned after his raft was tipped over. A body of water and an unexpected boating accident, the details of which I have since demonstrated are eerily represented in an ancient legend about a witch killing a man coming after her on a raft. Might this man, Isidore Josseau, have been the victim of one of these demonic spirit-ladies with the pale skin and blue eyes?

At the very least, I cannot help but suspect that the telluric currents and gravity anomalies of the geomorphologically formed 'world grid', so prevalent across and shockingly identical to Paulides' map of disappearances, have a lot to do with many of the strangest cases presented in his books. Because the telluric/gravity anomaly 'ley line' system as

[321]Mr Baumgarten and I were unable to schedule a meeting before the publication of this book, but he wants to show me a file relative to his disappearance. I will report on the details of this meeting once accomplished.

identified and examined by Sesh Heri and myself has shown direct association with sites characterized by symbols and themes of the Tuatha de Danann, I can't help but suspect their presence in these particularly strange disappearance cases, at least in the places in which they have happened. The legendary presence of the Miwok spirit entities who lure human prey to their death and devour their flesh, and specifically their physical description, demands a consideration that perhaps unsavory denizens of the same dimension as associated with the fairy lore at large in Yosemite, and perhaps elsewhere throughout the US National Park system.

Or at least someone who wants us to think so.

So how does any of this business with these energies and lines and geomorphology factor into the events and places of the *Secret Missions* series of books?

In the first volume, there is the speculation that a Templar vault may have been located inside Mt Rubidoux and that could have been from where Juan Cabrillo retrieved the sword of Joan of Arc. That is among the purest speculations of the book, of course. It is in the places Cabrillo's expedition explored where we find the world grid phenomena discussed in this chapter. Sesh Heri has long ago identified to me where the energy and gravity anomalies flow and intersect and gather along the California coast. These places include the Chumash *humqaq* at Point Conception, as well as the previously discussed circle near Indian Rock which I suspect may have been the occulted objective of secret exploration of San Francisco Bay. There is also the presence of these phenomena at and around Catalina Island where we are told Cabrillo died.

In the second volume of this series, there is Burton's time in the United States, crossing many of these telluric/gravity anomaly lines and their related phenomena, as well as my suspicion that his visit to Sacramento and then San Francisco, a ten day period there, provided ample time to visit Yosemite which he had previously stated was his desire. I suspect he indeed made the trip to Yosemite. Would Burton have known about the energy phenomena associated with the gravity anomalies intersection there? It's certainly possible but that remains unknown as we are left with an official assumption that he did not go, Burton allegedly being exhausted. This from the man who went on a solo expedition in India while he was recovering from illness and whom, in my examination, used being under the weather as a likely cover.

In the third volume, we have in 1866 the Hazen expedition for which Ambrose Bierce served as an army officer once more time after the war. This journey, overtly assigned to inspect US Army posts across the frontier plains, took Bierce across much of the same territory Burton had seen six years prior. That includes the telluric currents and gravity anomalies. Though Heri has not yet examined the geomorphology of Europe, we have to wonder about any such phenomena in the south of France where Bierce spent some time alone. There is the Languedoc and its Rennes le Chateau mystery to be considered where Bierce's curious tour is concerned. But probably the most interesting resonance with things discussed earlier in this chapter is that Bierce was fascinated with stories of strange disappearances. Was long time California resident Ambrose Bierce already familiar with such strange incidents as David Paulides has documented about Yosemite?

If my wild speculation that Bierce was somehow associated with the mystery airship milieu is correct, then we must wonder what he knew of the Sonora Aero Club and thus Yosemite, if such phenomena as telluric currents and gravity anomaly geomorphology are indeed linked to airship functions and operations (if real). It is also possible therefore that Bierce could have known about the same phenomena which had piqued Juan Cabrillo's curiosity. Because of Bierce's lack of clues, admittedly my offering on him is the most speculative of all in this series, so far. Yet, there he is in more than one place I have elsewhere linked to the phenomena discussed here.

Where Napoleon Bonaparte is concerned, he may have had the most significantly extraordinary experience of his life inside the Great Pyramid, itself located at that most celebrated of esoteric zones on the planet, the 33rd Latitude North. This possibility alone is enough to qualify in this discussion of high strangeness associated with the presence of geomorphological phenomena, but Napoleon was fascinated with places all around the world, specifically in the Americas. As with Cabrillo, Burton and Bierce, Napoleon's activities, known and suspected, find their way along and across these phenomena.

But it isn't merely a geographical presence in the suspected clandestine objectives of the figures examined in the *Secret Missions* series that is significant here, it is the presence of these curious phenomena in these places as they also relate to the search for the forgotten civilization. Each one of these men was an explorer, whether by profession or circumstances and certainly by nature. Each one of them were keenly interested in things off the beaten path of history and their personal journeys took them to these places. The pursuit of the lost past took Cabrillo, Burton, Napoleon and even Bierce to places associated with relics or legends of a forgotten civilization. For me, the obvious implication is that said forgotten civilization established its outposts and cities in these places for the very reason of their geomorphology – because these special phenomena were there to be tapped. You just had to know where to look and, a long time ago, somebody taught some of us how.

So who were they who knew the hidden secrets of the natural forces in the earth?

Chapter Nine

They Have Been With Us For A Very Long Time

The Tuatha de Danann discussed in this book are not those whom anthropologists smugly write off as tribes of Mediterranean invaders. Neither are they those ephemeral ornaments cherished by my witchy lady friends who see the Tuatha as quaint sprite-like figures. And they, as discussed here, are *not* mere anthropomorphic representations of the wind, the sun and the stars. The Tuatha as discussed in this book are those who have left an indelible presence upon the landscape of my research and who have specifically manifested themselves in odd personal experiences.

The Tuatha de Danann of my research and experiences themselves do not express their presence strictly in terms of trendy lore. There is syncretism and synchronicity alike. In an effort to go about this as an investigator, I choose to present this material as it has appeared to me because the manifestation is what counts, not a consensus mythology. I think that a being's own manifest expression suggests more truth than does human assumption which all too often boxes in something it doesn't really understand. The most we may know about them is only what they show of themselves to us, not what some scholar deep in his or her own weeds will presume, as filtered through their own preferences. I try my best to describe the Tuatha first in terms I have found evident in my research and then in terms of my personal experience with their known associations and symbols.

I only have three major points to present: Their presence is marked throughout the history which I have covered in my books, they remain here and available to us today, and I think I understand the purpose of what I've found and experienced. I will attempt to cover these points through a review of the Tuatha evidence as it appears in my books and then offer my wild-ass guess at what I think it means.

Who are the Tuatha de Danann?

The earliest record of them as such is in ancient Irish mythology, but that is only the record of them as encountered by one culture. Where they come from is unknown and the Tuatha we concern ourselves with here did not come from the Mediterranean. They came from a different world, whatever that actually means. The point is, one cannot limit their definition strictly to the *Lebor Gelen* therefore I will not concern myself with the Tuatha as popularly conceived because that is a long and winding dead end.

The Tuatha de Danann did not call themselves this Irish name. We don't know exactly what they called themselves as a group. What the ancient Irish called them could have been in error, so it is pointless to spend time and energy on further analysis of a name that has been dissected *ad nauseam* in other sources available to the reader.

An answer I will give, to the question posed, is that the Tuatha are a group or clan of beings who arrived from the sky in a great tumult of power and demonstrated their superior intellect and technology. They soon became described in terms of ethereal qualities. When they ultimately departed, it was to the underworld, be that literal or metaphysical and there is evidence for both.

The Tuatha may explain some of the more nagging questions of our times and all times. For instance, they have been associated with UFO encounters.[322] Their presence may certainly explain some reports of ghosts and other paranormal phenomena. Their ultimate purpose could involve things most people would rather not think about too much.[323] Other than that, I can only confidently present the Tuatha as I've encountered them as a research scholar and an experiencer.

I first documented their presence in the research for my first nonfiction book, *Latitude 33: Key to the Kingdom,* which presents my hypothesis that Disneyland was constructed to function as a psychotronic device.

In early 1981, I cannot recall if it was February or March, I went to Disneyland with some friends from high school. Three of us decided to ride King Arthur's Carrousel some time around nine o'clock that evening. As we were going round, I noticed a man standing in the area between the Dumbo and Mr.Toad rides, near the path that leads farther back into the park toward Tomorrowland.

---

[322]Refer to Jacques Vallee's work.
[323]Like death.

The man was wearing a black suit and a white shirt, no tie. At the time, I estimated his age to be around 70 years. His white hair and beard were cut close. This man stood there with wide eyes watching the carousel spin around several times before departing. I noticed him every time I went around and when he wasn't there anymore. Thinking nothing further of it, my friends and I got off the ride when it stopped and we went off in the direction of the aforementioned path in the direction of Tomorrowland.

As we were passing the Teacups, I noticed the old man seated on a bench under the monorail track near the Matterhorn. Something compelled me to approach the man and strike up a conversation. I asked if he was having fun and he said he was. He told us that this was his first time here. To this day, I cannot remember the sound of his voice, I remember that he said his name was Alfred.

What I gleaned from the conversation is that Alfred was almost out of tickets, which were standard in those days. He had only one remaining and we determined that he could ride 'It's A Small World' so I said we would ride it with him. My friends followed as I led Alfred to the ride which was nearby. As we rode, with Alfred seated in the front, I noticed how he looked at everything in awe and wonder. When it was all over and we stepped out of the boat, we meandered with the old man back in the direction of Fantasyland, stopping about where he had been seated when we approached.

That was the moment it struck me. I decided that since I live in Southern California and would be returning to the park many times again, I didn't need my passport ticket for the remaining two hours the park was open. I unpinned it from my shirt and pinned it to Alfred's lapel. I explained that with this special ticket, he could ride whatever he wanted as many times as he liked.

Alfred's eyes widened and his expression lit up. You would have thought I'd given him a pot of gold from the end of the rainbow. Thanking me profusely, he appeared overwhelmed by my small generosity. My friends and I bid him a good time and he departed in the direction of Fantasyland, eventually disappearing from our view. Feeling that I had done a nice thing for a nice old man, I turned with my friends and we wandered into Tomorrowland.

I never forgot about that night. Something about the encounter with Alfred stuck with me through the years. Especially when weird things began to happen the likes of which I've discussed in another book, *Confessions of A Spooky Mind.* But here, for the first time, I must admit to neglecting consideration of a particular detail that, though I have always recalled it, I never thought to analyze it for any hidden meaning. The pin to which I refer above was a Donald Duck pin and, when I finally bothered to look deeper into it, I found some interesting things.

First of all, I should have known back in 2011 when I was investigating imagery relative to the *Empire of the Wheel* material at Riverside's Mission Inn. I was only recently compelled to reconsider the significance of that Donald Duck pin when I looked again at the Bavarian Gooseman statue at the bottom of the Mission Inn rotunda. The third book on that series goes into the Gooseman more but I can't answer why it didn't dawn on me before now to reconsider the Donald Duck pin for deeper meaning relative to my Disneyland experience with the mysterious Alfred.

Ducks, to some Native Americans, represent a sort of fool who is subject to the treachery of the Trickster. They are also depicted as a sort of sacrificial victim in one native legend. In Chinese tradition, ducks are a symbol of love, both romantic and familial. In Christianity, ducks symbolize blessing, protection and enlightenment, as well as an inspiration to not be angered by provocation, you might say. Egypt uses the duck as a symbol of the creator god. But most significant to the examination here, because of the Irish context in which the Tuatha are best known, is the Celtic meaning of the duck symbolism: the duck is linked to migration and transition.[324]

This is quite intriguing. The migration aspect seems obvious, as water fowl migrate to warmer climes during the winter, but relative to my experience with Alfred, a man who appeared to represent a being from another dimension, the *transitional* aspect is most significant. My experience that night at Disneyland was apparently intended to be transitional for my consciousness, perhaps even for my soul. Still, the migration aspect remains intriguing for it suggests passage.

But to where?

---

[324]Garth C. Clifford, *Duck Symbolism & Meaning* (World Birds: Joy of Nature 11 Jan 2021)

I am still on that road so I don't know yet, but I suspect it may relate to where we go following physical death. This certainly makes sense to me when I consider my personal suspicion that the Queen of the Crossroads, Goddess of the Underworld herself is one of the Tuatha de Danann. We'll be discussing her shortly, but we have more to consider where these curious beings are concerned.

My Alfred encounter wasn't the only clue that the Tuatha had left their influence on the Magic Kingdom experience. In my book *Latitude 33*, I describe how their symbols, specifically of their Four Treasures, are to be found on the King Arthur Carrousel. Readers of that book will recall that the premise for Disneyland being engineered as a psychotronic device centers upon the carousel having been placed atop an intersection of three lines of gravity anomaly/telluric current. What followed my experience at Disneyland, and the book it motivated years later, was a research journey along one of those intersecting lines leading out of the Magic Kingdom and to the San Bernardino Valley, where I have spent a fair portion of my life. It was like following the footsteps of Dorothy along a brick road of a different color.

Suspicion nagged me, during my *Empire of the Wheel* years, that the Tuatha de Danann have been a guiding hand in the development of our current civilization. Observation of apparent symbols relative to the lore associated with them gave me this idea. For example, the giant arrowhead of San Bernardino.

I describe this feature of the local landscape in the first volume of the *Empire of the Wheel* trilogy and have also written an article about it published in WEX Magazine.[325] It is my opinion that this relic looks much more like a spearhead than an arrowhead. According to local native lore, it was placed there by a sorcerer wielding a magic rod in an incident long before their time. The tale reads like something from a fantasy adventure epic and the sorcerer could, for all the world, be one of the Tuatha himself. Interestingly, the second object which impresses upon me a suspicion of association to the Tuatha is one of known origin.

The giant cross atop Riverside's Mount Rubidoux, is discussed in *Empire of the Wheel 3: The Nameless Ones*. Having replaced an original rustic wooden cross placed by a local church to mark the peak of the hill (popularly referred to as a 'mount'), it also marks the spot where Easter services have been performed for decades. However, the newer cross resembles a sword every bit as much as it does a cross, its blade burrowed into the ground, hilt upward. When you consider how these objects actually look, as opposed to their popular descriptions, you see in them two of the Four Treasures of the Tuatha de Danann.

What are these Four Treasures? They are four magical objects associated with four island cities of the Tuatha homeland: the Spear, the Sword, the Stone and the Cauldron. Island cities are rather suggestive of an Atlantean or Lemurian civilization at play here, or perhaps survivors of those legendary places.

---

[325]World Explorer Magazine, Vol 6 No.4.

Within the context of this book where California is specifically concerned, Lemuria comes to mind. But why a spearhead that has been part of the San Bernardino Valley terrain throughout known history, and a sword stuck into a mountain-sized hill in modern times? How could the ancient and mysterious Tuatha have anything to do with *both* of these?

From this perspective, the giant arrowhead of San Bernardino represents the magical Spear of the Tuatha island city Gorias. It is sufficiently old enough that the legend of the rod-wielding sorcerer could represent *direct* Tuatha influence, their literal mark upon the terrain. The giant cross on Mt Rubidoux, however, could have been designed by someone knowledgeable of Tuatha lore and perhaps even knew something of their possible ancient presence in the area. Said individual, or group, may have styled the cross to look like the Sword of the Tuatha isle city, Finias. As I've discussed in EOTW3, there are stories linking Mount Rubidoux to an ancient tomb. The cross may have been co-opted to mark the general site as sacred to the Tuatha or their local followers, without the knowledge of the church associated with its construction. Let's say that's the case, we now have the Spear to the north, the Sword to the south. We are left with the Stone and the Cauldron and the east and the west.

Is there anything to suggest that these markers would be purposely associated with the cardinal points?

It is noted in *Empire of the Wheel 1* and *3* that the giant arrowhead of San Bernardino, our Tuatha Spear, is angled at 17 degrees or true north. The Sword on Mt Rubidoux is to the southwest, the arrowhead pointing almost directly to it. That adjusts our remaining points to northwest and southeast. I have been looking for corresponding objects that could represent the remaining treasures, the Stone and the Cauldron. I haven't found anything sufficient yet but I must note that my UFO experience comes into play here.

It is to the northwest of the San Bernardino Valley that the odd schematic I found over a decade ago is laid out upon a concrete surface. It incorporates a pyramidal shape and, like at Giza, it is missing the capstone. Subsequent experiments at this site have convinced me that an individual using this site fulfills the role of the capstone. The Stone of the Tuatha is alleged to 'cry out' when someone takes the throne of the blessed land. Might a 'throne' also be representative of the 'capstone' space 'atop' the pyramid? This curious site itself could represent the Stone, as a 'pyramid' is often a carefully stacked 'mountain' of stone blocks, though in this case a schematic painted on cement, further cementing the suggestion of a Stone of Falias.

But what of the Cauldron of Dagda from the city of Murias

The UFO I saw in December 2014 had elements that behaved like a cauldron, even spewing a molten golden-white substance over its sides as it glided away. It had been sighted coming from the northwest by the other witness, the direction in which one finds the curious schematic I suggest is the Stone. And that very day I had been to the Stone site to conduct some research. Coincidence? I do not personally think so.

The object we saw resembled a flying cauldron (with a domed top) and it is said that to see Dagda's Cauldron is to be blessed, for no one comes away from it unfulfilled.[326] The object paused over the house for several moments before moving off in a eastward/southeastward direction. Was it a blessing? Did it appear as a result of my activity at the site of the schematic earlier that very day?

More importantly here, does the Cauldron represent the missing Tuatha Treasure in this valley? I can only suggest it is so. I suspect there may be something to the east of my location that would associate with the Cauldron. Further east of the San Bernardino Valley is Yucca Valley and there you find Landers, a desert community and the home of the curious Integratron. Interestingly, the domed top of the Integratron is the same shape as the visible image of the UFO I saw. Was George Van Tassel actually instructed by the Tuatha or a group representing their knowledge in the construction of this curious structure?

The thing I saw that December night in 2014 moved from my house to the general direction of Landers. The Integratron itself, as it was allegedly designed to generate natural forces to extend human life, could serve as a technological version of the Cauldron of Dagda. Long healthy life is generally viewed as a blessing. Are the natural forces Van Tassell intended to tap into the telluric current/gravity anomaly energies of the Earth itself?

Sesh Heri's mapping indicates this may be so but Van Tassell didn't live long enough to finish the Integratron as designed.

---

[326] I must also add that Dagda has a special harp called Uaithne which sets the seasons right and also plays the music of dreaming. In *Shimmering Light* I discuss my experience with an overdose of guarana seed extract and the intensely vivid psychedelic dream I had from it. In this dream I heard a musical sound that remains the most pleasing sound I have ever heard or even imagined. Did I hear Uaithne?

We face the issue of an ancient object, the Spear (aka a giant 'arrowhead'), and three modern placed objects, the Sword (aka 'cross') and the Stone (pyramid schematic), and the Cauldron (The Integratron). The only explanation I can offer for now remains the aforementioned possibility that someone in our times, say the last 150 years, has been familiar with Tuatha lore and applied it in a practical manner, even if only via their influence upon the designers, at particular sites for whatever reason. Was the intention to bless the area in an ancient tradition? Or to claim it?

There may be yet another reason.

What's so special about the San Bernardino Valley that a hidden culture would claim it from ancient times to today? The greater Inland Empire is the butt of humor these days. However, it wasn't always this way.

As discussed in the first volume of the *Empire of the Wheel* series, Rick Spence and I point out that the San Bernardino Valley was once a very popular garden spot of Southern California early in the last century, and it maintained a status as a desirable place to live until the late 1980s when crime rose and industry faded. Sesh Heri, author and researcher associate of mine, believes the San Bernardino Valley was valued for its telluric current/gravity anomaly energy. He and I agree that this was channeled into the once great citrus empire that reigned here in the greater Inland Empire. Perhaps it is this very energy that attracted the Tuatha – or its influence – to this place. If the admittedly wild speculation that in ancient California were outposts of whatever the Lemurian civilization actually might have been is true, this might explain the Spear (giant arrowhead) and its relative positioning within the telluric/gravity anomaly grid system here in San Bernardino Valley.

A problem with that idea is that the Spear (giant arrowhead), explained away as natural formation by geologists, is the only suggested Tuatha marker of the four I propose that would be ancient. The cross on Rubidoux is late 20th Century, replacing a cross of less than a century before it. The proposed Cauldron (Integratron) in Landers dates back only between the original Sword (cross) on Rubidoux and the new one. Whoever laid down the Stone schematic I found to the northwest likely did it in the 1980s, based upon my local research. The Tuatha obviously didn't place three of these objects. But there is a possibility of association with the Tuatha, for these modern objects might have been placed where once original Tuatha relics were located.

In the case of Mt Rubidoux, we have the unsubstantiated tale of the 'sacred tomb' which might have once warranted a Tuatha treasure marker. In *Secret Missions* 1, I suggest that said 'sacred tomb' might have been the secret Templar vault. This would preclude the idea of any noticeable marker if intended to be kept secret. However, an ostentatious marker at the top of Mt Rubidoux might have served as a warning to keep away. Still there remains another reasonable possibility.

If the Templars who built said vault knew that Mt Rubidoux was an ancient Tuatha site, that could have been the reason they selected it for their vault in the first place. Therefore, Mt

Rubidoux as a Tuatha site, and the cross that looks like the half buried Tuatha treasure Sword atop it, remain in play here. Taking this wild ass speculation even further, George W Van Tassel might have been directed by mysterious representatives of the Tuatha, instead of government nor ET MiB agents as is popularly repeated, to build the Integratron (Tuatha Cauldron) on an ancient Tuatha treasure marker spot. Likewise with the Stone (pyramid schematic) I found in northwestern San Bernardino, itself a possible ancient marker spot of the mysterious race of beings. It may be that I have discovered the Four Treasures markers of the Tuatha de Danann laid out across the Inland Empire geography. With three of these being of modern incarnation, that clearly means I'm not the only one.

Again, for what purpose?

I am getting to that. Patience, dear reader.

It has long been my opinion that someone here has been carrying out an ancient tradition involving Tuatha symbols and lore, some of it in veneration of the goddess Hekate, whom I surmise is one of the Tuatha herself. Veneration suggests a human agency, in the general sense of the word, where this mystery is concerned, and thus a more down to earth possibility to consider. Simply put, there could be some group along the lines of a fraternal order that has been placing these things in accordance with their knowledge or mere interpretation of relative Tuatha history and lore. When you consider what we proposed in E*mpire of the Wheel Vol 1* regarding the San Bernardino Working having a role in Crowley's *Moonchild* novel, that suggests that perhaps another secret group exists in opposition. This makes San Bernardino Valley and the greater Inland Empire look like a hotbed of occult activity.

There remain for me those strange personal experiences with the Tuatha. I discuss this in my book *Confessions of A Spooky Mind*. Owls appearing at significant moments. Winged cryptids. A UFO. Raven visitations. Faces on the sides of mountains. These things were outside the reach of any fraternal order's clandestine influence over landmark placement. These things came loaded with personal and ancient associations, loaded with synchronicity, and brimming in numerology. There appears to be something going on here which transcends a mere extraterrestrial assumption.

The Tuatha, or perhaps simply their symbols, do something to our perception of reality. More specifically, these symbols and experiences seem to ignite something in the human psyche and they do this on an individual basis. If the markers are there for everyone to see, it depends upon whether the viewer knows what he is looking at, as to the overt effect it will have. When it comes to the more living symbols, the owl, the raven, the UFO, the cryptid – these may be the Tuatha leading us or it may be us bringing the Tuatha closer, or even both. Whatever the case, the Tuatha seem to prefer dealing with us as individuals, not as a collective.

There is another theme involved here and that is of death. Hekate is the Queen of the Crossroads and stands at the gate to the underworld. She is encountered by the souls of the deceased as they embark upon the journey into the afterlife. The Owl is her familiar, the Raven is another. I have come to know all three of them.

My first conscious encounter with Hekate's presence here was through investigating those seven mysterious deaths of 1915. One of my experiences with Owl happened around the time a relative passed away. On an earlier occasion, Raven led me to the Cora Stanton grave site back in 2008, which happened to be the year my father died. The winged cryptid I saw a few years later resembled a humanoid ibis, which is the description of Thoth[327] in the underworld of the Egyptian 'Book of the Dead'. My UFO sighting occurred on the same day I visited the pyramid schematic site and during that season someone instrumental in my early progress as a writer passed away. With Hekate and the Tuatha crossing lines in their respective lore, I can't help but associate the Tuatha with the Land of the Dead. Is this where they 'went underground'?

Are the Tuatha de Danann a race of beings whose abode can only be reached through our physical death? Are they actually able to exist on both sides of that veil between our living material world and whatever lies beyond death? Do the Tuatha communicate with us through that veil, from the Land of the Dead? Might this suggest that we have nothing to fear in that experience? If any of this is so, then we all have the Tuatha in common, for each of us dies. Why would they show themselves to us long before our own death?

Perhaps there is something the Tuatha wish to convey to us about life. Or it might be that they have personal messages to

[327]Is Thoth linked to the Tuatha? Thoth or 'Tehuti' = 'Tuatha'?

communicate which eliminates any one of us suggesting that there is anything special about those who experience and recognize contact with them. Whatever I gleaned from my suspected encounters with the Tuatha may be of little to no value to you or anyone else. Likewise regarding any experiences with them that you may have. The Tuatha do not appear to be in the business of guru-making. There seem to be as many different opinions of them as there are people offering those opinions. I prefer to rely upon my experiences more than within the strict and insistent dictates of a popular lore. If it's all in my mind, it's still *here* and manifests in external *realities*, or at least my interpretation of external realities which oddly choose to appear at just the right time to be interpreted as linked to or coming from the Tuatha.

Are the Tuatha de Danann who we become after we die?

This is a whole new territory that breathes fresh life into all the work I have done. I don't have all the answers and I suspect it might be that we never do until we cross that threshold and that, dear reader, means facing Hekate at the crossroads of the underworld. Thus do we come to her presence across the field of my research and experiences.

Don't worry, I haven't forgotten that nagging possibility relative to why the Tuatha would have marked the Inland Empire of Southern California. We will get there.

The conduit of the mystery I have been investigating for nearly fourteen years is Hekate. It has all come through her, flowing along the roads leading to the so called 'dark goddess'. Hekate is prevalent in every one of my books so far, usually obvious, sometimes cleverly shrouded, or at least alluded to. After several years of synchronicity and repeatedly finding her wherever I was looking at something seemingly unrelated – and often when I least expected it -- I must conclude that all my research involves some truth to which Hekate's presence points, at least metaphorically where not literally. Repeatedly have I said that I do not resort to her as an oracle, nor as an object of worship. However, I do acknowledge her presence and personally accept her existence. I have also come to understand her better than I did previously.

What does this mean? I question the popular depiction of Hekate as primarily the goddess of witchcraft and magic. I also reject the superstitious insistence that Hekate is a dark demonic figure representative of Satanic Hell. For the past several years of my life have I consciously experienced her presence in, and her influence upon, the mystery into which I have been immersed as a scholar and investigator. At no time has my experience with Hekate proven negative nor evil. On the contrary, the more I learned and the deeper I journeyed, the brighter and more positive a figure she became.

The truth as I have seen it? Hekate plays a specific role in our existence, in our individual lives, particularly in the journey of our souls. The ancient mythology has it that she is among the favored of Zeus. The manifestations of Hekate that I have observed, especially the dreams in which she has appeared, have appeared bright and positive in the way that Pallas Athena is toward Odysseus. Even the experiences with the Owl, as harbinger of a family death or in response to a personal query, have not been negative, likewise with the Raven, despite the gothic aspects of these experiences. Truths and understanding gleaned from my experience with Hekate and her familiars have, without fail, proven to be nothing to fear, untainted with anything evil, and in the most revealing case quite profoundly simple.

But that is mere testimony and my readers know what I think about relying solely upon testimony. The materialists demand more and I respect that, thus a quick but sufficient academic look at Hekate is in order, short because much of what people think they know is wrong and the rest remains murky and scant.

I know what you're thinking. This is where he says he knows more than the reader. The fact is, you would be wrong. This is where I point out the available facts from history and literature, none of it 'revealed' via mystical or prophetic means, as is somewhat popular to claim in this field of alternative research. The truth about Hekate is mostly to be found in some basic scholarly research, what remains after that is available to any and all who would conduct some inner reflection and rumination on personal experiences.

Hekate is popularly thought of and celebrated as the patron goddess of witchcraft. Her domain is usually identified as the steamy dark underworld of Hades or Hell, take your pick. Sources regularly describe Hekate as both good and evil and *'especially associated with witchcraft, magic...and creatures of the night such as hell-hounds and ghosts.'*[328] Depending upon the historian, the genealogies so confidently cited by them all

[328] 'Hekate' Mark Cartwright, *Ancient History Encyclopedia,* 22 June 2017

contradict one another. Hesiod says Hekate's parents were Perses and Asteria[329] while others assure us she is the daughter of Zeus and Demeter. Meanwhile, Euripides says her mother was Leto[330] and Pherecydes says her father was Aristaeus[331], yet not together. Tell me, which is it?

Though scholars tell us she is among the oldest goddesses and her origin is in the obscure past, Hekate's association with witchcraft, the dead, and other occult underworld delights is dated to the 5th Century BC and the first Greek historian to speak of her does so in high praise without a mention of anything to do with graveyards or ghosts or the horrors of Hell.[332] Seriously, ask anyone you know who fancies him or herself as a practitioner of the craft and some will, in all grim and pious assurance, tell you that Hekate is and always has been *their* patron goddess, probably with some variation of the phrase 'since time immemorial'.

Whereas I am in no way disputing Hekate's prominent presence in the traditions of witchcraft, it can also be that whom they thought was Hekate smiling down upon their skyclad reveries might sometimes have been someone else. Hekate's association with witchcraft and the like may be as syncretic as the Roman Catholic grafting of her attributes onto the completely fictionalized character of Saint Catherine of Alexandria. Perhaps not completely, when considering that a portion of the bogus saint's identity is lifted shamelessly from

---

[329] *Theogony*, Pragraph...; Cartwright
[330] Cartwright
[331] *Apollonius Rhodius, Argonautica*
[332] Hesiod; Various

the biography of the very real Hypatia of Alexandria, still Catherine the Saint of Alexandria as such never existed. The Greek assignation of Hekate to witches and the dark underworld of ritual magic might be recognized today as having made in response to an inconvenience.

Worship and recognition of Hekate prior to Greece describes a loving, protective entity very similar to Pallas Athena, yet with other attributes too similar to existing goddesses already established in the Greek pantheon. This would not do, so Hekate was given to the underworld where there was apparently plenty of room for another entity, and a lot of fun was had with her in this regard, applying accurate elements of Hekate's story to this dark reputation when the ancient Greeks inherited her from the Carians.

There is so much more to this goddess figure than I can summarize here so I will bring it back to her presence within a *Secret Missions* context but also relative to all my other books, and what it might suggest. One way or another, her appearance every step along the way in my overall investigation of Cabrillo, Burton, Bierce and Bonaparte and their more curious exploits is certainly trying to tell us something. That she is there, whether prominently or subtly, is communicating something.

I was finding data on Cabrillo simultaneously with my first steps into the *Empire of the Wheel* mystery, this during the same period of a few months when I first 'met' Hekate, albeit in her 'St Catherine of the Wheel' syncretic alias. Thus must I associate her equally to my Cabrillo research. As the fictitious

St Catherine (of Alexandria), Hekate is the namesake of Catalina Island off the coast of California, the island where some believe Cabrillo died. Hekate may also be found in the wheel symbolism of the Chumash, that ancient native tribe at the center of much mystery in California. It seems to me that her place in California has significance and perhaps obvious.

Montalvo's novel has Califia proclaiming that she is of an ancestry of unknown origin. This is exactly why Hekate is a cthonic goddess, her origin actually predates all of her commonly attributed origins. That a California island associated with ancient worship of an arcane deity is named after her also reflects this association with a race of murky lineage. That Riverside, California, displays a virtual Hekate shrine openly in the heart of its city center[333] and a St Catherine of the Wheel shrine in nearby Mission Inn cannot be dismissed. That the Church of St Catherine of Alexandria in Riverside appears to be linked geophysically to the murder site of one of the victims of the Zodiac Killer[334], as well as found within symbology and lore associated with the 1915 *Empire of the Wheel* mystery deaths in San Bernardino, can't be ignored.

The very goddess in the State Seal of California is Minerva aka Athena, herself sometimes linked to and likely an aspect identity of Hekate. A statue in the civic center of San Francisco features Minerva/Athena/Hekate with a bear. She is naturally featured in architecture, statuary and frescoes of the state

---

[333]*EOTW3: The Nameless Ones*.

[334]Cheri Jo Bates; *EOTW1*.

capitol and various museums. You might say that California is the realm of Minerva/Athena/Hekate in the United States.

Of course, these facts are the result of a conscious application of Minerva/Athena/Hekate on the part of explorers, settlers, and civic leaders. These individuals brought with them the lore and historical influences leading to such identifications in place name or symbolic veneration. Is there anything to suggest an actual presence of Hekate in California prior to the European arrival?

The obvious possibility that comes to mind is in whatever nugget of truth may have inspired Montalvo's novel linking the lost realm of the Amazons to the state. Is this novel a product of an actual knowledge that there was such a kingdom and it was ruled over by the queen of 'an unknown ancient lineage'? Was Hekate indeed of the Tuatha de Danann and did she claim what we know as California as hers when they ventured forth into the world following departure from Ireland? Is this what those hypothetical America-exploring Templars discovered when they ventured to the western shore of the New World?

I can't answer those questions definitively (yet) but they may lead to the evidence, or lack of it, that will. What I can offer are more possibilities in line with what has been traditionally associated with Hekate. For instance, she is associated with roses. It was while seated in a rose garden that I first addressed her, asking her to 'show me something' just minutes before happening upon the strange quarry discussed in the Empire of the Wheel series. There is also a circular (wheel shaped?) feature of a rose garden facing the statue of Hekate in downtown Riverside. Those are simply examples of a more pleasantly associated symbol, others are a bit darker.

That the island commonly linked to Cabrillo's death is named after Hekate/St Catherine is more in line with her primary identity, underworld goddess at the gate to the land of the dead. Her apparent presence in the details of the seven mystery deaths in 1915 San Bernardino reflects this. Her presence in the symbols used by the Zodiac Killer reflects death again. The Ambassador Hotel, site of the infamous assassination of Robert Kennedy, was bordered to the east by Catalina Street. The murder of Harvey Milk and Mayor Moscone in San Francisco happened on the city hall property, essentially where that statue of Minerva/Athena/Hekate stands. In the process of California gaining affiliation with the United States and subsequent statehood, thousands of native residents were killed or massacred, several by the previously discussed John C Fremont and his associates. Was Hekate spiritually responsbile for these deaths?

The answer to that is no, she isn't. Hekate is simply present where there is death because of her obvious role after death. Rather, the dead must go through her to pass on to their next place. However, the forces surrounding her in that shadowy realm of the Underworld tend to gather round those who are responsible for such things, if the reader would allow me to be philosophical about it. But this leads into aspects of her presence better served in a dedicated discussion best suited for another volume. The present focus is on why she may be present in the lives and exploits of the individuals this series presents.

In the first volume of this series, Hekate is most prevalent in the section about Joan of Arc, for obvious reasons. St Catherine of Alexandria/Hekate was the primary entity communicating with Joan. If my speculative hypothesis about Cabrillo looking for and taking custody of the sword of Joan of Arc is correct, it may be this very venture that brought Hekate directly to his consciousness, though Cabrillo simply taking on the expedition to the realm of Califia could easily have been the catalyst for interaction with the forces of the goddess. However it happened, it is my opinion that Cabrillo's curious behavior on the expedition, dangerously hugging the coastline, and what I am convinced is the lie that he missed the San Francisco Bay entirely, is evidence that he was searching for something specific, secret and likely arcane, as previously discussed. It is my suggestion that, if it was some relic of the Tuatha de Danann that he was looking for, Cabrillo would have been drawing the attention of Hekate to himself.

As discussed in the previous section on California's role in this greater mystery, I suspect that what Cabrillo was looking for was evidence of the Tuatha de Danann or its direct influence upon a lost civilization pre-dating the known history of the state. In my opinion, this would have to be relative to the Amazon lore linked to California, also discussed within the context of Montalvvo's novel and the idea that there was an Amazonian kingdom here. Do we have any present evidence that this is even possible?

The Chumash were matriarchal and they were the culture linked to that which inhabited Catalina Island, called both Pimu and Limu by California natives, the latter reflecting a possible association with what we know as 'Lemuria', whatever it actually may have been. But there is also the possibility that Africans made it as far west as California.

Various accounts indicate that Africans were already among the natives of the Americas by the time of Columbus' arrival (whether it be 1485 or 1492). There are the Olmec heads in Mexico which strongly resemble African facial features. The 9th Century historian Abu al-Hasan Ali al-Mas'udi wrote of an Arab explorer who crossed the Atlantic to an unknown land and returned to tell about it. Certainly among his crew were Africans and we can suggest that once they came to the New World they would likely have been followed by others. Historian Hui-lin Li of the 20th Century certainly agreed with the idea. These aren't the only diffusionist hypotheses of African travelers to the Americas. That a realm of dark-skinned women are described in Montalvo's *Esplandian*, as if they were Africans, provides us with enough margin to consider the possibility that there indeed was an African Amazonian civilization, or at least their colony, in ancient California.

But what about those 'combat griffins'? Perhaps they were an exaggeration of the California Condor which has the largest wingspan of any bird in North America. They also have been dated back to at least the Pleistocene Era. Between these giant birds and the history of the gold in California, it wouldn't be out of hand to seriously consider some nugget of truth to the

Amazonian presence in the state's lost history. If it's true, we can further speculate upon a Tuatha de Danann link, be it direct or merely a cultural influence. Throw into this mix the things I have found in the San Bernardino-Riverside area of Southern California's Inland Empire, the giant 'arrowhead', the 'cross' on Rubidoux that looks like a sword sunk into a stone, two potential representations from the Four Treasures, and one might argue a presence of the Tuatha all along the Pacific coast of the state.

At present, I state here my position that ancient California was inhabited by a now lost civilization and this is what Cabrillo suspected or knew and was what drove him on his expedition, not so much any Spanish directives.

Of course, in my opinion, where there are the Tuatha, there is Hekate and somewhere in this we may find the reason for how the sword of Joan of Arc would have been vaulted in California by the Templars. As I also propose that Juan Cabrillo did not die as popular history dictates, rather I say that his death was reported in a contrived manner to facilitate him taking on a new identity. It is my speculation that such a contrivance was framed within some variation of Templar ritual for the reasons specified in that previous book. As a result of this hypothesis, I presently conclude that Hekate's role in the Juan Cabrillo chapter of this series' greater context is associated to the issue of the special sword.

In the matter of Richard Francis Burton, we have Hekate linked to Oxford via Balliol College which I suspect was the source of clandestine recruitment of Burton during his university days.[335] Their patron saint is none other than Hekate herself in her guise as Catherine of Alexandria. It could then be argued that Burton would have recognized Hekate in any experience with Kali aspects while in India. As regards his 'lost expedition', the City of Manuscript 512, and Burton's general career long interest in ancient civilizations, we may rightfully suggest that he was looking for (and finding) the Tuatha de Danann, as was Cabrillo. Yet, we may have further still reason to link Burton to the Hekate influence and to Ambrose Bierce's subsequent activities in possible involvement with the Crystal Skull business.

Any search for relics or sites of the lost civilization might be, in essence, a search for the Tuatha civilization or its brand. But where Hekate is concerned, we might say that Bierce's familiarity was as intimate as Burton's.

With the documented suspicion that Bierce also had some connection to the acquisition of the notorious Crystal Skull[336] and its subsequent link to Sidney Burney who had obtained the ancient relief known as 'Queen of the Night', we have a milieu exposed to her symbols and trappings, and thus her presence.[337] But even more so, we have Bierce's literary works to argue in favor of the presence of Hekate in his psyche. The man wrote a lot of stuff about strange things and his best known contribution to that genre is Carcosa, that country in the land of the dead: Hekate's domain. In this one work we have the best evidence of

---

[335] *SM2:Burton*, Pgs 94-95.

[336] Sibley S. Morrill, *Ambrose Bierce, F. A. Mitchell-Hedges, and The Crystal Skull* (Cadleon Press 1972)

[337] *SM3:Destination Carcosa*, Pgs 132-149

her influence upon Bierce, but there is the question as to what extent he may have known of the secrets of San Bernardino in those years leading up to the *Empire of the Wheel* events[338] and we know her role in that.

Might any influence of Hekate on Bierce be associated with what he could have learned about Napoleon Bonaparte? Bierce's association with James Mortimer, the close friend of Napoleon III, raises the question as to what possible extent Bierce became privy to that milieu, and even more so what his trip to the south of France without his wife and family might really have been about. In this we might suspect that Hekate was connected to some curious and as yet still unknown business involving Bierce in the Languedoc. Was he getting mixed up in the Rennes-le-Chateau mystery?

In light of the earlier Poussin discussion, I wonder if Bierce could have been investigating some aspect of an association between the Hautpoul family and the Bonapartes or, given his particular literary proclivities, the subject of time phenomena and how it might factor into death and the afterlife.[339] This would most assuredly have brought Hekate to Bierce's door, so to speak. And I haven't even begun to analyze Hekate's possible presence in Chambers' *The King In Yellow*, much influenced by Bierce's *Carcosa.* Considering the aforementioned possibility that Bierce learned secrets about Napoleon I from Napoleon III or James Mortimer, could there

---

[338]Ibid. Bierce's father in law owned mining properties in San Bernardino County and Bierce had to travel there on at least one occasion relative to that, after the man died.

[339]Refer to the discussion of Poussin and Longfellow in *The Mystery of Ingersoll Lockwood* by Wood & Bosley.

be revealed a connection of a Hekate thread between the night Napoleon I spent in the pyramid and something about Colonel Hautpoul's family's secret?

Here is what makes it possible: Napoleon III was living in England while Bierce was there. We know about Bierce's friend James Mortimer, close friend of the banished emperor (like uncle, like nephew) but there is the issue of American Colonel Zebulon Benton who was a member of Napoleon III's immediate circle in England, living at Camden Place with the former emperor. Benton's wife was Caroline Christina Bonaparte – a daughter of 'Joseph' Bonaparte and his live-in American mistress, Annette Savage.[340] If my hypothesis about Napoleon and Joseph in the fourth volume of this series is correct, that makes Zebulon Benton the son-in-law of Napoleon Bonaparte I. Thus, through Mortimer, Ambrose Bierce very readily had an opportunity to become acquainted with Benton and could very reasonably have learned the truth about the switch in 1815 that allowed Napoleon to live in America after Waterloo. What else could Bierce have learned…?[341]

It's intriguing to think that Ambrose Bierce stood at an intersection of the lost secrets of California, Napoleon Bonaparte, Edgar Allan Poe, Rennes-le-Chateau, the 1890s

---

[340]Mark Meredith, HouseHistree June 2020.

[341]It should be noted that Benton was from Oxbow, New York. Consider Bierce's tale of a hanging, 'An Occurrence At Owl Creek Bridge', and the 1940 western lynching novel *The Ox-Bow Incident* by Walter Clark. Did Clark know something we don't about a possible Bierce and Benton association? Also note that author Clark was born in Maine and consider the whole Maine-and-Clark links to the airship mystery per the *Empire of the Wheel* books and *Origin*. We got us here a whole lotta implication.

Airship Mystery, and the San Bernardino Working. Like Etta Place, Bierce disappeared. Could all this be why?

Did Ambrose Bierce journey to the homeland of the Tuatha de Danann via Hekate's crossroads? Recall in *Destination: Carcosa* the discussion regarding what Clark Ashton Smith might have learned about Bierce's disappearance. His story *City of the Singing Flame* is about a geomorphological portal through which the narrator's friend passes into a hidden dimension.[342] Smith, who had been critically praised by Bierce but never got to meet him as planned, lived close enough to the Yosemite area to have been familiar with any tales of strange things going around back then. Smith also stood at an interesting crossroad between Bierce and Lovecraft, an associative landscape all quite reflective of the things of Hekate's underworld, not the least of which was Bierce's familial link to the San Bernardino Valley via mining claims (underworld).

Could Ambrose Bierce's secret expedition through Latin America, from which he never returned, have been inspired in any way by something he learned while in San Bernardino County? More specifically, by something he learned of Hekate's presence in all this?

I think it may be so, if one understands the true nature of Hekate. If one can decipher the true purpose of her role, one might understand her presence in certain places and perhaps even determine if she in any way had anything to do with the disappearance of Bierce, or even perhaps all the people who

[342]*SM3: Destination: Carcosa,* Pg 120.

disappear in the national parks, where the natural state of the planet reigns supreme, much like the jungles of South America. Personally, I think this may be the key to all of it.

What is Hekate's secret? Like the goddess Isis, the answer to that is something the seeker must pursue on his or her own and something about that quest changes a person's perspective. She is linked both to the lost civilization and to our present one. Juan Cabrillo, whether he died on Catalina or changed his identity and lived on, has never been found. He disappeared while exploring a strange new landscape where Hekate very much tread. Burton went looking for the answer, disappeared for several months, and never uttered a serious word about it for the remainder of his life. Napoleon Bonaparte may very well have encountered Hekate on her own turf that night in Egypt long ago. Bierce could have set off to face her at the very intersection where she waits, perhaps having figured out her secret. Hekate seems to call people to her and that road leads to revelation, with only a single caveat: *Tell No One*.

I have, through my own journey, determined that she waits for us all.

And what of that other possibility which could explain the presence of the Tuatha de Danann in this part of California? Why might Tuatha landmarks have been placed across Southern California's Inland Empire, specifically the greater San Bernardino Valley? What might be the purpose of such landmarks spanning the centuries? Why this place?

It may be that the Four Treasures of the Tuatha have been placed and maintained to keep something from getting out. This place has had a reputation for dark things for a century. Something lurks here, lying in wait, perhaps looking for a mountain pass to slip through. Whatever it is, it has been here a very long time. Bad things have been done in its name. To paraphrase what Rust Cohle says in 'True Detective': Maybe we need the 'dark' Goddess of the Underworld here to help keep the other dark things from our doorstep.

Even after glimpses of the darkness here for the past several years, I never considered that the Tuatha landmarks might be the prison gates keeping something inside this valley. I'm admittedly curious, like the men I've written about in this series.

I'm gonna have to take an even closer look.

Epilogue

"*The djong, jong, or jung (also called junk in English) is a type of ancient sailing ship originating from Java that was widely used by Javanese and Malay sailors. The word was and is spelled jong in its languages of origin, the "djong" spelling being the colonial Dutch romanisation. Djongs are used mainly as seagoing passenger and cargo vessels. They traveled as far as Ghana or even Brazil in ancient times...*" Wikipedia

Afonso de Albuquerque was born near Lisbon in 1453 and before he died, on the 15th day of December 1515AD, he had become an adventurous and heroic heroic figure in Portuguese history. A decade of crusading against North African Muslims taught him soldiering and subsequently he became a terror to Arab ports. Albuquerque was in the fight at the European conquest of Tangier. He conquered Goa and Malacca, establishing his reputation from India to the Malay Peninsula. He was also responsible for the establishment of Portuguese dominance of Eastern maritime trade routes and their superior power across Asia in the late 15th and early 16th Centuries.

When Albuquerque took Malacca, a map was seized from a Javanese navigator. The chart demonstrated the extent of Malay seafaring at that time and that included Brazil. This impressed

Afonso de Alburquerque greatly and in a letter to King Manuel of Portugal on 1 April 1512, Albuquerque expressed it.

Junks had crossed the oceans from ancient times. Claudius Ptolemaeus had written about it in his First Century AD work, *Geography*. These vessels continued to be acknowledged seafarers for centuries after that. There was no reason in 1939 to think a junk would not make it from Hong Kong to San Francisco.

Richard Halliburton was born in Tennessee in 1900. His father Wesley was an engineer and real estate developer. Richard grew up in Memphis where he became interested in history and geography. As a teenager, Halliburton developed a rapid heartbeat and spent time at the well known Battle Creek, Michigan, health mecca of John Harvey Kellogg. Halliburton's health was otherwise robust. He went on to focus on journalism and in 1921 graduated from Princeton where he had been on the editorial board of the university publication. But it was a sabbatical he took away from college in 1919 which defined Halliburton.

Signed aboard the freighter *Octorara*, Halliburton took a sea voyage from New Orleans to England, seeing London and Paris before returning to Princeton. He would graduate, of course, but the cast had been set. Halliburton craved more travel. He wanted to see the world, but not merely as a tourist. Richard Halliburton wanted adventure and to see the curiosities of the far off corners of the world. Swimming the entire length of the Panama Canal, living like Robinson Crusoe on the island of Tobago, and retracing the journey of Odysseus were some of his adventures. Halliburton's exploits earned him the respect of other travelers like Douglas Fairbanks Sr who became his friend.

In 1930, Halliburton embarked upon a trip around the world in an open cockpit Stearman biplane from England, over Europe, south to Africa then over the Middle East and on to India. As the pilot took them over Mt Everest, Halliburton unfastened his safety belt and rose from his seat to take the first aerial photograph of the world's tallest peak. That pilot was Moye Stephens, a co-founder of Northrop, who would go on to fly the N-1M, an early flying wing concept aircraft.[343] By 1934, Halliburton was writing about his unique travels under contract and one of his articles was about his time with the Seri tribe in California whom we discussed in a previous chapter as the source of claims that Vikings had sailed as far west as the Gulf of Baja. Halliburton wrote about them five years before the anthropologists Dane and Mary Coolidge did. What might Halliburton have learned about the Viking explorers of California?

Richard Halliburton would attempt to cross the Alps on an elephant. He would climb the Matterhorn, spend a night at the top of the Great Pyramid, encounter pirates and headhunters, and would leave behind a collection of essays and articles and books chronicling his escapades. He didn't travel as some American aristocrat, he saw the world mostly on a budget, inspiring generations of young travelers who had first seen the world through Halliburton's enthusiastic Clark Griswoldesque

[343] 1940.

style of expression which managed to irk a rather humorless Ernest Hemingway who hated him.

By the time 1937 rolled around, Halliburton was the owner of a custom built architectural wonder in Laguna Beach popularly referred to as the 'Hangover House' because it literally hung over a cliff. Among the visitors who admired the home was Ayn Rand who based the house in *The Fountainhead* on the place. She would also go on to write about a 'fictional' breakaway group in *Atlas Shrugged*. Between his time with the Seris in California, his association with Rand and pilot Stephens, I must wonder what Halliburton may have learned about the hidden secrets of the past and his present. He certainly had seen places affiliated with lost civilizations.

While Richard was away at college, during which time he had taken his seagoing adventure, his older cousin Erle was busy in 1919 founding the company we know today as 'Halliburton' which would one day employ Vice President Dick Cheney and make a lot of money as a contractor for the US government via its subsidiary Brown & Root, and all that goes with that. During Richard's days of traveling the world, the Halliburton company made its first foreign business deals in Burma and India, in 1926. Had Richard played any role in corporate intelligence gathering or brokering the deal? Most of Halliburton's foreign business got rolling after Richard was gone.

Which brings us to 1939.

Like other curious and strange things I have written about over the several years, this story involves an exposition, this one the Golden Gate International Exposition. Richard

Halliburton had departed from San Francisco in September 1938 to Hong Kong, from where he would attempt to sail a Chinese junk across the Pacific Ocean back to San Francisco. The vessel would be an exhibit at the expo held on Treasure Island. It was to be called the *Sea Dragon* and was a Wenchow-style junk, built to Richard's specs and 75 ft in length. Including Richard, the crew would total twelve, three of the men were Chinese, the rest Americans. The project was an early example of crowdfunding but was kicked off by an investment from Erle's wife. There were problems during construction of the *Sea Dragon* but Richard maintained his usual enthusiastic attitude. Finally, on 4 March 1939, the ship left port.

On 23 March, the *Sea Dragon* sailed into a typhoon. The nearest vessel was the *SS President Coolidge*, battling forty foot waves. The transmission that came from the Sea Dragon as she was fighting the unforgiving sea was perhaps reflective of Richard Halliburton's spirit: "*Having a wonderful time. Wish you were here instead of me...*". The next message heard from *Sea Dragon* was in regard to its position and speed, heavy rain squalls, high seas. "*All well*" was added.

But they were never heard from again.

That was 1,200 miles west of the Midway Islands.

The *Sea Dragon* had been unheard from for seventeen days before the US Coast Guard in Hawaii decided to respond to requests to look for her. They thought Halliburton was pulling a publicity stunt. The US Navy tasked ships and scout planes to look for the lost ship, but after over 150,000 miles of ocean were searched, all hope was lost. The junk and her crew were gone. Richard Halliburton was declared dead on October 5th.

The following year, a ship sighted a barnacle encrusted rudder suspected of being that of the *Sea Dragon*. In 1945, the skeletal remains of the hull of a Chinese design boat washed up in San Diego, but it was determined to be too big to be the *Sea Dragon*. It has been reported that Richard Halliburton haunts his former house in Laguna Beach.

If anyone lived an adventurous life, Richard Halliburton should be counted among them. At the time he and the crew of Sea Dragon disappeared, there was indeed a war going on. Amelia Earhart had disappeared two years prior and, like with her, some wondered if Halliburton and crew had been involved with spying. However, my questions come from another place when I look at his life of travels: What might Richard Halliburton have seen of the forgotten civilization? What might he have learned of the secrets of the past?

As it is so with Marco Polo, Giovanni Verrazzano, Juan Cabrillo, Napoleon Bonaparte, Jan Potocki, Richard Francis Burton, and Ambrose Bierce, we may never know the whole story of Richard Halliburton. But we should never stop trying. It's the least they would expect of us.

Pack your bag, lace up your boots, dear reader.

This mission ain't accomplished yet.

Additional Bibliography

Bawlf, Samuel *The Secret Voyage of Sir Francis Drake* (Penguin 2003)

Bernier, Francine *The Templars' Legacy in Montreal, the New Jerusalem* (Frontier Press/AUP 2001)

Bosley & Spence, *Empire of the Wheel: An Investigation of Occult Espionage and Murder* (Corvos 2011)

Bosley, *Empire of the Wheel 2: Friends From Sonora* (Corvos 2013)

Bosley, *Empire of the Wheel 3: The Nameless Ones* (Corvos 2014)

Bosley, *Latitude 33: Key to the Kingdom* (Corvos 2008)

Bosley, *Secret Missions: The Hidden Legacy of Old California* (Corvos 2014)

Bosley, *Secret Missions 2: The Lost Expedition of Sir Richard Francis Burton* (Corvos 2015)

Bosley, *Secret Missions 3: Destination Carcosa* (Corvos 2017)

Bosley, *Secret Missions 4: The Esoteric Napoleon Vol 1* (Corvos 2019)

Braghine, Alexander, *The Shadow of Atlantis* (1940, AUP Reprint 1997)

Childress, David, *Ancient Micronesia & The Lost City of Nan Madol* (AUP 1998)

Childress, David, *Lost Cities & Ancient Mysteries of the Southwest* (AUP 2009)

Childress, David, *The Lost World of the Cham: The Transpacific Voyages of the Champa* (AUP 2017)

Childress, David, *Pirates & The Lost Templar Fleet: The Secret Naval War Between the Knights Templar & The Vatican* (AUP 2018 Ed of 2003)

Churchward, Col. James, *The Lost Continent of MU* (BE Books & CW Daniel 1926, 2001 reprint)

Borle, Edwin, *The Royal Highway* (Bobbs-Merrill 1949)

Costanso, Miguel, *El Descubrimiento de la Bahia de San Francisco: La Expedicion de Portola de 1769-1770* (First published in 1911, Great West Books 1992 Edition)

De Erauso, Catalina, *Lieutenant Nun: Memoir of a Basque Transvestite in the New World* (1630, Beacon Press 1996 Edition)
Downey, Kirstin, *Isabella: The Warrior Queen* (Anchor Books 2014)
Durant, *The Age of Faith: a History of Medieval Civilization – Christian, Islamic and Judaic – From Constantine to Dante: AD 325 – 1300* (Simon & Schuster 1950)
Durant, *The Age of Louis XIV: A History of European Civilization in the Period of Pascal, Moliere, Cromwell, Milton, Peter the Great, Newton, and Spinoza: 1648-1715* (Simon & Schuster 1963)
Durant, *The Age of Napoleon: A History of European Civilization from 1789-1815* (Simon & Schuster 1975)
Durant, *The Age of Reason Begins: A History of European Civilization in the Period of Shakespeare, Bacon, Montaigne, Rembrandt, Galileo, and Descartes: 1558-1648* (Simon & Schuster 1961)
Durant, *The Age of Voltaire: A History of Civilization in Western Europe from 1715 to 1756, with Special Emphasis on the Conflict between Religion and Philosophy* (Simon & Schuster 1965)
Durant, *Our Oriental Heritage: Being A History of Civilization in Egypt and the Near East to the Death of Alexander, and in India, China and Japan From the Beginning To Our Own Day; With an Introduction On the Nature and Foundations of Civilization* (Simon & Schuster 1954)
Durant, *The Reformation: A History of European Civilization from Wyclif to Calvin: 1300-1564* (Simon & Schuster 1957)
Durant, *The Renaissance: A History of Civilization in Italy from 1304-1576 AD* (Simon & Schuster 1953)
Durant, *Rousseau and Revolution: A History of Civilization in France, England, and Germany from 1756, and in the Remainder of Europe from 1715, to 1789* (Simon & Schuster 1967)
Faivre, Antoine, *The Eternal Hermes: From Greek God to Alchemical Magus* (Phanes 1995)
Farrell, Joseph, *Babylon's Banksters: The Alchemy of Deep Physics, High Finance and Ancient Religion* (Feral House 2010)

Farrell, Joseph, *Financial Vipers of Venice: Alchemical Money, Magical Physics, and Banking in the Middle Ages and the Renaissance* (Feral House 2010)

Farrell & DeHart, *The Grid of the Gods: The Aftermath of the Cosmic War and the Physics of the Pyramid Peoples* (AUP 2011)

Farrell, Joseph, *Thrice Great Hermetica And The Janus Age: Hermetic Cosmology, Finance, Politics and Culture In the Middle Ages Through the Late Renaissance* (AUP 2014)

Fell, Barry, *America BC: Ancient Settlers in the New World* (Artisan 1989)

Goldstone, Nancy, *The Maid And The Queen: The Secret History of Joan of Arc* (Penguin 2012)

Halliburton, Richard, *The Royal Road To Romance* (1925, Traveler's Tales 2000 Ed)

Hapgood, Charles, *Maps of the Ancient Sea Kings; Evidence of Advanced Civilization in the Ice Age* (1966, Souvenir Press 1996 Reprint)

Hapgood, Charles, *Mystery In Acambaro: An Account of the Ceramic Collection of the Late Waldemar Julsrud in Acambaro Gto. Mexico* (1973, AUP 2000)

Jameson, W.C. , *Buried Treasures of California: Legends From California's Mountains, Deserts, Beaches, and Cities* (August House 1995)

Morris, Roy, *Ambrose Bierce: Alone In Bad Company* (Oxford Univ Press 1995)

Paulides, David, *Missing 411: Western United States & Canada: Unexplained Disappearances of North Americans That Have Never Been Solved* (David Paulides, Publisher, 2011)

Penfield, Thomas, *Dig Here! Lost Mines & Buried Treasure of the Southwest* (1962, AUP 2004)

Poe, Edgar Allan, *Complete Tales and Poems* (Barnes & Noble Books 1992)

Potocki, Jan, *The Manuscript Found In Saragossa* (1810,1814,1837, Viking 1992 Translation by Ian MacLean)

Silverman, Kenneth, *Edgar A. Poe: Mournful and Never-ending Remembrance* (Harper Perennial 1991)

Sora, Steven, *The Lost Colony of the Templars: Verrazano's Secret Mission To America* (Destiny Books 2004)
Stacy-Judd, Robert, *Atlantis: Mother of Empires* (1939, AUP reprint)
Starr, Kevin, *California: A History* (Modern Library 2005)
Whishaw, E. M., *Atlantis In Spain* (1928, AUP 1997)
Zapp & Erikson, *Atlantis in America: Navigators of the Ancient World* (AUP 1998)

Printed and bound by CPI Group (UK) Ltd, Croydon, CR0 4YY
29/03/2024
03756115-0003